THE
CONSCIOUS
RESISTANCE
TRILOGY

Jimmy Tomorrow,
Thanks brother for sharing your
inspiration to connecting with John
Trudell. I appreciate you being
here. —Derrick Broze

Discovery Publisher

Author: Derrick Broze, John Vibes

616 Corporate Way
Valley Cottage, New York
www.discoverypublisher.com
editors@discoverypublisher.com
Proudly not on Facebook or Twitter

New York • Paris • Dublin • Tokyo • Hong Kong

TABLE OF CONTENTS

Introduction   3

BOOK I: Reflections on Anarchy: & Spirituality   7

Part 1 – Naming the Path   8

Background   9

Chapter 1: What is the Conscious Resistance?   11

Chapter 2: Explorative Agnosticism   16

Chapter 3: Reality Beyond the 5 Senses: Beyond Logic, Beyond Reason   21

Chapter 4: Towards Panarchism: Anarchy Without Adjectives   26

Chapter 5: Healing the Inner Child Today Will Save the World Tomorrow   37

Chapter 6: Consciousness & Rights Applied to Animals, Plants, and Earth   42

Chapter 7: Conscious Healing   46

Chapter 8: Rites of Vigil and Solitude   55

Chapter 9: Are We All One? Collectivism vs. Individuality   59

Chapter 10: Balancing the Feminine and the Masculine   63

Part 2 – Anti-Authoritarianism: in World Traditions   69

Chapter 11: Intersections of Shamanism and Anarchism   70

Chapter 12: Intersections of Christianity and Anarchism   76

Chapter 13: Intersection of Judaism and Anarchism   80

Chapter 14: Intersections of Islam and Anarchism   82

Chapter 15: Intersections of Buddhism and Anarchism   88

Chapter 16: Intersections of Taoism and Anarchism   93

Chapter 17: Intersections of Anarchism and Confucianism   96

Chapter 18: The Art of Not Being Governed   98

BOOK II: Finding Freedom in an Age of Confusion   107

A Message From the Authors   108

Chapter 1: You are a Pioneer of Peace   109

Chapter 2: Reclaiming Your Self-Esteem 111

Chapter 3: You Are Divine 114

Chapter 4: Trust Yourself, Vacate the State 116

Chapter 5: You Are Not Alone 118

Chapter 6: Learn From Everyone, But Be Your Own Teacher 122

Chapter 7: Understanding Family and Friends 124

Chapter 8: The Rabbit Hole Trap 126

Chapter 9: The State is Not Invincible, It's Just a Bad Idea 130

Chapter 10: The Golden Age is Now 133

Chapter 11: The Sky is Falling, But It's Only a Storm 137

Chapter 12: The Illusion of Race 139

Chapter 13: Another Look at the Doomsday Myth 143

Chapter 14: There is Nothing Positive About Willful Ignorance 145

Tools for Action: NVC, Meditation, and Positive Affirmations 147

Chapter 15: What is Meditation and how do I meditate? 148

Chapter 16: Non-Violent Communication 151

Chapter 17: Affirming the Positive and Manifesting Reality 153

BOOK III: Manifesto of the Free Humans 159

A Note From Derrick & John 160

Part 1 – A Strategy for Defeating the State 162

Chapter 1: Overcoming the Fear of Freedom 163

Chapter 2: What is Agorism? 168

Chapter 3: Vertical and Horizontal Agorism 175

Chapter 4: Spontaneous Order 182

Chapter 5: Agorism is not Anarcho-Capitalism 188

Chapter 6: On Non-Voting 195

Part 2 – Our Vision of a Stateless Society 198

Chapter 7: Providing Public Services Peacefully 199

Chapter 8: Stewardship of the Earth 204

Chapter 9: The Authoritarian Right and Left 212

Chapter 10: Identifying the Alt-Right Infection 218

Chapter 11: On the Use of Force   227

Chapter 12: Panarchist Experiments: Can Propertarians &
            Non-Propertarians Coexist?   231

Chapter 13: The Revolutionary Potential of "Illegal" Immigrants   236

Part 3 – Creating Conscious Agoras   241

Chapter 14: Sovereignty of the Individual   243

Chapter 15: PermAgora   246

Chapter 16: Strong Hearts and Revolutionary Minds   249

Chapter 17: Mobility vs. Homesteading   253

Chapter 18: Getting Off the Control Grid and Defending the Agora   255

Part 4 – Understanding Holistic Anarchism   259

Chapter 19: Defining Holistic Activism / Anarchism   260

Chapter 20: The Intersection of Holistic and Relational Anarchism 266

About the Authors, Acknowledgements & : suggested reading list 273

About the Authors & Acknowledgements   274

Suggested Reading List   275

THE
CONSCIOUS
RESISTANCE

TRILOGY

Introduction

It has been five years since we first wrote The Conscious Resistance trilogy. The original intention of this work was to open the doors to conversation regarding the intersection of anti-authoritarian political philosophy and the spiritual search for meaning. Since the release of the trilogy, we have witnessed an explosion of interest in these two topics. Where discussions on Anarchism and religion once almost exclusively revolved around atheism, we now see an abundance of conversations bridging the gap between the spiritual and anarchist worlds.

We have seen these changes manifest in the many Anarchist and spiritual/transformational conferences and festivals. Events which previously exclusively focused on anarchism or political debates, now regularly feature speakers and workshops discussing permaculture and personal/spiritual development. At the same time, transformational events which already understand the need for empowerment and spiritual healing, are opening up to the concept of holistic anarchism, which we have spent the last few years promoting.

While we are thankful to see this growing melting pot of anarchism and spirituality, we also recognize that the world has undergone rapid changes in the last five years. The State has continued to expand, politics is dividing friends and neighbors, and corporations continue to place profit before life. Yes, the search for meaning has led many to question these systems and to begin working on healing their own trauma, but where do the spiritual anarchists fit in all of this apparent chaos? *How do the ideas of The Conscious Resistance fit into the world of 2020 and beyond?*

We believe these works are more important now than they were when we first wrote and released them into the world. As we write this expansion to our original work, the world is facing a growth in authoritarian forces from the left and the right sides of the political spectrum. This authoritarian creep has also caused previously sleeping minds to wake from slumber. As we take solace in the fact that many people have lost faith in government institutions, we also see how some are falling prey to the allure of the "strongman" archetype or are simply waiting for some savior to ride in on a white horse. Simultaneously, the COVID-19 pandemic is bringing the world as we know it to a halt. Governments are using the crisis to expand their tyrannical grip on the people and install even more surveillance grid measures.

We are in the early stages of a decade that is sure to see an increase in government power, and this power grab reinforces the need for introspection and deep healing. *Why do people in positions of government always seem to seek more control over the lives of others? Why do we, the public, often focus on pointing our fingers at the authorities, solely placing the blame on their shoulders, while ignoring the role we play in manifesting our reality?*

We attempted to answer these questions in our original trilogy. From our perspective the different books in the Conscious Resistance series represent individual pieces of a larger whole. Book one, *Reflections on Anarchy and Spirituality*, represents an introduction to our philosophy and the foundation of our ideas. This could be seen as "the body." When we wrote *Finding Freedom In An Age of Confusion* we wanted to focus on the more emotional or heart-centered aspects of our philosophy; thus this represents the heart of our work. Finally, *Manifesto of the Free Humans* represents the mind, where we explore the intellectual arguments that free thinkers often find themselves in when discussing the possibility of a stateless society. Taken together, these works symbolize the movement that we call *The Conscious Resistance*.

In the midst of our rapidly changing world, we have discovered exciting new ways to illustrate our philosophical perspective and we have additional knowledge which has added nuance to our view of the world. While we proudly stand by the entirety of the previous versions of this book, we feel that we have collected sufficient information to provide more supporting evidence for our arguments and cover new topics that have entered the collective consciousness in recent years. There are even some areas where our perspectives have evolved.

We recognize that these books are not the final word on this subject. Since we embarked on this series, our main goal was to start a conversation we thought it was incredibly important to all lives on this planet, and we encourage anyone who feels inspired by our words to add their own thoughts to the discussion. We welcome personal critiques on our philosophy. We don't claim or wish to be an authority on anything, we merely want to be a part of the conversation. We hope you will join the conversation too.

In previous centuries anarchists and free thinkers would put forth ideas for consideration and welcome responses and even debunking of their concepts. In this same spirit, we hope those who find our work intriguing (or infuriating) will take the time to propose alternatives to what we have written. If we truly hope to create a better world—one where self-ownership, individual liberty, truth, and justice are respected—it will require a collaborative effort between the free hearts and minds of the world.

Thank you for joining this journey.

John & Derrick
November 2020

BOOK I

...

REFLECTIONS ON ANARCHY
& SPIRITUALITY

PART 1—NAMING THE PATH

Background

The first seeds of this project were planted in late 2012, when Derrick traveled from his home in Houston to take a media internship near Washington, DC. During that trip, Derrick and John met through a mutual friend. Almost immediately the two burgeoning anarchists dove deep into conversation and were quickly talking about future collaborations. When Derrick returned home from DC, John made a few recommendations to his new connections in the independent media and helped Derrick land his first writing job. Over the next few months, John made a series of appearances on Derrick's online radio show, "The Conscious Resistance," to discuss some of the issues that they felt were being undervalued, both in the mainstream and in the counterculture.

The main topic they kept returning to was the lack of open dialogue regarding the spiritual aspect of the global struggle against tyranny. Many anarchists considered themselves logical, rational people who avoided conversations about God, spirit, and other often unexplained phenomena. Some of these materialists dismissed the world beyond the five senses as "woo" and closed their minds and hearts to the world of spirit. However, as John and Derrick began exploring these concepts from an anarchist perspective, looking for intersections to explore, they noticed there was a hunger for more content of this nature. Those early podcasts formed the foundation for *Reflections on Anarchy and Spirituality*.

Another piece of the puzzle was found in April 2013, when Derrick spoke in New York City at the Anarchy in the NYC conference. This was Derrick's first time engaging in public speaking outside of his community in Houston. His short talk focused on the intersection of Buddhism and Anarchism, which would later be the foundation for a chapter in this book. Despite sharing the stage with speakers who were vocal atheists, Derrick was pleasantly surprised by a round of applause and immediate interest from those listening. Some anarchists in the audience wanted more details on the thesis of the intersection of spirituality and anarchism, while others shared their favorite meditation practices.

During that same talk Derrick also coined a phrase which would perfectly illustrate the comparison between religion and spirituality, and the state and anarchism. *Anarchy is to Statism as Spirituality is to Religion.* This concept would also make its way into *Reflections*:

"Anarchy is the physical manifestation of freedom, and spirituality is a mental manifestation of freedom. In contrast, statism is control in the physical sense, and

religion is control in the mental or spiritual sense."

This was a turning point in spreading the message of The Conscious Resistance. It was some time after this that the two decided to write a book.

In 2014, John traveled to Houston to speak at a music and arts festival Derrick organized in the city, and to start writing their initial thoughts on paper. They worked all day, and late into the night to prepare the outline for what would become the first installment of The Conscious Resistance series. Throughout the rest of the year, they used a shared cloud document to collaborate on the project and were able to finish in time to present the finished work at the 2015 Free Your Mind Conference in Philadelphia. After giving a presentation on *Reflections on Anarchy and Spirituality,* John and Derrick gave away hundreds of copies for free to all of the attendees.

Five years have passed since the original release. In this new version, most of the chapters remain the same, with some additional text and footnotes. Brand-new chapters are marked on the table of contents. Although the book ended up being the first in a trilogy, we originally wrote as if it was the conclusion of our thoughts on these topics. The book is meant to be an introduction to many intersecting topics, but it is also representative of the threads of our two lives. These are the paths we have walked as we pursue knowledge and healing. This was our first message to the world. Please read these words as they stand here, without expectations for the other books. Thank you for your support.

Chapter 1
What is the Conscious Resistance?

There is a persistent struggle in this world that dates back thousands of years and has created an untold amount of suffering. It is a struggle towards freedom and peace which continues to unfold in the so-called civilizations of the world, which are ravaged by slavery, genocide, and war. Today, many of us live under the illusion that these horrors are a thing of the past or the problems of some faraway land, but they are just as real today as they were in the days of our ancestors, and they are just as real in America as they are in the rest of the world.

There are many social and political changes that must take place to heal the widespread suffering in this world. The entire structure of our societies must change in order to achieve peace and freedom for all people. While a truly utopian world is likely impossible, a world without systematic and socially acceptable violence would certainly be a paradise compared to what we have now.

To create the social and political changes necessary to end the violence, we must use a different method than those tried in the past. We cannot simply storm the gates of the castle and hang the masters from the highest trees, as tempting as that may be. This will only result in a new master sitting on the same throne, exactly as we have seen throughout history repeatedly.

A real lasting change comes from within. In order to stop this cycle of madness, we need an evolution of consciousness. The state and all of its predatory appendages, including the corporate and military industrial complexes, are more than groups of people with weapons that need to be overthrown—they are bad ideas that can be rendered obsolete with the right combination of good ideas.

As the fight for freedom has evolved, so has humanity's understanding of what "*freedom*" actually means. The desire to understand the pursuit of *freedom* has existed for as long as conscious beings have been on this planet. Different cultures throughout history have had their own ideas and visions of how freedom manifests itself. Throughout this book, we will be careful to define important terms that may have different meanings for different people.

There are two ways to define philosophical and political terms like *government, statism, democracy, capitalism, communism, freedom, slavery*, etc. We can define these terms according to how they are supposed to operate in theory, or we can define them according to how they operate in reality.

For example, many people now recognize the word *propaganda* as a pejorative term used to describe psychological manipulation. Thanks to Edward Bernays and his propaganda of the 1920s, most people now understand the word to mean something designed to manipulate or influence in a negative fashion. However, propaganda can also be used as another word for "*media.*" There are many modern words that are largely defined by their theoretical definition rather than how they operate in reality. When we define terms throughout this book, we will not only be looking at the standard dictionary definition but will also break down what the word has truly represented throughout history.

Since "*freedom*" is the very basis of this conversation, it is important to be clear about how we are defining the term. Freedom is defined by *Merriam-Webster's* dictionary as follows:

```
"the quality or state of being free:

a : the absence of necessity, coercion, or constraint
in choice or action b : liberation from slavery or
restraint or from the power of another

: INDEPENDENCE

c : the quality or state of being exempt or released
usually from something onerous <freedom from care>"
```

Pay attention to the first definition of "*free*" — "*the absence of necessity, coercion, or constraint in choice or action.*" It is this definition on which we base our vision of freedom. We advocate not only a voluntary society free of coercion but also that each individual has the utmost control over their own life and affairs.

This view that humanity can and will flourish when the boot of tyranny and authoritarianism is lifted off our collective necks is sometimes known as negative liberty. The concept was popularized by Isaiah Berlin in his 1958 lecture, "Two Concepts of Liberty." According to Berlin, negative liberty is the idea that freedom is to be free from constraints and interference. This is contrasted by positive liberty which deals with the ability of an individual to act upon their free will. It has often been interpreted by philosophers as a support for collectivism or the ability of the people to participate in the government to achieve change. Essentially, those who believe in negative liberty want to be free from restrictions and limits, and those who support positive liberty believe that freedom means the ability to have or possess something which they believe empowers them (i.e., free healthcare, education, etc.)...

With this definition of freedom, we can begin to analyze the history of humanity and decide whether we are living in a state of relative freedom or in varying levels of slavery. By studying philosophy, logic, rhetoric, economics, politics, and history, we can determine whether humankind is freer than it was in the past or if we have been slowly losing our freedom over time.

From our perspective, the opposite of freedom or liberty is slavery. Of course, slavery can be defined in a large number of ways, depending on the context, the environment, and the individual's personal subjective experience. We find it helpful to see slavery as a spectrum, with complete slavery (mental, physical, spiritual) on one end and various shades of liberation that a person experiences as they move away from complete slavery. One manifestation of this slavery is statism.

Statism has been defined numerous times in anti-authoritarian, libertarian, and anarchist literature. First, when we use the term state we are describing the institution or organization which establishes a monopoly on law and control of a territory. This is no longer beholden to a power structure that makes their lives worse in the long run.

As anarchists, we reject the desire to work for or with government institutions. We recognize that using the government as a tool to achieve change, even small change, works against our larger goals of reducing and eliminating the violence and coercion in the world. We do believe that in the coming seven generations some of humanity will desire a life free of institutionalized state theft and violence. Some of our brothers and sisters will be a living example of liberty by thriving in the absence of corporate-state power and other forms of authoritarianism. Despite the commonly held belief that humanity would regress to a barbaric state without government, we propose that the individual who governs himself is better equipped to create a free and enjoyable life.

In the following pages, we propose that it is not only humanity's physical struggles for freedom that should be studied but also our daily internal struggle for freedom. We believe there is a vastly deeper and extremely personal "fight" for freedom taking place every moment. This is the internal struggle, the mental battle, the war waged between our desire for our "highest good" and our doubt and self-imposed limitations perpetuated by our internal tyrants. It is on this field where humanity's greatest war is fought.

Due to our research and experience, we have come to the conclusion that it is essential and necessary to challenge and expose the physical manifestations of power. Equally important is our ability to face and challenge our doubts, fears, insecurities, and pain.

No matter how hard and long humans try to establish a freer world, we are doomed to repeat the same mistakes of the past if we cannot conquer our inner demons. Poverty, corrupt governments, environmental degradation, and wars are manifestations of our inner struggles, and the fact that we al low these travesties to carry on shows we are a species in need of deep healing. Until that healing takes place, humanity will be ripe for control by an external source or "*leader*," and, in fact, people will continue to beg for that control.

It is with this thought in mind that The Conscious Resistance was born. "*Consciously resisting*" means being willing to engage in self-reflection. We believe without knowing our doubts, hopes, fears, dreams, insecurities, and strengths, we cannot truly know what freedom means to us as individuals.

Becoming conscious of your actions is one of the most important steps towards understanding and claiming your own freedom. From that clear state of mind, one can lead by example and help others in their own pursuit of self-discovery and freedom.

This book is aimed at those who already possess some level of understanding about the search for freedom but are ready to challenge long-held beliefs about where freedom begins and ends. These essays are for those who live as free humans in the physical realm but desire a deeper, fuller experience of liberty. The words are also written for the spiritually curious—the researchers and wayfarers who value themselves spiritually but may have yet to consider how to achieve physical freedom or may be intimidated by some of the darker aspects of our five sense reality that need to be overcome.

We would also like to make it clear that this book is not meant to be the final word on ANY of the topics discussed. Rather, we hope to broach the conversation and spark healthy debate about how far one should take their desire for freedom. None of the ideas expressed should be taken as arguments for a monopoly or a "*one size fits all*" model of freedom.

In the *New Libertarian Manifesto*, Samuel E. Konkin III, founder of Agorism, wrote:

> "*There is no One Way, one straight line graph to Liberty, to be sure. But there is a family of graphs, a Space filled with lines, which will take the libertarian to his goal of the free society, and that Space can be described.*"

There are a variety of excuses that are commonly used to justify the existence of governments and the involuntary relationships they have with their subjects. The vast majority of these excuses are based on the idea that humanity is psychologically incapable of peaceful self-governance, and too greedy or self-interested to allocate the resources needed for community services and social safety nets. To make the situation even more complicated, these limiting ideas are unwittingly reinforced by activists who set out to fight the system. By voting or petitioning the ruling class for changes, these activists' efforts are used as an example that the people are apparently free to redress their grievances and thus they are free. The structures of power have faced with riots, political campaigns and peaceful protests for centuries, and while these strategies can sometimes achieve short-term goals, they rarely create lasting changes. The ruling class has a time-tested playbook for subverting these efforts, demonizing activists, and channeling the public attention in a direction that suits their agenda. The "powers-that-wish-they-were" know how to deal with the traditional threats, but they don't know how to deal with obsolescence. Millions of people support the paternalistic relationship that the ruling class takes with the rest of society and believe they are getting a fair deal because they are not emotionally ready for the responsibility that comes with a life of freedom. Furthermore, many people recognize that their neighbors are not ready either, which means that many of us do not even have sufficient trust in one another to believe a free society is possible. So long as people are unhealthy (mentally, physically, and spiritually) and dependent on the ruling class, they will continue to give their energy, support, and, sometimes, their lives to the establishment. A psychologically healthy population that has its needs met elsewhere would not support a ruling class which works against its best interests. This is why it is important to strike at the root of our oppression, by empowering those around us.

We believe that The Conscious Resistance—the coupling of self—governance with a sense of self-reflection—is the best path towards the goal of a free society.

Chapter 2
Explorative Agnosticism

M odern culture is defined by the experience of the five sense world. Experiences we can physically quantify and measure set the parameters of reality. Without a doubt, there are phenomena that can be observed and proven by the five senses. Also, there are concepts in this world that are objective. Still, this does not necessarily mean that everyone shares one uniform consensus on the nature of reality.

There is a vast world beyond our five senses. Despite a lack of understanding of what this world beyond the five senses is composed of, there is a mountain of evidence that proves it exists. It is better for everyone to personally interpret what lies beyond the five senses and respect the interpretations of others instead of fighting over something that will not likely be proven in our lifetime.

When pursuing a spiritual path, even if an individual's intuition isn't *real* or *true* in the quantifiable sense, the experience they are having and the information they bring back from their journey—even if it is simply a journey into the deepest reaches of their own mind—can still provide value and facilitate positive growth in this world.

That being said, it appears the most logical spiritual path to take is an agnostic one. Before we go forward, it is important to define some of these terms, especially "*spirituality*" and "*agnosticism*."

We define Spirituality as:

"An individual's personal set of beliefs about the great mysteries of life and the world beyond the five senses."

Traditionally, the idea of spirituality has been attached to the concept of religion. However, "*spirituality*" and "*religion*" actually represent two entirely different philosophies. A religion is a one-size-fits-all worldview with a hierarchy, a set of rules, and often, a priest class to enforce it all.

Spirituality is a free and personal interpretation or connection with a spirit realm, higher power, or whatever that person wants to call it. Spirituality is a practice that brings an individual closer to their essence, where essence means a set of attributes that make an object, "what it is." To use a comparison, anarchy is to statism as spirituality is to religion. Anarchy is the physical manifestation of freedom, and spirituality is a mental manifestation of freedom. In contrast, statism is control in the physical sense, and religion is control in the mental or spiritual sense.

The organized religions of the world have caused untold suffering and manufactured wars around the world. They have spread propaganda, instigated genocide, and justified slavery. These facts cannot be ignored. However, despite these flaws, the major religions have much to teach us. All of the world's religious teachings, from those that border on historical fact to those that are obviously myths, contain a wealth of knowledge that should be considered.

As Aristotle said, *"It is the mark of an educated mind to be able to entertain a thought without accepting it."*

Different cultures have different belief structures based on the lessons taught in their particular region of the Earth, yet every religion tells essentially the same story, using different words to accommodate whichever culture the tale originates.

In the following chapters, we delve into the history of specific religions and their roots in anti-authoritarian teachings. We are not advocating these religions nor are we excusing the political organizations that represent them. We also do not seek to judge anyone who participates in these religions. In fact, we hope to communicate that many religions are rooted in the same spirit of anti-authoritarianism and can coexist peacefully.

We hold the perspective that religious organizations have taken legitimate ancient spiritual teachings and corrupted them with their own political ideologies. This is why many religions seem to have the same basic truths but also much of the same poison and disinformation. A positive spiritual philosophy usually turns into a violent control mechanism when it is corrupted by an authority figure. It is at this point that everything changes: The goals are no longer to discover powerful truths but to fear the future and cling to the past in order to serve some master.

At our current stage of evolution, we have about the same chance of understanding the spirit realm as a goldfish has of understanding quantum physics, so it's absolutely insane for us to be killing each other in the name of God. At the heart of this ignorance is fear—fear our oppressors have stirred up and manipulated for many generations. They have preyed upon our natural fears of the unknown, of change, and of death while only giving us fractions of information about our existence.

We can now look back throughout history and see that most wars and crusades in the name of religion were actually wars over land, resources, and empire expansion. The rulers of the time used their subjects' deep fear of God to manipulate them into going on crusades, just as our rulers today use fear tactics to con us into fighting and dying in wars. Like pawns on a chessboard, men and women are sent out to war by an almighty authority who believes they are expendable. This kind of senseless carnage is still taking place without much questioning from the public. Insignificant differences among common people of all nations are still used by those in power for the sake of conquest. Regardless of whether those differences are based on religion, race, economic status or culture, they are used as justifications to commit atrocities.

Technically speaking, agnosticism is the perspective that supernatural matters cannot be proved or disproved. Agnosticism is defined by Webster's dictionary as

```
the view that any ultimate reality (as God) is unknown
and probably unknowable; broadly

: one who is not committed to believing in either the
existence or the nonexistence of God or a god
```

Historically, agnostics have chosen to stay away from supernatural topics altogether. The position we advocate in this book takes a more hands-on approach. We believe there is wisdom and self-discovery to be gained from seeking to understand and participate in the world beyond the five senses.

Explorative Agnosticism is strongly different from atheism because there is no claim of truth beyond the five senses, and there is no expectation as to what other people believe. While atheism claims to be a non-religion, some of its loudest advocates seem as concerned with evangelism as born-again Christians. Militant atheists are very intent on changing people's minds about whether anything lies beyond the five senses and will often form their opinions of others based on whether they believe in a higher power. The same can be said of fundamentalists of any faith. This, of course, does not apply to all atheists. A fundamentalist of any religion will claim their perception is superior, so this is surely a view held by some atheists. Without a doubt, some atheists act in the same manner as dogmatic true believers of any other religion.

Agnostics, on the other hand, feel it doesn't really matter what people believe about anything that goes on beyond the five senses because none of it can be proven. There is no expectation of what others should believe, and there is no personal investment in philosophical conversations. While mainstream religions and even modern atheist philosophies rely on the masses for validation, agnostics' personal connection with nature, the universe or god(s) is validated only by their own intuition and doesn't depend upon the approval of others. Following that same standard, there is no need to take a role in validating or judging others as long as they commit no physical transgressions. Agnostic atheists may have their own atheistic beliefs but also understand that their beliefs are just as fallible as an ancient myth.

We find agnosticism to be the most logical position to hold. However, this does not mean that the realm of the supernatural is not worth exploring.

This is why the term "Explorative Agnosticism" is so important to this discussion. While supernatural phenomena cannot be measured or proven, exploration of these realms is a worthwhile quest and necessary for the advancement of our species on this planet.

Of course, we cannot define what supernatural realms look or feel like or how an individual should interpret them. We are simply advocating an open-minded approach to the information presented in this book. While we understand and value rational thinking and logic, we also understand that sometimes humans are better served by intuition and imagination. In fact, humans are best served when there is a balance of these two polarities.

It is in the world of imagination, creation, self-reflection and deep connection to the non-physical that rational thinking often proves insufficient. You might experience a transcendental state of meditation leading to insight about your path, but the rational side of your brain may tell you to disregard gnosis gained from such states of *"incoherence."*

Perhaps you participate in a sweat lodge and drumming ceremony and find yourself carried away on a cloud to a distant location to communicate with animal spirits. Logic may tell you to disregard these experiences as nothing more than irrelevant dreams or outright fabrications.

We, however, believe it is not up to the collective to decide what is *"real"* and valuable for another person in their experience on their path.

To illustrate this, we like to imagine four individuals standing in a meadow witnessing the scene from four different perspectives. We could call these perspectives the objective, subjective, symbolic, and holistic.

In the Objective world, you might notice the physical aspects of the scene. The colors of the plants, soil and sky, the square footage, the variety of plant life, and so on. In this world, the fundamental belief or assumption is that everything is separate.

From the Subjective world, one may have an understanding of the interdependence of the natural world and the mutually supportive roles played by all its elements and creatures. This Subjective world is a deeper experience than the Objective world where you may be able to commune with plants and animals. The fundamental assumption in this world is that everything is connected.

Looking from the meadow of Symbolic perspective, you are now seeing nature as a representation of yourself. The open meadow is your openness to life, and you may feel called to express yourself artistically with this symbolic perspective. You come to know that everything is a part of a pattern and exists in relationship to something else—and that everything means what you decide it means. In this world, you know that everything is symbolic.

From the Holistic world, you have transcended from standing in front of the meadow and observing it to becoming one with the meadow. Now you are the meadow as the sunlight is shining on your leaves and being turned into energy via photosynthesis. The bees are gathering your pollen as you experience the moment as a flower. You feel the sensation of drinking the nectar as the bee. The fundamental assumption in this realm is that everything is one.

In our view, every individual experience is valid, regardless of the world in which it takes place. Further, what rings true and factual in the Objective World will not be so for those experiencing life from one of the other realms.

Someone stuck in a strictly rational, materialist, reductionist mindset will not understand the reality experienced by someone operating in a more intuitive state.

Lastly, it's important to remember that the biggest obstacle to successfully moving between these worlds—thus improving our ability to communicate with a wide range of people—is interference of critical analysis from other levels.

This is the frontal lobe, the analytical part of you that is difficult to quiet during meditation. This is the part of you that will likely doubt the legitimacy of self-reflection and might tell you "This silly hippy stuff isn't going to do anything for you! You should stop reading now!"

In order to gain a better understanding of ourselves, our world, and what it means to be a free human being, we must practice removing our assumptions and doubts. We recommend remembering this when moving between worlds, whether physical or ethereal. From this standpoint, we believe Exploitative Agnosticism to be a beneficial position.

As free people, our beliefs about the world should not be limited or controlled by the collective. As such, we do not care if others doubt or deny our beliefs because we make no effort to doubt or demean their beliefs about the spiritual, non-physical world. Quite simply, our interpretations of the world beyond the five senses are not dependent on any one person, institution, or book.

If we are to know ourselves as spiritually liberated beings, we must open our hearts and minds to the possibilities that wait outside the quantifiable world.

Chapter 3
Reality Beyond the 5 Senses: Beyond Logic, Beyond Reason

The religion of materialism is the dogma that rules modern popular culture and the realm of mainstream science. The Materialist believes only that which we can see, touch, smell, taste, feel and measure quantifies reality. The materialist also believes that any discussion of what lies beyond the five senses is foolish and not worthy of consideration. This worldview is shaped by the unproven assumptions of mainstream science, which is important not to confuse with the scientific method.

The scientific method describes a process of experimentation in which theories are tested and either proven or disproved. This is a great concept that helps us to better understand the five-sense world of matter, but the political establishment that we know today as mainstream science is no longer rooted in the scientific method. Instead, it has arguably become a new religion. However, there is a blind spot in this point of view. Much to the dismay of materialists, science has many times helped humans unveil the world of superstition by confirming truths that were once opposed by the scientific establishment.

Many of the experiments carried out today in government labs begin with their conclusions pre-planned, and many topics are entirely off-limits for scientists to explore. For example, it is taboo for an archeologist or anthropologist to present an alternative view of history with their scientific findings. Scientists have dismissed researchers like John Anthony West and Graham Hancock, who presented evidence that the mainstream view of Egyptian history was entirely misdated and incorrect.

These researchers had significant evidence that many structures in Egypt date back much farther than scientists initially projected. Mainstream science dates the construction of the Sphinx to around 10,000 years ago, while West and Hancock proved that certain significant weathering on the structures must have occurred at least 30,000 years ago. Despite this ground-breaking discovery, mainstream science rejected their evidence because it didn't fit in with the official narrative.

Another rebel who has been challenging the unproven assumptions of materialism is scientist Rupert Sheldrake. Sheldrake courageously conducts his own independent experiments, based in the scientific method, that set out to explore areas that are too 'weird' or taboo for mainstream science to take seriously.

One of Sheldrake's experiments provided compelling evidence that many pet owners have a telepathic connection with their animals. In the experiment, dogs were observed waiting for their owners to come home. Every dog would become excited moments before they received any physical indication that their owner was nearby. Sheldrake would have the owners take different ways home at different times of the day, drive different cars, take the bus, walk, and wear different shoes or an unfamiliar aftershave or perfume, etc. This ruled out the possibility that the dogs were simply using their heightened sense of smell or hearing. Regardless of how the experiment was framed, the animals were always able to sense when their owners were coming home. While this does not definitively prove a telepathic connection, it does show a strong connection between humans and animals, which suggests that this is a point of view at least worth considering.

Sheldrake also assembled some compelling evidence for the case of crop circles. Crop circles are patterns created by flattening crops. While the mainstream view is that they are a hoax perpetrated by two hoaxers, there is much more to the story. In a brilliant experiment, Sheldrake hoped to gauge how talented human crop circle artists actually were. If it were possible to see the best job a human could do with a crop circle, then it would be much easier to deduce whether other random crop circles had been created by a human hand or some other technology. To get to the bottom of this question, Sheldrake hosted a contest with a massive cash prize for the best crop circle, and participants entered from around the world. Though they created incredibly elaborate crop circles, they were still not as elaborate as others that have been recorded in the countryside around the world.

Another field we feel the scientific establishment needs to catch up with is the idea of reincarnation, or remembrance of past life experiences. Traditional thought says that when a human body expires, so does the conscious experience. However, there is abundant anecdotal evidence indicating that children are sometimes born with memories of formerly lived lives.

Take, for example, the story of James Leininger. James is the focus of the book *Soul Survivor: The Reincarnation of a World War II Fighter Pilot*. The book discusses how Leininger began having nightmares, recalling violent scenes of planes being shot down and his own ensuing death. He was only two years old when these nightmares began. Leininger's parents say he would draw incredibly detailed pictures of battle scenes complete with fighter jets from America and an enemy that seemed to be Japanese.

James's parents began searching for clues as to what their son was speaking about and whether or not he was experiencing some type of mental delusion. The two-year-old child exhibited an uncommon knowledge of the mechanics of World War II planes and would even detail memories of what he said was a past life as James, WWII fighter pilot.

After researching some of James's claims, his parents were able to confirm the names of several people he said he had fought alongside. Eventually, the family learned that James Leininger somehow had detailed memories of James Huston, a fighter pilot who crashed into the ocean near Iwo Jima after being fired upon by the Japanese. When asked for specifics about his memories, the young child was able to identify his ship as the Natoma. James Leininger also correctly identified the name of Jack Larsen, a friend of Huston's and the pilot who was flying next to Huston when he was shot down.

Upon meeting veterans of the USS Natoma Bay, James Leininger was able to recite specific names and places from the war. The Leininger family went even further and contacted the family of James Huston. James met the sister of James Huston and told a story of a painting done by Huston's mother. This painting had not been seen by anyone other than the Huston's deceased mother and the siblings. Huston's remaining family was amazed at the detail the young boy was able to recall nearly 60 years after James Huston had died.

Jim Tucker, a professor of psychiatry and neurobehavioral sciences at the University of Virginia, has studied over 2,500 cases of children who report memories of past lives. In a January 2014 interview with *National Public Radio*, Tucker described the difficulty in fitting these phenomena into a strictly materialist worldview:

"I think it's very difficult to just map these cases onto a materialist understanding of reality. I mean, if physical matter, if the physical world is all there is, then I don't know how you can accept these cases and believe in them. But I think there are good reasons to think that consciousness can be considered a separate entity from physical reality."

Tucker references Max Planck, the father of quantum theory. Planck believed consciousness was fundamental and that matter was derived from it. This could indicate that consciousness and superconsciousness, or experiences of higher consciousness, are not necessarily dependent on a physical body or brain.

So, what exactly is consciousness? Before we delve deeper into expanding on consciousness, we should take a moment to define the word, as we have defined other key terms.

Consciousness is defined as:

: the condition of being conscious : the normal state of being awake and able to understand what is happening around you

: a person's mind and thoughts

: knowledge that is shared by a group of people

As we have noted, the mainstream view of science operates from a place of ignorance when it comes to what consciousness is or where it resides. The accepted dogma is: Matter is life, and anything beyond the physically measurable world is irrelevant to scientific pursuits.

Rather than ignoring or condemning that which is unknown by the scientific community or the rational mind, we believe in remaining open to the endless possibilities.

The topic of consciousness is a highly contentious field. Beyond just what and where consciousness is, there are also questions of animal and plant consciousness that we will explore in more detail later.

One area where spirit and science align is the topic of quartz crystals. Quartz crystals are often used in *"New Age"* circles for trading, ceremony, and, some believe, healing. Though a rational person may dismiss these trinkets as fantasy, they have both a scientific and cultural relevance. There are several types of quartz crystals. These include amethyst, citrine, rose, smoky, and clear quartz. The crystals are composed of silicon dioxide molecules and other "impurities." Crystals containing only silicon dioxide are known as clear quartz. The atoms within crystals vibrate at a stable frequency, making them excellent receptors and emitters of electromagnetic waves.

Quartz crystals are piezoelectric, meaning they can turn energy from one form into another when pressure is applied. When mechanical pressure is applied to a quartz crystal, it vibrates, producing a voltage that can be converted from mechanical forces into electrical signals. Quartz crystals have been used in many common items, including radios, watches, sonar and ultrasonic generators, and hearing aids. They can also be used to make glass, mortar, grindstones, sandpaper, and cleaning compounds.

One of the first people to recognize the uses of quartz was Nobel prize winner Marcel Vogel. Vogel was a research scientist for IBM when he discovered that crystals can be programmed as silicon chips in a computer. He came to believe that crystals could be programmed through thought.

He wrote that thoughts are a form of energy that can be directed through intentions. Specifically, he created devices that he told allowed users to program their intentions onto a crystal and then transfer them to water. He likened the process to the way an inductor in electronics creates an energy field in components in proximity to the field. Despite, or perhaps because of, his prolific work and extreme foresight, his work was denounced as pseudoscience.

We now know that Quartz has a place in both the modern scientific and mechanical worlds. However, scientists and mechanics were not the first to acknowledge the power of crystals. Quartz crystals have been popular for centuries—and possibly millennia—with indigenous peoples around the world. Amazonian shamans and healers communicate with spirits they believe live within the crystals. In his book, *The Cosmic Serpent*, anthropologist Jeremy Narby writes about the use of crystals by indigenous peoples and a possible relation to DNA. Narby discusses how Australian Aborigines believe life was created by *"the Rainbow Snake,"* symbolized by quartz crystals. He also mentions the Desana of the Amazon, who believe an anaconda created life. They symbolize the creator with a quartz crystal.

Narby goes on to inquire about how these varied cultures, separated by time and space, could have possibly come to such similar conclusions. He suggests that these cultures may have been aware, from their perspective and understanding, of what modern science and its tools of measurement have yet to discover. Perhaps, he proposes, the spirits communicating with these cultures using hallucinogenic plants and altered states of mind was a form of direct communication with DNA, what Narby calls the Cosmic Serpent.

DNA itself has a historical connection to crystals. In the modern scientific community, Erwin Schrödinger was the first physicist to propose the idea that an aperiodic crystal contains genetic information. DNA had already been discovered, but its helical structure and role in reproduction had not. Schrödinger proposed the existence of a hereditary material responsible for all life. He called this an aperiodic crystal, which, unlike a standard crystal, does not repeat itself and can produce an infinite number of possibilities with limited atoms.

These examples offer starkly different viewpoints on what crystals and DNA are—and what purpose they serve. Different cultures and researchers from vastly different backgrounds, using tools both modern and archaic, physical and intuitive, arrive at similar conclusions. They are unable to recognize the similarity of their discoveries due to an experiential barrier. The information could be identical, yet the presentation and reception of the information are dependent on the one receiving said information.

As Narby noticed while living among indigenous communities in Brazil, the objective mind often cannot rationalize or fathom that which has not yet been uncovered. He spoke of the importance of de-focalizing the gaze, and specifically, he learned to take the word of the natives he worked with, regardless if what they said made objective sense. He spoke of "*objectifying one's own objectifying relationship,*" or "*becom[ing] aware of one's own gaze.*" We should remember this valuable lesson as we consider information that may be beyond our current understanding or comprehension.

Chapter 4
Towards Panarchism: Anarchy Without Adjectives

Since "anarchy" is one of the most maligned and misunderstood words in the English language, we are going to use a concise definition that gets straight to the point. Simply put, anarchy is a social arrangement in which there are no "rulers." A ruler is defined as a person who claims nonconsensual authority over another life. Anarchy is a lived experience which lacks oppression from state or corporate power, as well as oppressive and manipulative behaviors which happen in our interpersonal relationships. Anarchism is the school of political thought which attempts to uncover methods to achieve this goal via economic, social, and political means.

Sadly, there cannot be a master without a slave, and by the nature of the relationship, the slave is physically and morally obligated to obey the commands of the master. Many people believe this relationship is the stitch that holds the fabric of civilized society together, while in reality, nothing has caused more pain and suffering in this world than corrupt authority and the concept of rulers and slaves.

These social relationships are the manifestations of the internal struggles that exist within us. The relationships between rulers and slaves, kings and subjects, and even presidents and citizens do not exist in reality. They are mental constructs that allow some people to harm and openly take advantage of others while maintaining moral superiority. This is far more dangerous than the relationship of a common criminal to his victims. When someone holds you at gunpoint and takes your wallet you see the criminal, you have a direct experience of being robbed and threatened.

However, when someone attacks from a position of authority with perceived moral justification, their crimes will go unpunished, and their power will be amplified as a result. This is why police brutality and government corruption have been a part of every civilization since before ancient Rome. The relationship of authority breeds and encourages corruption.

That being said, to achieve anarchy—or the abolition of masters and slaves—the solution is far more complicated than simply having a revolution and taking on the current establishment in physical combat, though some argue this will be a part of the process. This has been attempted many times before, and each time power has shifted hands, but the cycle of violence and slavery has continued.

This cycle has been in constant repetition for generations. While power has

Derrick **Broze** · John **Vibes**

shifted hands over time, little has changed about how our species views the world, how we view one another, or how we view ourselves as individuals. This is not by mistake. Mountains of propaganda have been released over the centuries to reinforce the old ways and to keep people from thinking outside of the box.

Thankfully, there were many brave philosophers and revolutionaries who recognized this dynamic and worked to construct a philosophy of anti-authoritarianism, which came to be known as *"anarchism."* The earliest anarchist-themed writings can be found in Lao-Tzu from the 6th century and there are those who believe Christ was an anarchist or at the least, an anti-authoritarian.

More recently, William Godwin, a writer in France during the 1790s, is said to have been the first philosophical anarchist with his book *Political Justice*. The first person to publicly proclaim himself an anarchist was Pierre-Joseph Proudhon with the publication of his seminal work *What Is Property?* in 1840.[1]

In the mid-1800s in America, anarchism was taking roots in the abolition movement. Many abolitionists recognized that slavery and government were essentially the same thing and that slavery will exist in one form or another, so long as government exists. One of the main pioneers in American anarchist thought was outspoken entrepreneur and abolitionist Lysander Spooner.

Unlike many other anarchist philosophers in Europe, Spooner's breed of anarchism was strictly individualistic with a strong emphasis on markets and property rights. Spooner was extremely critical of collectivist ideas like democracy and constitutionalism, so his work was heavily focused on deconstructing these concepts and exposing them as deceptive forms of oppression.

Spooner thought of a way to put his philosophy into action by creating his own businesses that would directly compete with government services. One of his most ground-breaking entrepreneurial achievements was forming the *"American Letter Company,"* a letter and package delivery business that competed with the US Postal Service and proved that people didn't need the government to deliver mail. More than a hundred years later, this strategy was identified by Samuel Edward Konkin III as *"agorism,"* a philosophy of non-compliance that uses underground markets as a means of making the state obsolete. We will be exploring the potential of agorism throughout this book.

As with many other popular schools of thought, anarchism has evolved and even splintered off over the years in various directions, creating various sub-sects within the philosophy. In the 1870s, Europe saw a great divide between anarcho-communists and anarcho-collectivists. Around the same time,

---

1. For a thorough examination of the history of international anarchist thought see Robert Graham's three-part anthology, *Anarchism: A Documentary History of Libertarian Ideas* and *No Gods, No Masters: An Anthology of Anarchism* by Daniel Guerin, and for the American Anarchist's read *Men Against the State*.

American anarchists were debating the pros and cons of individualist and anarcho-communist thought. As a result, anarchist philosophers in Europe and America began calling for "anarchism without adjectives," which was essentially an acceptance of all those who believe in self-governance and a lack of coercion regardless of their particular economic solution.

Most recently, the libertarian activist and writer Karl Hess discussed the need for what he called "*Anarchism Without Hyphens.*" Hess was well known for working in and out of political circles with anarchists on both the left and the right. In 1980, he outlined his argument for anarchy without hyphens:

"There is only one kind of anarchists. Not two. Just one. An anarchist, the only kind, as defined by the long tradition and literature of the position itself, is a person in opposition to authority imposed through the hierarchical power of the state. The only expansion of this that seems to me to be reasonable is to say that an anarchist stands in opposition to any imposed authority.

"An anarchist is a voluntarist.

"Now, beyond that, anarchists also are people and, as such, contain the billion-faceted varieties of human reference. Some are anarchists who march, voluntarily, to the Cross of Christ. Some are anarchists who flock, voluntarily, to the communities of beloved, inspirational father figures. Some are anarchists who seek to establish the syndics of voluntary industrial production. Some are anarchists who voluntarily seek to establish the rural production of the kibbutzim. Some are anarchists who, voluntarily, seek to disestablish everything including their own association with other people, the hermits. Some are anarchists who deal, voluntarily, only in gold, will never cooperate, and swirl their capes. Some are anarchists who, voluntarily, worship the sun and its energy, build domes, eat only vegetables, and play the dulcimer. Some are anarchists who worship the power of algorithms, play strange games, and infiltrate strange temples. Some are anarchists who only see the stars. Some are anarchists who only see the mud.

"They spring from a single seed, no matter the flowering of their ideas. The seed is liberty. And that is all it is. It is not a socialist seed. It is not a capitalist seed. It is not a mystical seed. It is not a determinist seed. It is simply a statement. We can be free. After that it's all choice and chance.

"Anarchism, liberty, does not tell you a thing about how free people will behave or what arrangements they will make. It simply says that people have the capacity to make arrangements.

"Anarchism is not normative. It does not say how to be free. It says only that freedom, liberty, can exist."

We understand that because of its anti-capitalist roots, many anarchist thinkers on the left might say that anarchism without adjectives or hyphens remains anti-capitalist and thus schools of thought like anarcho-capitalism should be excluded. On the other hand, there are many market anarchists and anarcho-capitalists who point to the coercion that is inherent in democracy and authoritarian socialism, showing that these ideas are essentially nothing more than government. In short, among anarcho-capitalists and anarcho-communists, there is a great deal of debate about who is a "real anarchist" and who is not.

There is truth in both of these viewpoints. Although market activity is peaceful and voluntary, the social system that has traditionally been called *"capitalism"* is far from a free and voluntary market. Capitalism has used state power as its primary mechanism of operation, so it is not fair to associate this term with a free and open market. Likewise, most traditional democratic and socialist societies have been ruled by a very few rich people despite the notion that these systems are created for and by the common people. Even the more egalitarian democratic societies sometimes fall victim to the tyranny of the majority as citizens are forced to live at the whim of their neighbors and change their lives because a vote was held in their community or country. Entire populations of free humans are made subjects of the majority, regardless of their opinion.

Capitalism, communism, and socialism are all loaded terms that have so many different definitions to different people that they are nearly impossible to communicate about. There is no hope in "saving" or "reclaiming" any of these words. They have been tainted by state influence for generations, searing their assumed definitions into the minds of billions of people.

In advocating for an entirely new and different way of life, using the names of old social systems and old ways of doing things seems counterproductive. Of course, there is value in bringing the old terms into the conversation for the sake of comparison, but social philosophies by the names of capitalism and socialism have been around for centuries and have ultimately been government-based economic systems.

For us, the definition given by Kevin Carson, author of *The Iron Fist of the Invisible Hand: Corporate Capitalism as a State Guaranteed System of Privilege*, best defines the rise of Capitalism over the centuries:

"[I]ndustrial capitalism, to the same extent as manorialism or slavery, was founded on force. Like its predecessors (crony) capitalism could not have survived at any point in its history without state intervention.

Coercive state measures at every step have denied workers access to capital, forced them to sell their labor in a buyer's market, and protected the centers of economic power from the dangers of the free market. To quote Benjamin Tucker again, landlords and capitalists cannot extract surplus value from labor without help of the state. The modern worker, like the slave or the serf, is the victim of ongoing robbery; he works in an enterprise built from past stolen labor."

In that sense, we are against crony capitalism, or the state's subsidization and protection of business interactions. This is, of course, because states require force and theft to maintain control. On the other hand, we are also against involuntary democracy and forced socialism, where people are forced into associations with others because they happen to share the same geography.

Many pioneers of the anarcho-capitalist philosophy have made strong arguments for the importance and morality of markets, property, and trade, bringing a new perspective to the growing culture of anarchism. To be certain, the anarcho-capitalists have been rejected by most left-wing anarchists and are not seen as a proper part of anarchist history. Regardless, the anti-state ancaps deserves some mention.

Economist Murray Rothbard coined the term *"anarcho-capitalism"* in 1949 or 1950. Rothbard's writing on banking, property rights, and the history of war was ground-breaking and highly academic, but he did not have the same knack for public relations and marketing as he did for economics and history.

Rothbard had some valuable ideas, but he also had some blind spots when it came to social issues and the problem of poverty. For a self-proclaimed capitalist, he wasn't really the best salesperson either, as the marketing strategy for his philosophy combined the two most hated words in the English language. Rothbard also made several strategic mistakes throughout his career, namely teaming up with politicians and Washington lobbyists with the hope of changing the system from the inside.

The most inspiring work done by Murray Rothbard was during his time collaborating with the emerging radical New Left and the burgeoning American Libertarian movement. In the 1950s and 60s Rothbard worked with student groups as he spread his specific anti-state philosophy. In the late 1960s Rothbard worked with Karl Hess on the Journal of Left and Right, which was an active publication focusing on issues that concerned the radical students from left and right. Eventually, Rothbard would sour on a left-right anarchist alliance and move further to the right. This move would set the tone for the American Libertarian movement for the coming decades. From our perspective, Rothbard's downfall was his later focus on paleoconservatism, which would also poison the roots of the American Libertarian Party by closing off many of its followers to the wide spectrum of anti-authoritarian ideas that exist to the left of Rothbard.

While both of us have definitely learned from our experiences working with Rothbard's material and his supporters, and would recommend his work for a full picture of anarchist thought, we ultimately believe his decision to abandon unity with anti-authoritarians outside of the ring-wing sphere laid the foundation for further division between anarchists that still exists to this day.

Rothbard's work was built primarily upon the work of Ludwig Von Mises, the founder of what came to be known as the Austrian School of economics.

Mises was not explicitly an anarchist, and he too, had no problem forming alliances with aristocrats and politicians. However, the work he did throughout his life explained exactly how market activity could make the state obsolete. Rothbard later applied these ideas to his anarchist philosophy.

Today, there are anarchist economists of all varieties who devote years of research to developing stateless solutions and voluntary ways to provide goods, services, and charity. Meanwhile, there are many mutualists and anarcho-syndicalists who are working to tackle some of the pre-existing state influences that create widespread inequality in our world, and they are finding ways to run worker-owned cooperatives.

Modern anarchists are split into different camps which are based mostly on different perspectives of property. We feel there is something to learn when considering each side of this debate. Anarchists who oppose the concept of owning property often point to governments' enforcement of property titles and the huge disparity of land ownership in the world and argue that property is a tool of oppression. They make valid points about the need to reconsider how to deal with property in a free society, and the disparities that exist in our world today, but they do not adequately make the case for ruling out property as a concept altogether.

In today's economic atmosphere, property rights understandably have a negative stigma due to the offensive amount of government-protected land and resources that have been acquired through force, theft, fraud, and coercion. This is an understandable objection, but since the property was illegitimately acquired, it should legally be considered stolen property. The insane amount of land that is unjustly owned by the royal families and governments of the world creates the illusion of scarcity of land when there is actually abundance. Furthermore, it is virtually impossible for such small groups of people to control and maintain such large areas of land unless they have a large-scale military or police force.

The problems in wealth disparity we see today do not indicate a problem with property as a concept, but they do indicate that the control of property is being used as a method of systematic oppression. The fact that the aristocracy unjustly controls much of the world's land today shows that mass reparations and restitution are in order, but it does not make a case for the abolition of property altogether. This lack of nuance has left economic discourse among anarchists stagnant for decades, and this problem is not limited to the property debate. For example, the state's monopolization of the currency and its centralization of the economy is often held up as evidence that currency itself is a harmful idea, or that economies are inherently oppressive. However, free currencies can be an ethical and efficient way of allocating resources, and economic activity can help to bring abundance to the world's impoverished people.

It is typically said that economies wouldn't exist without governments, but quite the opposite is true, the economy functions very much in spite of government. A world of abundance could be created if the spontaneous order of human interaction were to be allowed to flourish freely, but our society creeps further towards total control. Despite all this control, it is still impossible for any one central organization to have the necessary information to successfully "run" an economy. Also, at the end of the day you don't own anything if the state and their criminal thugs can come take it from you. If you must pay rent (property taxes) for the rest of your life, you do not own it.

Our views on property have become more refined in the five years since the first printing of this book, but they are essentially the same. We believe that the concept of private property in the modern world has value, but it is also worth exploring how the control of property has been used to perpetuate systems of oppression. Essentially, the idea is that in a society which accepts the principles of self-ownership and personal responsibility it follows that what a person produces with their body or obtains via voluntary and consensual agreements is an extension of them. It is their private property. We believe protecting and defending such private property is legitimate. However, the more time we have spent connecting with indigenous teachings and learning from our elders, the more we understand that the concept of property is a modern illusion, a construct of modern men who seek to divide up the earth to profit off of it. We do not believe there is a way to "go back" to pre-private property times or to reclaim the practices of our ancestors, but it is possible to reimagine our concept of property without these corruptions.

Despite the many differences between the various anarchist philosophies, there is actually a lot of common ground to explore — if only each side engaged in polite conversations on the issues at hand. For example, a great opportunity exists in studying the similarities between the philosophies of agorism and mutualism.

Mutualism is the school of thought that seeks to give individuals, rather than the state, control over a piece of the means of production. In *The Practicability of Mutualism*, Clarence Lee Swartz writes, *"Mutualism is a social system based on reciprocal and non-invasive relations among free individuals. The Mutualist standards are*

- *Individual: Equal Freedom for each — without invasion of others*

- *Economic: Untrammeled reciprocity, freedom of exchange and contract — without monopoly or privilege*

- *Social: Complete freedom of voluntary associations — without coercive organization"*

Mutualist economies might manifest as mutual credit banks or worker-owned cooperative farms.

Agorism is the philosophy of creating alternative institutions to directly compete with the state. Samuel Konkin III called for participation in Counter-Economics, or economic activity that is typically seen as illegal or unregulated by the state. This includes competing currencies, community gardening schemes, tax resistance, and operating businesses without licenses. Agorism also extends to the creation of alternative education programs, free schools or skill shares, and independent media ventures. Also essential to agorism is support of entrepreneurs who actively do business outside of the state's license and regulations.

The agorist-mutualist alliance represents an opportunity for anarchists of all stripes to focus on common ground and build institutions that can help us live free now. Both philosophies reject non-defensive violence, politics, and monopolies. Neither philosophy wishes to use the force of the state or some "*dictatorship of the proletariat*" to meet their goals. Both philosophies support the experimentation of a variety of communities working outside the state to create institutions that give our brothers and sisters who remain in the state's grasp another option outside the corporate-state monopoly.

The concept of creating alternative institutions does not end with the economy. We would do well to support alternative forms of food production, community defense, education, governance, media, and open-source technologies, as well, all of which give the people a choice that extends outside the state and weakens its power over time.

The concept of homesteading is often an area of common ground between anarchists who disagree on the subject of property. With the concept of direct homesteading, property belongs to whoever is living in or making use of a piece of land or property. If homesteading had been applied to slave plantations in colonial America, the slaves would technically be considered part owners of the plantation or each would own an individual piece of the plantation because they were the ones physically living and working on the land. Claiming large areas of land by planting flags or drawing lines on a map is not a legitimate way to homestead property, but it is how much of the property in the world was claimed. This is an especially important concept because it is a nonviolent way of ensuring that there is some kind of natural limit on how much space one person can control.

There is value in all anti-authoritarian literature and philosophy, though each side of the argument also has numerous blind spots. We believe in panarchy, which can be defined as the ability to freely decide which government's laws and jurisdiction you choose to live under. It also indicates an acceptance of all the anarchist schools of thought (and their potential economic solutions) as long as they are absent of force.[1] This would allow for all individuals who

1. In 1860, Paul Émile de Puydt published an article with the first exposition of panarchy:

claim their right to self-governance and seek the absence of coercion to break free from the state with other free humans with similar goals. We choose to find common ground with other anarchists to move past the state and then allow for free experimentation with all communities and all economies.

Furthermore, it is important to encourage everyone to accept the idea that people do not need to be forced into associations and relationships with one another because they happen to live in the same area. In some circumstances, it may be necessary to migrate to the same area to create a commune or a type of protected community. However, as long as it is logistically possible for people to arrange themselves peacefully in the same geographical region, they should still be able to subscribe to different views on economics, spirituality, or any other controversial topic that divides people politically. The only common thread that needs to tie communities together is the mutual understanding that they have no right to force their beliefs on anyone else.

Voluntaryism is the idea of mutual non-aggression. You may notice us refer to this term throughout the book. On the surface, voluntaryism is just another word for anarchism. However, it denotes specific philosophical principles that take the definition of anarchism a step further. A voluntaryist not only believes in a world without rulers and slaves but also advocates for a society built on a culture of peace, non-aggression, and a general "*live and let live*" atmosphere.

The Voluntaryist newsletter has defined the philosophy in the following way:

"Voluntaryists are advocates of non-political, non-violent strategies to achieve a free society. We reject electoral politics, in theory and in practice, as incompatible with libertarian principles. Governments must cloak their actions in an aura of moral legitimacy in order to sustain their power, and political methods invariably strengthen that legitimacy. Voluntaryists seek instead to delegitimize the State through education, and we advocate withdrawal of the cooperation and tacit consent on which State power ultimately depends."

When exposed to this philosophy for the first time, people often ask for "proof" of its validity. We are conditioned to having our worldview crafted by sacred tomes written by long-dead authority or hero figures. This is not how freedom works. Waiting to be told what to do by a self-interested authority will never lead to a peaceful society.

As we have briefly discussed in this chapter, the philosophy of freedom is a

---

a political philosophy that emphasizes each individual's right to freely join and leave the jurisdiction of any governments they choose. Puydt wrote that "governmental competition" would let "as many regularly competing governments as have ever been conceived and will ever be invented" exist simultaneously. In 1909, anarchist Max Nettlau revived the concept with his essay, "Panarchy: A Forgotten Idea of 1860." More recently, writers like John Zube and panarchy.org are keeping the concept alive. We suggest reading the panarchy essays from Puydt, Nettlau, and Zube.

giant web of dissenting viewpoints that have continually evolved over generations. There is no ultimate authority on what freedom should or will look like. It is important to remember that these are merely a collection of ideas spread by brave individuals who dared to think differently and stand against the slavery of their times.

However, even though there is an apparent lack of "proof" or official doctrine, the principles of voluntaryism are self-evident in human behavior, human desire, human history, and possibly in the animal kingdom. The vast majority of human beings desire peace. Even the nasty people in the world desire peace for themselves if not for others. Those who want peace and freedom from harm are obligated to allow the same for others. In other words, by placing the expectation of peacefulness on others, you are automatically accepting the obligation not to harm them.

Furthermore, if you harm or threaten another person, you are breaking your end of the bargain and forfeiting your own right to peace, allowing them the moral right to use defensive force against your attacks.

Of course, these expectations and obligations will be broken from time to time, even in a free society. However, the random violence in a free society is manageable on a case-by-case basis, while the systematic violence in today's world—which operates under the color of law and false moral superiority—is far more dangerous because it goes unquestioned. Also, when these obligations are broken, the injured or threatened party is morally justified to defend themselves with force if necessary. Various researchers and economists have studied how things are handled when these rules are broken, and many possible solutions have been suggested. However, these are just predicted solutions; the real solutions will come when millions of minds start working together on these issues and solve problems that stand in their paths. It is through this process of spontaneous order that brilliant solutions will be pulled from the human consciousness.

While the term voluntaryism is only a recent development in the language of freedom, the philosophy it embodies is age-old. As we will explore in later chapters, many of the world's ancient teachings hold this philosophy as their key value.

The Buddha is quoted as saying, "*The wise harm no one. They are masters of their bodies and they go to the boundless country—beyond sorrow.*" In the early teachings of Christianity, these ideas came in the form of the golden rule, or "*Do to others as you would have them do to you.*" In Islam there is "*La ikrah fi deen,*" or no compulsion in religion. This philosophy runs deeply through many of the world's ancient teachings.

Imagine a panarchistic region of the world where voluntaryism is the norm: anarcho-communists, anarcho-capitalists, Muslims, Christians, and free people of all varieties would live among one another, or within a very close geo-graphical distance, with very few issues. Neither side would imagine they have the moral right to use force or threats against people who did them no harm. When members of the community fail to reach a mutual understanding, ide-ally they would not hurt one another, so long as they still lived according to voluntaryist principles. Instead, they could freely disassociate from people who they have conflicts with. Free communities of the near-future will need to understand that the struggle for a freer world is not just one against the physical state, but also a struggle with our idiosyncrasies which can manifest as authoritarian tendencies. This possibility is mentioned because a free so-ciety would not be a utopia, though it may appear to be when compared to what we see today because there would be no such thing as morally justified violence except in defense one's own liberty.

The root of the many traumas, pain and suffering that the human family has both inflicted and endured is almost always morally justified violence. Human sacrifice, genocide, torture, arranged marriages, and all forms of slavery are examples of morally justified violence — violence that someone in authority either allowed or enforced. If we want to affect long-lasting change as freedom seekers, we must challenge the very nature of morally justified violence instead of analyzing the person on the throne and the policies they make.

Chapter 5
Healing the Inner Child Today Will Save the World Tomorrow

When speaking of freedom and enslavement, it's important to acknowledge the abysmal albeit improving, relationship between children and adults. Generations of conditioning have caused many adults to become bitter and hostile. This happens because of generations of parents treating children like wild beasts to be tamed, or slaves to be controlled. It should come as no surprise that these children eventually become adults who emulate this attitude of domination and spend their lives attempting to tame and control the external world.

The bond between parent and child is one of the strongest human relationships, and children have learned valuable life lessons from their families since the beginning of time. Because of this, many authoritarian societies have guided the structure of the family to mold future generations, even before those generations could enter the indoctrination centers we have come to know as public education. The establishment's most effective form of propaganda is the ability to impose their values on impressionable young children through their parents.

Using the methods of propaganda that exist via the media, education systems, and religious institutions, the establishment has created a society where authoritarianism and domination is a part of everyday life. When parents raise their children, they draw from a lifetime of propaganda and feel a great sense of guilt when their child doesn't accept the established norms in society. Children are free and full of spirit. Parents often forget what it's like to be a child and simply don't understand. Their oppressive culture and its abhorrent values have brought them so far away from their spirit that they feel something is wrong if their child does not conform to the establishment's ideals.

This causes some parents to be authoritarian with their children in the hopes of encouraging conformity. What they are really doing is breaking their children's spirits and preparing them to live in an oppressive world and submit to authority. Parents take this aggressive route due to the example that has been set by the established control systems. In our society, it is commonplace for authority figures to be controlling and close-minded. When an individual is treated as a slave rather than a free human, they often tend to behave in the same fashion if they find themselves in a position of authority themselves. Many good people who only want the best for their families put themselves and their children through a lot of pain and turmoil because they believe their child must live a certain way in order to obtain happiness. All of this stress and oppression is often carried out with the best of intentions, but it is with corrupted perceptions that parents are projecting society's ideals onto their children.

Many modern parents aren't passing earthly knowledge and wisdom to their children but are instead passing down a long list of cultural assumptions, idiosyncrasies, and misconceptions. They are passing along the aggressive, materialistic message of the aristocracy, which has been instilled in them through years of propaganda and indoctrination. Even worse is the fact that these false values are instilled through constant emotional—and sometimes physical—abuse. This has resulted in a situation where many children have been psychologically abused. With millions of children experiencing some form of trauma during childhood, is it any surprise that most of the adults in our society behave in such irrational ways?

As the empire's facade crumbles and the middle class disappears, it is becoming more obvious that the ideals of our society are rotten with corruption. It is important that we don't instill the same set of ideals in future generations, or we will be doomed to repeat this cycle of dominance and propaganda yet again. We should be protecting our children from the toxic culture that surrounds us instead of forcing them to conform to it. The values that drive our culture are the reason for a great deal of suffering across the world. These values not only have a detrimental personal impact but also lead other human beings to project the same oppressive, predator energy that is destroying our planet and our species.

Despite the existence of economic inequality, and continuing propaganda aimed at the minds of the youth, each new generation of children generally appear to be more widely respected. This has especially been the case since the 20th century. Physical child abuse, infanticide, pedophilia, and child slavery have been widespread throughout history. However, in the past century or so, society has become more conscious of the value of human life, and those horrors are much less common. Physical child abuse still takes place today, but it is more isolated due to the fear of legal punishment and its recent taboo nature.

There is still a great deal of emotional and psychological abuse that is dished out to most children, even by the most well-intentioned adults. Children are a minority group who remain second-class citizens in the eyes of most of the world. Their actions are scrutinized, their opinions are ignored, and their existence is seen as not much more than a burden. Many adults appear to secretly, and perhaps subconsciously, fear and envy children. This is because the child is a free spirit that represents change, which the adult has been trained to fear. They suppress their fear by attempting to tame and train the child just as they were tamed and trained.

This "taming" process is extremely confusing and traumatizing for the child, but unfortunately, most parents feel that it is their duty to mold their child to obey authority. Not many have questioned the morality or efficiency of this parenting strategy, but it is a question of extreme importance. Our children are the future of this world, and if they are not treated with respect and given freedom, there will never be freedom or respect in our societies. That's not to say that children should be allowed to do whatever they want, but it means that they should not be treated like animals to be trained and controlled.

Our goal here is not to criticize anyone who uses a "mainstream" parenting strategy. Rather, we want to stress the significance of how we treat children and how that is directly related to the kind of adults we see in our society. There is an adage that says, "*The hand that rocks the cradle rules the world.*" This phrase points to why it is so important to reevaluate how we treat young people. In the context of spirituality and social philosophy, it is important to allow a child to choose their own path. Parents can and should teach their children all they know, but should be careful not to take it personally if their children want to explore other social or spiritual philosophies.

Throughout the course of our lives, we develop baggage from the various environments we encounter. We come into this world as pure souls with a clean slate, and as we grow we adopt various beliefs and idiosyncrasies from our culture, which eventually manifest as our personal identities. Whether it is race, class, occupation, or belief structure, people identify with cultural labels and use those labels to build their personal model of reality.

Children see the natural world with a clearer perspective because their perception is not yet clouded by cultural conventions and other prejudices. This is why concepts like money, time, and authority make no sense to children—and rightfully so. These are all man-made cultural abstractions. Young minds are typically condemned in authoritarian societies because they have not yet been corrupted and molded into obedient, mechanized citizens. If the youth of any oppressive nation were given freedom to grow without being indoctrinated into the cultural control system, the whole system could radically transform within a single generation. The establishment's stranglehold on the human race is unnatural, immoral, and insane, which is why their ideals are always met with resistance by the youth culture.

This brings us to the concept of the inner child. In psychology, the inner child is your connection to your childlike behaviors and habits. This includes what a person learns as a young child. The inner child is sometimes imagined as a semi-independent subpersonality, usually working under the direction of waking conscious mind. However, sometimes the inner child takes over and you might exhibit a habit you have carried with you since childhood. This could be something like running away from uncomfortable discussions because that is what you learned as a child. It could also be communicating in a healthy way if your parents established healthy dialogue as the norm during your early years. Other examples include hiding, pouting, fantasizing and ignoring reality, etc. Each of these behaviors are not inherently wrong, but could be seen as an indication you picked up the behavior as a coping mechanism as a child. Simply put, the inner child is the opportunity to connect to your joy, imagination, and creativity, as well as the chance to act out (and heal!) the fears, traumas, and doubts of your childhood.

The ruling class knows their only hope of maintaining political dominance is to confuse, distract, and divide their citizens until they have been indoctrinated into the system. In other words, until they "grow up." What this is really about is disconnecting you from the joyous, creative aspects of your inner child. Instead, the system, the void left by this disconnect is often filled with the fear and insecurity of the inner child. However, the human mind is resilient, and many of us can slip into adulthood with minimal psychological corruption. This growing portion of society may not be popular, but they are very often the source of the positive progress that has taken place throughout history. Some of the greatest minds to have walked the earth have recognized that the ideas of "growing up" and "fitting in" place people in invisible cultural prisons and corrupt their natural personal philosophies.

One of the most brilliant thinkers of the 20th century, Albert Einstein, was one of these people. Einstein believed that imagination is much more important than knowledge and that *"common sense is the collection of prejudices acquired by age eighteen."* He was well aware of the cultural games being played with people's minds. When he was 16 years old, one of his school teachers told him he would never amount to anything because of his unorthodox, rebellious attitude. So this free-thinking revolutionary dropped out of school and immediately sought opportunities at universities of higher learning. Einstein went on to become one of the greatest scientists of all time and maintained his rebellious attitude throughout his entire life. Einstein was against war, elitism, and authority—although it does appear he supported socialism. If it was not for his incredible contributions to science, he might have been considered insane or an enemy of the state by the establishment. Einstein was successful because he allowed himself to be imaginative and by doing so he maintained a relationship with his inner child.

Many creative and rebellious people who are in touch with their inner children receive overwhelmingly negative feedback from family and peers that they consciously submit to a culture that makes no sense to them. When someone does make it out of childhood without being corrupted, they are usually called naive and told their unorthodox point of view isn't welcome in society. This is exactly why you must be a certain age in order to vote or run for political office. The system makes sure to give people enough time to submit to the established cultural model of reality before they are able to have any impact on the direction of the society.

There are many cases where we do have much to learn from our elders, and it is true that skills we depend upon for survival have been passed down through the generations. Our elders are an oft-forgotten resource which offer a wealth of knowledge and wisdom for the younger generation. However, the government should not be seen as a parental figure. When it comes to a government setting cultural norms, we cannot deny the existence of an ulterior motive. That motive is always the same– to maintain the control of the population and defend the power of the established institutions so they endure for the next generation. It is possible to learn and mature without "growing up" and limiting yourself with cultural prejudices. Being responsible, respectful, and peaceful is what makes you a mature adult. It has nothing to do with fitting into the established dominant culture.

This brings us back to the importance of imagination, something that tends to have heightened potency within the minds of the youth. It is through imagination that we weave our dreams and intentions for the future. A powerful imagination and a relinquishing of fear and doubt can help one experience deep states of meditation and shamanic visioning that remain unavailable to the doubting mind that lacks the imagination needed for creative visualization and, ultimately, manifestation. If we allow our imagination, our thirst for knowledge and our youthful passion to be extinguished, then we allow a piece of ourselves and of the human collective to be forgotten. By recognizing the importance of this passion and taking steps today to cultivate empowering relationships and experiences for future generations, we ensure a more peaceful tomorrow.

Chapter 6
Consciousness & Rights Applied to Animals, Plants, and Earth

The topic of consciousness is controversial in the fields of philosophy and science. For hundreds of years, the debate has raged on in search of a commonly accepted definition of "Consciousness." The term has been associated with or defined at various times as subjectivity, awareness, sentience, or simply the ability to experience or to feel.

The idea that animals possess some level of sentience, or the ability to feel, and express themselves in a way that humans can measure has proven even more difficult to discuss in mainstream science than human consciousness. Despite a growing body of evidence which indicates animals have awareness at varying levels, people prefer to deny the possibilities and implications of the idea. Scientist Victoria Braithwaite, author of *Do Fish Feel Pain?* explored the topic and offered compelling evidence that fish in fact do feel pain and are sentient beings.

Marc Bekoff, emeritus professor at the University of Colorado, Boulder, is one of the pioneering cognitive ethnologists in the United States. In his paper, *"Aquatic Animals, Cognitive Ethology, and Ethics,"* Bekoff compiled a review of the literature on sentience in fish and other water-dwelling animals. Additionally, the World Society for the Protection of Animals released a systematic review of the scientific literature on animal sentience. The effort used a list of 174 keywords, and the team reviewed more than 2,500 articles. The evidence gathered by Bekoff and the World Society for the Protection of Animals overwhelmingly indicate the existence of conscious action on the part of animals.

The ego-based human perception of animals, especially insects, is that they are emotionless creatures that have no distinct personalities. However, new studies have shown that even cockroaches have unique personalities. In the study *"Group Personality During Collective Decision-Making,"* scientists in Brussels, Belgium, found that cockroaches behave very differently, even when in the same environment, due to their unique personalities. In the study, 304 cockroaches with RFID chips placed on their backs were led through a variety of settings, both light and dark. The scientists measured how quickly the cockroaches were able to find food and shelter. They discovered the cockroaches would all behave differently even when subjected to the same external stimulation.

On July 7, 2012, a prominent international group of cognitive neuroscientists, neuropharmacologists, neurophysiologists, neuroanatomists, and computational neuroscientists gathered at the University of Cambridge to assess the conscious experience and related behaviors in human and non-human animals. The statement they wrote is known as the Cambridge Declaration on Consciousness. This international team of scientists stated that "*Convergent evidence indicates that non-human animals have the neuroanatomical, neurochemical and neurophysiological substrates of conscious states along with the capacity to exhibit intentional behaviors.*"

The evidence consequently indicates that humans are not unique in possessing the neurological substrates that generate consciousness. Non-human animals, including mammals, birds, and many marine creatures, including octopuses, also possess these neurological substrates.

Scientists believe animals communicate and make vocalizations to communicate certain stressors in their environment. For example, researchers at the Wolf Science Center in Austria published a paper called "*Wolf Howling Is Mediated by Relationship Quality Rather Than Underlying Emotional Stress,*" which demonstrated that wolves voluntarily choose their vocal communications, specifically howling and barking. To study the physiological stress response due to social separation, the scientists separated one wolf at a time from the other wolves in their enclosures. The teams collected saliva from the remaining pack mates 20 minutes after removing the first wolf. During this period, all the wolves' vocalizations were also recorded.

The wolves would always howl whenever they were separated. However, the researchers found that the wolves would howl more often for a close friend than for the removed socially dominant wolf. Although the stress was measurable with an increase in salivary cortisol in all cases, the wolves appear to focus on friendship over social dominance, which indicates some level of cognition and choice rather than an inflexible, automatic response.

If animals can feel pain, use tools, and make choices about how they communicate with one another, is it that difficult to imagine them as aware, complex beings with emotions and thought processes?

In 2014, an Argentine court ruled that Sandra, a 29-year-old Sumatran orangutan, was a "*non-human person*" unlawfully deprived of her freedom and that she must be freed from the zoo and transferred to a sanctuary. The Association of Officials and Lawyers for Animal Rights (AFADA) argued that Sandra exhibited cognitive functions and deserved the right to a freer life. This ruling has the potential to ignite a huge shift in the treatment of animals in captivity. We look to the future to see how court rulings on animals might redefine the human-animal relationship.

Currently, there is a huge disconnect in the modern Western world in our diets and our treatment of animals. Many people consume unhealthy animal products that contain antibiotics and other harmful steroids and purchase meat from the Farming-Industrial Complex (aka the Meatrix). In doing so, they are supporting the mistreatment of the animals as well as damage to the environment caused by factory farming. Many people have begun referring to this industry as "*The Animal Holocaust.*"

To be clear, we are not asking everyone to become vegetarian or vegan or advocating some form of eco-fascism. Rather, we are asking free individuals to reconsider their level of respect toward the life that surrounds us always. We prefer if every individual takes an active part in their diet, especially if you choose to be a carnivore. If you have the option, hunt your meal yourself. Spend the time, sweat, and energy it takes to claim your meal. At the very least, buy your meat from a local vendor with "humane practices" (this is debatable, depending on your view) that you know or can visit in person. Take the time to give thanks to the life that is passing, the life that will allow you to continue to exist. This is the type of thinking that has permeated indigenous cultures for thousands of years and allowed them to live in relative harmony with the planet.

Whether by growing our own food, hunting animals on our own, or simply showing respect to the animals we encounter on a daily basis, we believe cultivating a stronger relationship with the life that surrounds us will strengthen the bonds within our human family and push us closer to a freer, more interconnected planet.

However, animals and humans are not the only conscious beings on this planet. Recent studies have found that plants have their own form of communication. Researchers with the University of Western Australia found that corn plants emit and respond to particular sounds. In their study *Towards Understanding Plant Bioacoustics*, the team discovered that when plants are played a continuous sound at 220 Hz, they grow toward the sound. This frequency range is similar to the clicking sound made by the plants themselves. Another study entitled "Plant Communication from Biosemiotic Perspective" reported:

"Plants are sessile, highly sensitive organisms that actively compete for environmental resources both above and below the ground. They assess their surroundings, estimate how much energy they need for particular goals, and then realize the optimum variant. They take measures to control certain environmental resources. They perceive themselves and can distinguish between self and non-self. This capability allows them to protect their territory. They process and evaluate information and then modify their behavior accordingly."

The ground-breaking 2014 study, *Plants Respond to Leaf Vibrations Caused by Insect Herbivore Chewing,* published in *Oecologia* by researchers at the University of Missouri, found that the Arabidopsis plant can sense when it is being eaten and secretes an increased amount of mustard oil as a defense mechanism to deter insect attackers. In the study, researchers recorded caterpillars's chewing vibrations and then played them to one group of plants while leaving another group in silence. The plants that could hear the chewing vibrations released the mustard oil.

If we have scientific evidence of plants and animals making rational decisions based on analysis and not simply emotion, perhaps we should reexamine our relationship with our fellow inhabitants of this planet, as well as the planet itself? Groups like the International Tribunal for the Rights of Nature believe that corporations and governments around the world have violated the rights of nature.

The tribunal and similar groups not only promote the rights of nature, but some also believe in a sort of "*Nature Supremacy,*" or that the fate of the planet should be put ahead of humanity and, in some extreme cases, that force should be used against humans for the good of the planet. We do not advocate such a position but hope to encourage a debate on how our ideas of a freer world will deal with problems involving the planet and our species.

The pursuit of humanity's coexistence with (or submission to) the Earth has manifested in a wide range of beliefs and opinions on how to interact with the planet and its inhabitants. From one side of the spectrum, there is a complete denial of animal or plant consciousness or any possibility of "rights" or mutual respect. In the middle, we see a healthy level of respect and compassion towards other forms of life– animals, humans, plants and minerals coexisting. On the other extreme side of the spectrum, there are those who advocate for a dismantling of all technology and "civilization" (anarcho-primitivism), the freeing of animals from research labs and the destruction of such labs (Animal Liberation Front), and the destruction of property and occupying of lands slated for destruction or "development" (Earth Liberation Front).

Another key part of the animal rights issue goes back to property. If an individual believes that pets are property, they may feel entitled to do as they please with the said "property." This could include violent abuse. This individual might claim that someone intervening during the animal abuse has committed a violation of property rights. However, we could also foresee a case where animals are given the same "rights" awarded to humans with diminished mental capacity. Also, one might conclude that since humans are animals, an attack on another animal is an attack on family, thus justifying the intervention. We will expand on this topic further in book 3 in this series, *Manifesto of the Free Humans.*

Indigenous communities throughout the world believe that life exists in all forms: plant, stone, human, animal and inanimate forces. We believe the closer we move to respecting all life, the deeper our understanding of liberty becomes. It is not only about pursuing freedom in terms of our individual paths, but recognizing the importance of allowing others to operate under their own freedom of action. Many of us already speak to our pets as children or companions. *Why not acknowledge the life in plants, animals, crystals, and the earth that surrounds us?*

Chapter 7
Conscious Healing

We understand it may be difficult to look at the current state of the world and imagine the world that we have described. Anarchy and spiritual awareness may seem like a distant pipe dream considering the unsustainable practices of the world's governments and industries. We do not deny these realities.

We also understand that humanity must experience deep personal healing on an individual level before the ills of the world can begin to transform. All the negativity we see manifested in the physical realm is a result of our own internal fears and pains. Once we are ready and willing to face ourselves and begin the healing process, we will see an increase in compassion, cooperation, and creation.

By choosing to reflect on our doubts, fears, insecurities, hopes, and dreams, we can come to know ourselves more deeply and begin to understand the ways we are limiting ourselves. As a result, our knowledge and application of freedom will become fuller. How can we truly know what freedom means to us as a people if we do not understand ourselves? The truth is we cannot. We may educate ourselves on the failures of the state—and maybe even overthrow that state through competition and peaceful resistance—but we will find ourselves facing similar conditions within a couple hundred years or so if we continue to operate at the same level of consciousness. If we do not deal with the root causes of humanity's pain, we are only applying Band-Aids to a gaping wound that desperately needs healing.

Imagine a post-revolution world without a spiritual transformation—educated groups of anarchists running around battling each other's egos due to a lack of empathy and unresolved internal conflict. A revolution without healing is a recipe for disaster. We need to evolve forward—not continue to go in circles.

In light of the need for spiritual healing, we would like to offer several methods that we, through our research and experience, have found extremely valuable. These include techniques that are not typically considered by the strictly rational, materialist individual. As we will discuss later, shamans and healers of all sorts have long known the potential of the ecstatic transformation created in altered states. Plant medicine, psychedelics, repetitive drumming, flotation tanks, and deep states of meditation can all induce altered states. In these altered states, we are able to access information that may have been hidden in the recesses of our mind and unavailable to the daily waking mind.

As we explore these paths to self-reflection, note that we are not concerned

Derrick **Broze** · John **Vibes**

with proving or disproving any other human experience in the pursuit of healing. Why should we care if someone's wild vision of facing down a demonic representation of his or her pain is real? It does not affect our paths if another free mind describes an experience beyond our current understanding. If the experience is of value to your path and produces healing while respecting the rights of other free humans, we have no place to condemn your journey. David Nichols, an emeritus professor of pharmacology at Purdue University, elaborates on this point when discussing psychedelic research on terminally ill patients.

"If it gives them peace, if it helps people die peacefully with their friends and family at their side, I don't care if it's real or an illusion."

Indeed, researchers of the effects of psychedelic medicines such as psilocybin mushrooms, LSD and MDMA (commonly known as ecstasy), are currently experiencing a renaissance of sorts. Throughout the 1950s and 60s, studies were conducted on alcoholics and terminally ill cancer patients, to examine the effects of MDMA on depression. By the 60s, LSD and psychedelics had broken free from the laboratory and entered the mainstream through the counterculture's free love movement. The human psyche was greatly expanded by the introduction of these tools to the Western world.

As many people know, our species has a long history of using psychedelics for self-healing, meditation, and the achievement of enlightening experiences. Our ancestors would take psychoactive substances in group settings, often while playing music and dancing around a campfire. Today's rave culture could be considered a modern form of this type of shamanic activity. While some cultures still carry on these practices the old-fashioned way, the Western world has manifested shamanic culture in a way that is uniquely fitted to its society. Under the influence of psychoactive substances, our ancestors danced in the woods around a fire playing primitive musical instruments. However, in the present day we often dance in clubs with flashing lights and loud electronic music. We are returning to the ancestral experience of warmth, light, and community.

This idea is important in the times we are facing today because in so many ways the oppressive traditions and culture we have inherited from the conquerors of our ancestors are still causing us to engage in irrational behaviors. Psychedelics allow us to think outside the cultural boxes we have spent our lives inside and often help us recognize the irrational nature of our own actions, allowing us to manage and overcome them properly.

That being said, it's important to remember the big picture when dealing with self-healing and empowerment. We need to share with others what we learn from the psychedelic experience and use that knowledge to brainstorm workable solutions for the problems going on in the physical world.

While we believe in the potential of the psychedelic experience, we cannot deny the early modern history of the tools and the culture. Therapists were not the only ones interested in these medicines. In fact, the US government spent millions of dollars studying the effects of psilocybin and LSD. In one of the most famous cases, the government attempted to use LSD as a mind-control drug. As part of Project MKUltra, the CIA and the US Army manipulated people's states of mind with LSD, hypnosis, sensory deprivation, and more.

The project was officially exposed in 1975 by a Church Committee investigation of CIA activity within the United States. Other programs such as MKDelta, Project CHATTER, Project BLUEBIRD, and Project ARTICHOKE were aimed at mind control and behavior modification. MKULTRA , which was later renamed MKSEARCH, focused on the development of a truth serum for interrogating spies. Many of the documents related to MKULTRA have been declassified. However, Richard Helms, director of the CIA at that time, destroyed the majority of the documents in 1973.

The introduction of psychedelics ripped conservative America from its comfort zone as many people began to express themselves for the first time freely. However, it is important to point out that the federal government introduced many elements of the 1960s counterculture; even the celebrated LSD guru and Harvard professor Timothy Leary stated that the CIA was involved in the funding of the dissemination of LSD. It is an incontrovertible fact that the state infiltrates creative movements by attempting to subvert influential leaders in music, arts, politics, and philosophy. Even so, agents of the US government who had a hand in the initial release of LSD, psilocybin and other medicines quickly discovered they could not control them. Whether the funding came from the CIA, the FBI, or independent sources is inconsequential to the potential these medicines offer. The experiences and enlightenment gained through altered states are invaluable regardless of the source of funding over 50 years ago. Earth-shaking revelations provided under the influence of external medicines should not be discarded simply because of the state's attempts to manipulate these beautifully empowering tools.

With the growing acceptance of the use of medicinal cannabis, psychedelics are experiencing a revival in academic research. In 2006, Roland Griffiths, a psychopharmacologist at Johns Hopkins University School of Medicine, and a team of researchers published an article in the *Journal of Psychopharmacology* entitled *"Psilocybin Can Occasion Mystical-Type Experiences Having Substantial and Sustained Personal Meaning and Spiritual Significance."* The paper concluded that *"psilocybin occasioned experiences similar to spontaneously occurring mystical experiences."* Two thirds of those involved in the sessions said they were among the most meaningful experiences of their lives. After that, Griffith's lab conducted a pilot study examining the possibility of treating nicotine addiction with psilocybin. In this study, the participants had three psilocybin sessions and three cognitive-behavioral therapy sessions to diminish cravings.

Eighty percent of those who received the psilocybin treatments abstained from nicotine for over six months, while less than 7 percent of those who received traditional nicotine-replacement therapy were successful for more than six months. Those who reported a mystical experience had the most success in breaking their addiction.

Some describe the mystical experience as the ability to step back and view one's life path and decisions as an observer. Imagine a camera pulling back and showing you your life in the grand scheme of existence. Griffiths believes this therapeutic experience leads to long-lasting change in individual behavior following a psychedelic session. Terminally ill patients involved in a New York University study reported a renewed thirst for life as well as less fear of their impending death. Under the right conditions, these tools can be guides for healing and transformation.

There is also great danger in not respecting the potential of these medicines. One should be weary of individuals who claim an external substance will lead to everlasting enlightenment. Despite the great opportunity for growth and the fact that the medicines can open *the doors of perception* and facilitate deep healing, we should not rely on them as a cure-all. Ultimately, the healing must come from a personal decision and the determination to face all that waits within your mind.

The enlightenment gained from these transformative moments is part of the reason the state has condemned psychedelics and those who promote them for so long. As Griffiths notes, "*There is such a sense of authority that comes out of the primary mystical experience that it can be threatening to existing hierarchical structures. We ended up demonizing these compounds. Can you think of another area of science regarded as dangerous and taboo that all research gets shut down for decades? It's unprecedented in modern science.*"[1]

When it comes to healing from addiction and trauma, psilocybin is not the only alternative to standard psychotropic drugs. MDMA has also been studied by psychologists for its many potential benefits. In 2012, the Multidisciplinary Association for Psychedelic Studies (MAPS) sponsored a long-term study on the benefits of MDMA. As recently as April 2014, researchers with the University of Connecticut's School of Pharmacy concluded that MDMA assisted psychotherapy could be useful for treating Post Traumatic Stress Disorder (PTSD).

Also growing in popularity in the modern Western world are the medicines ayahuasca and ibogaine. Ayahuasca, or yagé, is a medicinal brew made with the Banisteriopsis caapi vine and other plants that contain dimethyltryptamine, or DMT. Shamans of the Amazon have long used the brew to enter into a psychedelic state for deep healing and communion with the spirit world. First introduced to the West in the 1950s, ayahuasca has since inspired a massive tour-

1. The New Yorker, February 9, 2015, *The Trip Treatment.*

ism industry created around the thirst for a night with the healing medicine.

Although modern Internet-educated chemists have learned to synthesize and smoke DMT in the comfort of their homes, the brew is not known as ayahuasca without the Banisteriopsis caapi vine. Drinking ayahuasca and smoking DMT produce a similar experience but are different in intensity and length. Ayahuasca produces an intense trip that lasts several hours and often involves throwing up. Smoking DMT will produce a short trip of around 3-5 minutes with after effects lasting around 20 to 30 minutes.

Studies have found that the human brain produces DMT during dreams, near-death experiences and death. This connection between a random plant medicine in the Amazon and a naturally occurring chemical in the human brain has caused some to believe humans are meant to ingest these medicines. Indeed, when the indigenous peoples of the Amazon were asked where they learned to combine these two random plants from the pharmacy of the rainforest, they said the spirits of the plants themselves instructed them. Both versions of the medicine can produce powerful visions, including contact and conversation with spirits, entities, or alien life forms. No one can say for certain what they will endure as it is a deeply personal experience, but there are some common threads. Users often report a mystical transformation and a renewed vigor for life. Ibogaine, or iboga, is another plant medicine that is quickly gaining popularity. The Bwiti people of Africa have long ingested the plant for healing ceremonies. With modern medicine, we have been able to isolate ibogaine from the plant and use it to help treat opiate addiction, depression, and PTSD. Per usual, Ibogaine was studied by the governments of the world and then banned, supposedly for having no medicinal use. If you are interested in healing from deep traumas and addictions you must escape the clutches of the State and seek out an iboga retreat center.

There is also much strength in yoga for spiritual growth and healing. In the study "*Breathing-Based Meditation Decreases Posttraumatic Stress Disorder Symptoms in U.S. Military Veterans*," University of Wisconsin-Madison researchers found that a practice known as Sudarshan Kriya Yoga can help those with PTSD better manage their symptoms. The idea behind this is that breathing affects the autonomous nervous system, so a consistent breathing practice as seen in yoga can help manage symptoms of PTSD such as hyperarousal.

Despite the apparent differences in the practices, meditation, yogic breathing, and the trance produced through shamanic exercises seem to create a similar state of mind. Meditation itself is a practice as old as human life. As long as human beings have existed, we have come to nature for quiet contemplation and reflection. Over time, a large number of meditation practices have been developed, each with its own instructions and insights. While we value and respect these individual methods, we note that nearly any experience can be meditative. There is something to be said for a balanced posture and proper breathing, but a bike ride, a walk under the stars, writing poetry, or any practice that offers individual quiet time within your own heart and mind can be considered a form of meditation. The consistent application of bringing one's attention to the present moment is key to any form of meditation. Remaining in the present moment, either through counting breaths, mantras, or contemplative thought, allows long-dormant emotions to rise to the surface. From that point, an individual can assess how best to deal with the new data.

In the same way that meditation reinforces the endless "now," certain yogic breathing practices allow an individual to become cognizant of the subtlety that is breathing. Although yoga is better known in the Western world for yogic postures, or asanas, the original intention was a system of healing that involved deep states of mind to protect one from external distraction. Patañjali first recorded the yoga sutras as a guide for those seeking enlightenment and a path towards true liberation. Through meditative practice, physical movement, and control of breath, or prana, one can achieve internal peace.

Flotation therapy is an alternative healing method that involves spending time in flotation or isolation tanks. American neuroscientist John C. Lily was the first person to develop what was known at the time as a *"sensory deprivation,"* or isolation tank. An employee of the US government, Lily developed the first isolation tank in 1954 at the National Institute of Mental Health. He and his colleagues became the first test subjects in their research of the tanks. Eventually, the experience came to be known as Restricted Environmental Stimulation Technique (REST).

In float therapy (REST), you are suspended in a dark, bubble-like tank. Earplugs prevent you from hearing much of anything while you float in complete darkness. The tank is filled with 12 inches of salt water set to a temperature of 93.5 degrees, the temperature of your skin. The matching of temperatures causes you to lose your sense where your body ends and the water begins. A typical float session lasts an hour to an hour and a half. Within that time span, your brain may be racing to worry about what exactly you are supposed to be feeling, or it may remain in thoughts of mundane everyday activity. Typically, that goes away after the first ten to fifteen minutes and, as with traditional meditation, you can relax more easily with repeated floats.

With no external stimuli to focus on such as light or sound, you are free to float without gravity or restriction of thought. After a period of ten to fifteen minutes, you may experience auditory hallucinations, swirling lines or visions, or you may simply find yourself in a deep state of relaxation. This form of meditation has been shown to facilitate great healing and insight.

Military veterans with are now pursuing float therapy as a way of coping with PTSD. A veteran at an Austin, Texas flotation facility told local news, *"[Flotation therapy] allows me not to be distracted by everything else around me and purely focus on what's going on with me."*

Scientists have studied flotation-REST for some years, with many concluding that the therapy reduces stress, anxiety, and depression while improving sleep quality. For those seeking further study of flotation therapy, we recommend *The Book of Floating* by Michael Hutchison. There has also been interest in the potential benefits of gardening therapy treatments for PTSD. Obviously, escaping the busy life in cities or suburbs for a weekend of nature is a common practice for many of us. We yearn to be close to something organic and more connected than man-made structures often allow.

Music also plays a powerful role in facilitating healing experiences. Indigenous cultures that predate modern musical instruments have long understood the power of rhythm. The drumming and shaking of rattles produce the same effect that pulls meditators and yogis into deep trances.

In his essay "*Shamans, Yogis and Bodhisattvas,*" Gary Doore refers to this as "*entrainment,*" or "*the induction of altered states of consciousness by the fixation of attention on a regularly repeating pattern of stimuli.*" [1]

When Patañjali writes of pratyahara he is speaking of removing the effects of external stimuli on the senses. This withdrawal from external stimuli allows one to bring their attention inward, moment by moment. A meditative practice that focuses on centering one's attention allows for states of entrancement similar to the shaman and the yogi. Ultimately, these three practices offer their own unique paths toward healing.

Other powerful tools worth mentioning are creative visualization, positive affirmation, and manifestation. For some, these words represent the latest fad for the "New Age" crowd or simply the denial of a bleak reality through the repetition of uplifting statements. However, these practices, which seem most effective in conjunction, are a very simple way of creating the reality you seek. First, creative visualization reinforces the power of imagination and the importance of remaining connected to your inner child. By creating "vision boards" with words and images that represent our desired goals, or by simply meditating on what we would like to see in our lives, we remind ourselves of the steps we must take to achieve those goals. By sitting in quiet reflection and allowing our minds to clear of distraction, we can achieve all we desire. Through visualization we can see, smell, taste, hear, and touch the ideal situation we are trying to manifest and work through the difficult problems we may be facing.

Once you are comfortable with visualizing your path, it is important to affirm the path. This is where positive affirmation comes into play. Positive affirmation is a highly effective method of programming oneself. We face external programming every day through the corporate media, the government, and those we communicate with. One way or another, whether by our own doing or some external force, we will be programmed. The mind is much like

---

1. *Shamans Path*, page 217

a computer that can be loaded with a variety of programs. Many of us buy into cultural and environmental programming that does not empower us as individuals, but rather, teaches us to doubt our potential and capabilities. We must take steps to deprogram ourselves from such destructive thinking.

With daily affirmations we can create a positive, compassionate view of ourselves and of the world around us. By using affirming statements such as "*I AM…,*" we allow our minds to let go of negative habits and begin to rewrite the pathways our thoughts take. For example, perhaps your insecurities are a constant prison, a paralysis that limits your social life as much as your internal world. By changing your internal self-talk that says you are incapable of certain tasks or that other humans view you in a negative light, and affirming, "*I am capable, I am deserving of love and compassion,*" you can overcome a lifetime of unnecessary insecurities and doubts. Over time, this reprogramming of your mind becomes habit. Rather than buying into the limiting thoughts when they appear, you are able to say, "*No, thank you, I no longer need you!*" and instead tell yourself, "*I am capable, I am loved, I am becoming stronger every day in every way.*" This simple act can have long-lasting, life-changing effects. Through creative visualization and daily affirmations, we are not only changing our state of mind and the way we look at our world but also energetically altering the course of our lives.

Manifestation is the power of watching an idea go from a seed in your mind to a daily focus to a physical reality. Manifestation is the culmination of an empowered individual understanding what they want, making a conscious choice to pursue that goal, calling out to the universe for assistance, and taking steps in the physical world to bring that idea into reality. These tools are not simply a method of praying or wishing away the problems we face. We must remember that the power of the mind is assisted by actions taken by the physical body. Through personal responsibility, determination, and a focused work ethic, we can produce the results we seek and have everything we desire.

As previously mentioned, we are all faced with external programming from a number of sources. Without breaking through that propaganda, the tools we have mentioned will lack their full potential. If you are trying to clear your mind for meditation and all you can think of is how silly you feel, you won't get very far. If you find your inner voice continuously berating you as you attempt to visualize your way through an emotionally damaging relationship, the likelihood of success is greatly decreased. To combat our internal tyrant we must learn to change our subconscious thoughts. This can be done through consistent application of Conscious Language.

In his book, *Conscious Language: The Logos of Now*, Robert Tennyson Stevens outlines the power of carefully choosing words that empower rather than hurt. Stevens explains how it is possible to upgrade the *"Human Operating System"* through words. One method is to catch yourself thinking or speaking limiting thoughts and then transform the words into powerful tools for growth. One example is to do away with actions that do not fulfill your highest good. For example, you may have trouble being punctual and say to yourself, "*I am always late.*" With Conscious Language, we learn to put those behaviors where they belong—in the past. We then affirm what we want to create in the present moment. Rather than saying, "*I am always late,*" you might try, "*In the past I have been late often, however, in the future, I will be on time.*" Maybe you often feel rushed, like you never have time for all of your daily pursuits. Rather than stressing yourself out and focusing on how limited your time is, you could instead affirm, "*I have time and energy for everything I need.*"

These are two very simplified examples of using Conscious Language. We encourage each individual to pursue their own research on the topic.

As with anything, practice makes habits. By learning to speak compassionately and consciously to yourself, you can create a more positive and fulfilling physical reality. It is important for our spiritual well-being to create the world we want and express gratitude through our words. In the study "Gratitude and Depressive Symptoms: the Role of Positive Reframing and Positive Emotion," researchers with Brigham Young University confirmed that positive thinking is related to lower signs of depression. As always, you are the master of your reality and experiences.

When cultivating a conscious mind, it is also important to maintain a healthy and well-nourished body. Among average people's diets, there is a culture of poor eating habits. This is usually the result of ignorance and financial disadvantage, as well as propaganda from state and corporate media. However, since this information has broken through to the mainstream in recent years, different researchers are now promoting a variety of alternative diets. Our intention here is not to tell you how to eat, but rather, to tell you to be conscious about what you eat. Unfortunately, most of the food that is popular and readily available in modern society can hardly be classified as food. The abundance of processed foods and toxic pesticides has made diligent research necessary when considering your diet.

It is not our job to tell you which path to choose. That is something every individual is free to choose for themselves. When individuals are less than conscious about their lifestyle and health choices, we see a degradation in the overall human experience. This breakdown of balance in our internal and external worlds manifests itself in the traumas we see in our world. We have the power to change this with our habits. We can choose to heal and contribute to the overall healing of our species.

Chapter 8
Rites of Vigil and Solitude

This essay features personal anecdotes from Derrick. We offer his experiences as a way of highlighting the role that solitude can play in spiritual growth.

"Nowhere can man find a quieter or more untroubled retreat than in his own soul." —Marcus Aurelius

"No man is free who is not master of himself." —Epictetus

When I contemplate the idea of freedom, the notion that human beings can possess critical thinking skills and a sense of self-determination and compassion for their fellow humans, a number of questions run through my head. *What does it take for one to be free? What are the necessities for freedom? In what ways do our unique ideas of freedom differ from one another? In what ways do we create artificial boundaries for ourselves?*

We must consider all of these questions to truly understand what freedom means and how to achieve it. While there is not one single road that leads to freedom, our individual experiences provide us with insights that serve as helpful hints, tips, and guidance for our brothers and sisters on their individual paths. It is with that in mind that I offer some of my perspectives with the hope that we may learn from each other.

I want to focus on the need for occasional solitary sessions or extended solo journeys. My experience with solitude has led to deep personal insights and a better understanding of my doubts, fears, and insecurities. The idea behind the conscious resistance is to create a population that encourages self-knowledge, individuality, compassion, awareness, and solutions. I believe that until we choose to know ourselves and our motivations and aspirations, we will continue to be ruled over by a small group of people who are not working on behalf of the best interests of the whole. In fact, if this "resistance" were to spread, that same small group of people might even have a powerful spiritual experience that could lead to an understanding of their place in the whole and a restoration of balance.

Solitary Paths

Twice in my life the universe provided me with opportunities for reflection and meditation, each vastly different from the other. The first involved my incarceration for possession of a controlled substance in 2005. I was less than a month from turning 21 and had been battling addictions to a variety of drugs for the better part of three years. At that point, the substance wreaking havoc in my life was crystal methamphetamine. Despite my current beliefs that people should not be arrested and caged for victimless crimes such as drug use, I now know that my drug use at that particular time was an effort to escape and self-medicate my depression and general lack of understanding of the world.

Upon my arrest and imprisonment, I resisted the environment and fought like hell to maintain a connection to the "free world." Eventually, however, I had to accept that I was going to spend the next 18 months behind bars. There was not a family member, friend, or lawyer who could do anything for me. The only choice was to sit, be with myself, and take moments to consider how I found myself in that predicament. I spent the next year and a half writing pages and pages of notes, stream of consciousness rants and ideas on how to take my life in a better direction. A family member began sending me Buddhist literature, and I started to meditate. This was the beginning of a major life change for me. The steps I took in those days have directly led to my present space.

While I wrote mountains of manifestations, I began to notice my handwriting becoming slower, more precise. As my thoughts slowed down and reflection became the norm, my physical world started to reflect the internal changes. Learning to meditate in an environment filled with false ego and posturing was not an easy task. I persisted and found many moments of peace despite being physically caged.

In the years following my incarceration, I struggled to stay connected to that feeling of pure being, of truly existing in the moment and accepting that I could not control the outside world. The best I could do was to work on my spirit. When I would slip, I'd pick myself back up. Eventually, I found myself released from parole and creating a new life with a new passion for knowledge and community.

In 2011, I decided to complete my journey and celebrate my newfound sense of freedom by taking a cross-country bicycle tour. I had long been plotting an adventure that would give me the ultimate sense of a restriction-free lifestyle and the wonder that comes with the open road. I took my bike, some books, and some supplies and traveled across Texas and into New Mexico. For three months I camped, rode, and volunteered on farms.

It was during this time that I once again found myself humbled by the lessons that came my way. I met many beautiful people, each of whom imparted a bit of their own experience to me. I slept under more stars than I had ever seen, howling along with the coyotes and laughing at how dirty but free I was. In those three months I laughed, I cried, I challenged myself like never before, and I decided to see every part of the journey as a magnificent piece of the puzzle, waiting for me to put it together.

I remembered the peace that I had found while behind razor wire and recognized how the isolation had allowed my mind to receive clarity and be washed clean. It was these two experiences that have played the most significant role in my awakening and growth. When given the time with my own mind—whether by force or choice—I began to understand my fears and my hopes. I saw my failures and witnessed the destructive nature of my past actions. I had a vision of a crossroads, a divided road. One way would take me further into darkness, and the other could be the journey of a lifetime. I pondered long and hard, asking myself what it is about these two unique experiences that sparked a quest within.

I have found that I, like many modern humans, was living a busy life cluttered with plenty of ways to ignore myself and slap on a façade of joy and happiness. I found that I had been doing anything and everything possible to avoid sitting down for five minutes and communicating with my own mind. I had lost touch with whom I identified as my self. In the process, I had lost a connection with my own humanity and heart. By having no other option but to sit—in a prison bed or on an isolated back road—I had an opportunity to understand my deepest pains and to begin healing them. It is this healing that will help bring our species back in alignment with the planet and its inhabitants.

Learning to Find Balance

Humans seek refuge from the big city in a number of ways. We take weekend camping trips to get away from the light and noise pollution, the smog, and the people. As much as we are communal creatures with a desire to form relationships, we also seek to break away and reconnect with nature and the simple life. In those spaces, we find the time to sit with ourselves and begin "checking in" with our mind to form healthy relationships with those closest to us.

The history books are filled with stories of individuals who sought out the rugged, dangerous, lonely, beautiful life that the solitary road offers. From Everett Reuss to Christopher McCandless, humans have pursued adventure and communion with nature for a variety of reasons. Many of these adventurers (myself included) have learned that community and familial experiences are equally as important as our personal vision quests. Life is balance. If you find yourself in the company of others solely to avoid dealing with your personal situations and hard truths, it might be time to spend a weekend alone. On the other hand, if you have spent the majority of your time in quiet reflection, try going out into the community and making connections with other people.

In the end, we are each other's greatest asset for finding out what freedom means, how to achieve it, and what role the global community will play. By opting to spend time examining ourselves, we become more capable of having positive, encouraging relationships and helping those who may be struggling to know themselves. For me, it was these two experiences that allowed me to discover the empowerment that waited in quiet contemplation. Being behind bars and in the wilderness also showed me that regardless of where I was in the physical sense, happiness, and thus liberation, could be attained by choosing to go within.

Indigenous people from a variety of cultures have understood and taught the power of solitude and the necessity of journeying. "Vision Quests" may take place in myriad forms, whether in the physical world involving several days or weeks of surviving among the elements or something internal such as a deeply introspective meditation session fostered by repetitive drums, rattles, and chants. Whether a physical or mental journey, they represent a quest for knowledge and understanding of the self and how it relates to the physical and spiritual worlds.

As we move from activity to activity in our busy daily lives, we often ignore or forget trauma and valuable insights we have gathered along our path. By taking time to do the difficult work of self-examination and healing, we contribute to making our individual lives more enjoyable and encourage others to go within. By promoting a more balanced state of mind and spirit, we are contributing to the cause of freedom and helping create a more compassionate tomorrow.

Chapter 9
Are We All One? Collectivism vs. Individuality

"We are all one," is a phrase often spoken in spiritual circles to describe the interconnectedness of all life on the planet—human, plant, animal, insect, and beyond. Many anarchists who value their individuality and free choice tend to be apprehensive about this seemingly collectivist worldview. However, it is possible for one to believe in a path that is in harmony with nature and its creatures while simultaneously believing in the right to be a free individual and freedom of association.

Throughout most of the world, people are taught to look at reality in a very polarized way. When certain issues are presented to us through mainstream circles, they are usually oversimplified into black or white concepts. For example, all people are either good or bad—with no in between. In reality, life is much more complicated than that. There are usually many different ways of looking at a situation and many different sides to any story.

This is especially true in the study of philosophy because terms are constantly being redefined. Ideas are constantly reexamined with every new generation of philosophers to accommodate the new insight and information that has become available over time.

One concept that is vastly misunderstood and oversimplified by the general population is that of individualism and collectivism. While there are many different ideas about what these words mean, the true value of any concept is determined by the consequences that arise in society as a result of its implementation.

At face value, collectivism has been a philosophy with cheery rhetoric but unpleasant outcomes. This is because it has traditionally been implemented coercively through politics. Collectivist philosophers have spoken of noble goals like making sacrifices for the group and working together and cooperating. They have said that these are things that people should do. It very well may be true that people should behave in these ways, but the problem is that politicians come along and use this philosophy as a way of telling people what they *must* do.

The mainstream stereotype of an individualist is someone who is a selfish person with no desire to participate in the community whatsoever. The contrasting view of a collectivist is someone who cares about the tribe as a whole, so much so that they are willing to sacrifice their own well-being for the sake of the tribe. However, individualism has nothing to do with selfishness. It is simply a way of looking at people without separating them into various groups by race, nationality, gender, religion, or social status.

When people are seen as groups instead of individuals, large numbers of them are often held responsible for things that individuals among them have done. There is also a great danger in the idea that an individual needs permission from the group to exercise his or her free will, which is exactly the type of worldview on which collectivist concepts like "democracy" and "consensus" were built.

We have often found that well-meaning spiritually inclined individuals buy into "New Age" messages that operate under the guise of helping out the whole human species while truly continuing to support statism. This could be a small group of wealthy individuals promoting a reduction in the population or forced sterilization for the supposed good of the whole. An anarchist perusing some modern spiritual material might be turned off by the prevalence of statist and collectivist language. Compassionate individuals may find themselves wrapped up in philosophies that claim to be about a greater good but end up harming the individual and thus the community as a whole. In contrast, Anarchists may be so independent they completely ignore the importance of community and turn away those who want liberation for all.

It's time we recognize each individual as a sacred being. To respect the whole, we must first respect the individual. For an individual to be truly free, he or she must not have physical obligations to anyone else. Rather, an individual must be able to freely choose whom to interact with in a meaningful and peaceful way. In this manner, he or she can then become truly fulfilled and free. At the very least, mutual respect for other free individuals' life choices will go a long way.

One of the most powerful examples of interdependence comes from the Avatamsaka Sūtra of the Mahayana Buddhist philosophy. The Huayan, or Flower Garland School of Mahayana, was founded on the ideas expressed in the Avatamsaka Sūtra, also known as the Flower Garland Sutra or Flower Ornament Scripture. This sutra centers on the ideas of interdependence and an interpenetrating reality. It describes worlds upon worlds, overlapping and coexisting within each other.

This concept is best expressed in the story of the jeweled net of Indra. Indra was a god who was said to possess a net that extends infinitely in all directions. The net contained individual shimmering diamonds that spread out in all directions. Each individual diamond was perfect on its own, but the individual pieces also reflected the beauty and light of the surrounding diamonds.

Thomas Cleary, a renowned translator of Eastern texts, describes the beauty of the tale of Indra's net in his book *Entry Into the Inconceivable: An Introduction to Hua-Yen Buddhism*. Cleary writes:

"*The seventh gate is called the realm of Indra's net. The net of Indra is a net of jewels: not only does each jewel reflect all the other jewels but the reflections of all the jewels in each jewel also contain the reflections of all the other jewels, ad infinitum. This "infinity of infinities" represents the interidentification and interpenetration of all things as illustrated in the preceding gates.*

"*To illustrate the net of Indra principle with a simplistic example from everyday life, we might consider the cost of a commodity as representing a nexus of various conditions. For the sake of simplicity, let us say the cost of something reflects (1) the cost of raw materials, (2) the cost of energy required for its manufacture, (3) the cost of labor involved in its production, and (4) the cost of transportation for distribution.*

"*Turning our attention to raw materials, the first element, we can see that the cost of raw materials also involves the cost of energy required for their extraction, the cost of labor involved in their extraction, and the cost of transportation of the raw materials to the processing site. The cost of energy involves the cost of raw materials from which energy is produced as well as raw materials for the devices involved, the cost of labor involved in producing energy, and the cost of distribution of energy. The cost of labor reflects the cost of goods, energy, and transportation necessary for the workforce. The cost of transportation involves the cost of materials, energy, and labor necessary to the manufacture and operation of transportation systems. Thus each element in this analysis reflects and contains every other element.*

"*While this example is rudimentary, using an oversimplified scheme of analysis and stopping at only one level of subanalysis, it illustrates how the net of Indra concept may be applied to the development of a balanced view of a complex of phenomena. The analytic framework may be usefully applied in economics, socioeconomics, group and individual psychology, and ecology. While it may be said that the net of Indra does not necessarily reveal anything startlingly new—it is, after all, merely an articulation of a principle inherent in an interdependent nexus of phenomena—still it is a valuable instrument for the achievement of balance and depth in understanding and, moreover, for the avoidance of one-sided views.*"[1]

We see value in understanding this parable and its call for unity without ignoring diversity. The sutra paints an image of a world in which one is simultaneously dependent on others and depended on by others. The whole is considered in relation to each individual, and each individual is seen in relation to other individuals. Again, Cleary offers clarity:

"*The ethic of the Hua-yen teaching Is based on this fundamental theme of universal interdependence; while the so-called bodhisattva, the person devoted to enlightenment, constantly nourishes aspiration and will going beyond the world, nevertheless the striving for completion and perfection, the development of ever greater awareness, knowledge, freedom, and capability, is continually reinvested, as*

---

1. pp. 37-38.

it were, in the world, dedicated to the liberation and enlightenment of all beings."[1]

While Huayan Buddhism hints at the power of interdependence and the importance of the individual, certain native communities believe that individuality in the Western world has played a role in the breaking down of the social fabric. While we cannot deny that a lack of awareness and concern for the fellow humans of the global community allows certain individuals to make destructive choices, we believe overall that the individual and the community are both valuable. You should not necessarily give yourself up to the will of the collective but instead remain willing to examine your behavior and recognize whether you are doing more harm than good.

Since we share this planet with billions of humans, animals, plants, stones, and countless other life forms, it is advisable to find ways to work together. We are connected through DNA, through our energetic bodies, and through our current position in time and space. By learning to value and love ourselves, we can move to a place of valuing and loving those with whom we share our local and global communities.

1. p. 2.

Chapter 10
Balancing the Feminine and the Masculine

For millennia, the human species has been pitted against each other. When brute strength was the only requirement to rule over another life, men would kill and enslave each other and often take women as slaves, using force to meet their every need. This imbalanced state, combined with the disconnect from nature we have discussed, created a world full of inequality and pain. Historically, governments, religions and popular culture promoted the idea that women were inferior. This is evident in fathers owning their wives and daughters and the fact that women were not allowed to own property or make any choices of their own until very recently on the historical timeline.

Anthropological evidence indicates that societies operated in a much more egalitarian fashion before the innovation of agriculture and domestication of communities. In *The Origins of Fatherhood: An Ancient Family Process* Sebastian Kraemer writes that the patriarchal mindset came about around 6,000 years ago with the growing concept of fatherhood.

Even the ancient philosopher Aristotle believed that women were inferior to men in intellect, morality, and physical ability. Regardless of how it began, we can clearly see an imbalance in the way women have been treated for thousands of years. To be clear, most people on this planet, of all genders, have been subject to enslavement by whatever authority ruled over their particular landmass, but even among male peasants and slaves throughout history, the pervading attitude was that women were born to be subservient to men.

However, there have been exceptions to this point of view. Greek historian Herodotus wrote about the differences between Egyptian and Greek women, specifically how Egyptian women contrasted with Greek women by maintaining employment in a variety of trades. Herodotus noted that Egyptian women were often found in positions of power and were able to inherit property and secure loans—privileges unheard of for women in Greece in his time.

Beyond simple employment opportunities, there is a rich history of goddess and femininity worship. There are thousands of female statues dating back 5,000 years before the current era, found in the Mehrgarh area of Pakistan, as well as a mother goddess statue in India that has been carbon-dated to 20,000 years before the current era. These seem to indicate a certain respect, if not worship, of the feminine form. Examples of female deities can be found all over the world.

The Pueblo and Hopi peoples of the American Southwest speak of Grandmother

Spider, a protective force involved in creation stories. In Inca mythology there is Pachamama, a fertility goddess who watches over the Earth and harvests.

There is also Shaktism, a branch of Hinduism that focuses devotional efforts on Shakti or Devi, the Hindu Divine Mother. In ancient Greece, Gaia was the name of the mother of all life, the great Greek mother goddess who gave birth to the earth and the universe. More recently we have seen goddess movements such as Dianicc Wicca and terms like "sacred" or "divine" feminine, a New Age spin on the Hindu Shakti teachings.

Despite isolated historical examples of equality, the dominant mentality has been one of male supremacy. Rejection of this system and pursuit of equality is known as feminism. At various points in history, women and men have both sought to empower women and establish practices of equality. Although there have been discussions of equal rights since the 14th century, there is no agreed upon beginning of the feminist philosophy. Most scholars agree that American feminism has had three waves, each concerned with different aspects of freedom for women. The first wave of feminism came in the 18th and 19th centuries and focused on women's suffrage, the right of women to vote and hold political office. In America, the women's suffrage movement began to gain ground in the 18th century as women pursued the right to vote.

Second-wave feminism came about during the 1960s and lasted until the 1980s, and broadened the feminist movement's focus to examine gender roles and culturally ingrained inequalities. The third and current wave of feminism includes a wide range of philosophies, including rejections of past schools of feminist thought and an evolution of first and second-wave feminism.

Out of the struggles of the second wave of feminism emerged radical feminism. Radical feminism focused on dismantling the patriarchy through opposition of gender roles. It considered how social class, race, sexual preference, and socioeconomic status play into the treatment of women and men. Many radical feminists had prior experience in the civil rights battles of the 1960s. These movements were focused on direct action and did not necessarily push for political solutions to the inequalities they opposed.

In the late 19th and early 20th centuries, a portion of the American feminism movement merged with the principles of anarchy to form what some call Anarcha-feminism.

Prominent Anarchist thinker Emma Goldman is seen as a founder of Anarcha-feminism. For Goldman, the opposition to male supremacy was essential in the struggle against state power. She was also a huge advocate of reproductive rights, sex education, and access to contraception. Before many other radicals accepted homosexuality, Goldman was publicly defending the rights of gay men and lesbian women to love as they pleased.

Goldman criticized voting as a legitimate form of fighting the State. She believed it foolish to assume that giving women the right to vote would halt the crimes of the State. *"To assume, therefore, that she would succeed in purifying something which is not susceptible of purification, is to credit her with supernatural powers,"* she wrote in "Woman's Suffrage."

Another prominent figure in American anarcha-feminism was Voltairine de Cleyre. De Cleyre was critical of traditional beauty ideals, gender roles, and the marriage laws that allowed men to rape their wives without fear of legal consequence. She wrote for Benjamin Tucker's classic newsletter *Liberty*. In addition to being a feminist, Voltairine was an advocate of anarchism without adjectives. In her 1901 essay, "Anarchism," she wrote of the need for anarchists of all economic schools to work together in free experimentation. She concluded:

"There Is nothing un-Anarchistic about any of them until the element of compulsion enters and obliges unwilling persons to remain in a community whose economic arrangements they do not agree to."

One of the more contentious areas feminists have explored is the question of whether gender roles are a valid concept or simply a social construct. Western cultures tend to accept two genders, male or female, while cultures around the world have accepted three or more genders throughout history. These include the mahu of the Kanaka Maoli indigenous. The mahu were seen as sacred educators of ancient traditions and could be either male or female with a gender somewhere in between or sharing traits both masculine and feminine. The Bugi people of the Sulawesi island of Indonesia recognize five genders. The Bugi support the idea of men, women, calabai, calalai, and bissu. Calabai are biological males who take on the role of a heterosexual female. Their dress and gender expression are feminine. Calalai are biological females who identify with a male gender. Bissu are healers or mediums who "transcend" gender and encompass aspects of all five in order to form a whole. Several American Indian tribes also have similar concepts. The Lakota word winyanktehca can be translated as "two-souls-person," or "to be as a woman." The term is applied to biological males who are transgender. The "winkte" are an important part of the spiritual community. The Navajo also have a similar concept in the Nádleehí, which could be translated as "one who constantly transforms."

Gender roles are imposed on each gender according to certain qualities that are deemed acceptable and those that are not. Queer theory proposes a deconstruction of gender-identity to get to the roots of oppression.

Psychologist Cordelia Fine believes there are inherent biological differences between the minds of men and women. However, she also believes that cultural traditions are responsible for shaping these apparent differences between the sexes. Professor Dianne Halpern writes that social and biological factors are equally responsible and cannot be separated. In *Sex Differences in Cognitive*

Abilities, Halpern writes that cultural traditions and biology both play a role in determining gender identity. She discusses how the influence of testosterone on a male brain gives men a slight advantage in tasks such as building with blocks. This could lead a male to seek opportunities to exercise similar skills, such as sports. Over time, these activities are labeled as male specific and become ingrained into the culture itself. However, these culturally accepted norms are not absolute and should not be used as a barometer for socially accepted behavior by either sex.

We believe a conversation on balancing the feminine and masculine is incomplete without discussing gender roles as possible tools for oppression of the freedom of expression and the freedom to love. The notion that all men are supposed to be tough, brave, fearless, and unemotional has caused untold harm to the human race. Just as dangerous is the notion that all women should be emotionally open, compassionate, easily scared, delicate, and passive. These concepts reinforce division among the masses and allow the authorities to pit people against one another based on their gender. Rather than seeing each other as equals capable of great things, we are taught to buy into and support false versions of the male-female dynamic, which includes the male-female binary itself.

Our roles in society have not only been predetermined by those in positions of authority but our private relationships with one another have also been heavily manipulated. For centuries, church and state have dictated what human relationships should look like based on their own political interests. In the past, this control was more apparent with arranged marriages and laws against certain types of partnerships, but the influence of these traditions persists in the form of social and cultural norms that many people accept as natural defaults.

As popular opinion has shifted towards inclusion, traditionalists have been forced to recognize that people who are different from them have a right to exist. However, among some traditionalists, there is a deep fear that traditionalism will fall into obsolescence unless their way of life is upheld as the only moral and socially acceptable option. This is why there is extreme cultural pressure on those of us who step outside of any cultural norms to hide in shame. This is also why we face such resistance when we attempt to live our lives proudly and publicly, or when our lifestyles are shown in the media. There is a vast opposition to the "normalization" of the diverse lifestyle paths that have long been forbidden by entrenched cultural traditions, but when you oppose the normalization of a person's existence, you are essentially demanding that they live in shame as second-class citizens.

The societal norms regarding relationships are still heavily rooted in traditions that were created by figures of authority many ages ago. This is now becoming somewhat obvious with gender and sexuality, but it hasn't always been this way. Until quite recently, finding love in a same-sex relationship or choosing a different gender than the one assigned at birth was not represented as a viable option. There have also been taboos against interracial or interfaith relationships, which have prevented people building the lives that could bring them true fulfillment. People usually aren't even aware that these barriers exist until they witness someone else living happily outside of them, but luckily, younger generations are having more courage than ever to step outside of their culture's expectations.

While humanity has made progress, there are still many unquestioned cultural expectations that shape our lives without our full understanding. One of the latest frontiers in this cultural expansion is questioning the philosophy of monogamy, the idea that a romantic partnership should be exclusively between two people. In monogamy each person abstains from emotional and sexual relations outside of their relationship. Of course, this is an arrangement that many people prefer—and that is perfectly fine. However, instead of consciously choosing that path against other potential lifestyles, most people don't realize that other options are available. Even if they are aware, the social stigmas against deviating from the norm are often strong enough to prevent people from exploring, or even discussing those other options.

When entering relationships, the vast majority of people simply go through the motions and do what society expects of them without ever stopping to discuss or even consider that they have the freedom to decide what their relationship will look like as long as each person is on the same page. When given the option, some people would choose monogamy, while others may choose polyamory, a philosophy that allows for multiple emotional and/or sexual partners. It does not matter which path is chosen, what matters is that each person in the relationship is able to choose the framework of their partnership freely, without cultural baggage influencing their decision.

For all of its merits and successes in the last hundred years, some would argue that feminism in the Internet age has become divisive. Modern American feminists have been criticized for promoting "female supremacy" rather than equality. Other criticisms include accusations of first world feminists forgetting about their struggling counterparts in Third World nations who are also dealing with oppressive, patriarchal regimes. Additionally, there is a tendency for some feminists to use the state to enforce equality. While some feminists may lobby for government granted privileges in the name of Feminism, Anarchafeminists truly seek equality by not attempting to use state power to achieve their goals. An anarchist view of feminism recognizes that the state does more harm than good by reinforcing traditional gender roles. The State pushes the idea that a liberated woman is a woman who has joined the workforce, pays taxes, and votes for her master. Governments love to declare that liberation has been achieved by incorporating women into their tax farm. We work towards acceptance of all individual choices, not declarations of equality enforced by governments. One reason women may be inclined to trust and seek assistance from government support systems is a lack of private alternatives. This is why building and creating alternative institutions that recognize the value of all life, regardless of sexual orientation, gender, or race, is of the utmost importance.

Efforts to use the government as a tool for equality has often resulted in "state feminism," which uses the force of government to grant rights and outlaw discrimination based on gender. In the past, using the state as a tool for equality has backfired and led to other forms of control, including limiting the free speech of important feminist leaders who are critical of government policies.

Men and women have been divided throughout our history on this planet. We have also experienced periods of great unity. The human species will benefit immensely from the promotion of free expressions of love and acceptance of all individual's right to live their lives to their contentment.

To achieve this goal, we must eradicate institutionalized oppression, including patriarchy. Still, the answer to millennia of abuse towards women is not shaming and condemning men. Once again, we stress the importance of balance. We support individual accountability, education, and expulsion of bigots of all types. If we are to truly move past the divisive and harmful ideas that have poisoned our species for so long, we must begin to accept the role that we each play in continuation of this toxic cycle. Only as well adjusted, emotionally balanced individuals can we create a truly free and compassionate society that respects all life.

PART 2 — ANTI-AUTHORITARIANISM IN WORLD TRADITIONS

In the following chapters, we will explore some of the popular spiritual traditions of the world to find their anti-authoritarian roots. We will also consider how these traditions were often institutionalized and turned into systems of control in the form of religion.

The ideas we cover in this book are merely scratching the surface and are intended to jump-start a conversation that is long overdue. We admit that in some areas we possess limited knowledge, so we are approaching these topics as students with curiosity and are more than happy to have other people expand on these ideas.

Chapter 11
Intersections of Shamanism and Anarchism

A discussion on the concepts of freedom would not be complete without an understanding of the shaman and their spiritual teachings. A shaman is quite simply a teacher and a student. A shaman is an individual who uses a variety of methods to communicate with the universe and the spiritual world. Shamans have been known as leaders of the community and communicators of divine messages for personal growth. A shaman experiences "religious ecstasy" when he or she accesses realms unseen to the physical world.

Shamans are said to travel between the physical and spiritual world to bring back knowledge for themselves and the community. Some actions taken by a shaman include tunneling to an underworld of spirits, experiencing altered states through drumming, meditation, or ingesting substances such as plant concoctions, and healing ailments by finding their root cause(s) on the spiritual plane.

We want to be clear that these definitions are based on our experiences with shamanic practices. The truth is that anthropologists themselves do not have one accepted definition for the term. Some define shamans as anyone who accesses the spirit world in altered states of consciousness, while others compare shamans to witch doctors or prophets. Others define shamans as schizophrenics.

The term itself has been attributed to the Evenki word saman, spoken by the indigenous peoples of Siberia. The word is thought by some scholars to mean, "to know," however, this and the true origin of the word are often contested.

Some critics of the word believe it to be a racist umbrella term that ignores the vast diversity and richness of the belief systems it attempts to describe. In the same way the term Native American has been applied to all the indigenous peoples of the North American landmass, the term shamanism is insufficient when describing such vastly different peoples and ideas. Most indigenous cultures do not even have a word for shaman. We use the term with respect to all the beautifully diverse cultures which maintain their connection to nature, promote spiritual growth, and predate the Abrahamic religions.

Western Europe and the Americas were first introduced to the term in the late 17th century, but no one really knows exactly when shamanism began. Shamanism has been called the aboriginal root of religion. All over the world, throughout history, aborigines were deeply connected to nature and used practices some of us in the modern world would consider insane. Through the use of hallucinogenic plants, drums, or meditation, one could experience a spiritual cleansing and a connection to a deeper understanding of self. This is also done through shamanic journeys — deeply personal journeys sometimes performed in the mind and sometimes performed in the wilderness for days or weeks.

Looking at anthropological studies of shamanism from cultures around the world, one finds an amazing connection to anarchy. In *Shaman's Path*, controversial anthropologist Michael Harner details why shamanism was a threat to the ruling classes:

"A reason it was wiped out is because it undermines the authority of the state and church. To have hundreds of thousands of prophets running around on the loose, in shamanism everyone is his or her own prophet, getting spiritual validation directly from the highest sources. Such people rock the boat; they are subversive. After all, if everyone is an authority, there is little possibility of creating a monopolistic business based on privileged access or right to interpret the words of a few official prophets or holy books." ("What is a Shaman?" in *Shaman's Path*, page 10).

Shamanism is the anarchism of the spiritual world. In the same way State authorities fear an educated, organized populace, the church authorities fear an independent, spiritually aware congregation. With its loose traditions and models for connecting to the realm beyond the five senses, shamanism completely bypasses the monopoly on God encouraged by all political church bodies. Throughout the history of colonization, the religious establishment has been the aggressor against the free-spirited pursuits of indigenous people and shamans.

Many ancient cultures held beliefs that fell within the realm of shamanism. From the indigenous tribes of America to the Celtic tribes of Western Europe, ancient civilizations shared many commonalities in their spiritual practices.

Before the royal oligarchies gave spirituality a strict set of rules and guidelines, indigenous cultures had a much more personal and open religious tradition. Through shamanism, these cultures were able to advance their spiritual knowledge with every age that passed because each generation played an active role in building their culture's understanding of the universe. Much how our scientific research is conducted today, generation after generation would put in work to slowly chip away at the mysteries they were trying to uncover.

Shamanism operates in a similar way, but it deals with exploring the realm of the spirit instead of the material realm of science. Generations of scientific research have allowed our species to create incredible technology, but our spiritual growth is absolutely crippled due to lack of exploration.

For the last few thousand years, much of the modern world has stopped exploring the spirit realm. The religious institutions that have had control of the spiritual dialogue for the past few millennia have completely forbidden any research into these realms.

They tell us there are no new questions to be asked because they already have all the answers, and to ask any questions is heresy. It is this strict stubbornness and arrogance that has caused many people to have a complete disinterest in spirituality. The fact that these institutions are trying to keep us from asking questions should tell us that they are not to be trusted. They do not want us to think philosophically because it could threaten their political power and influence.

Shamanism is different from our modern religious institutions because, in most cases, there is no agenda or hierarchy. There are no cloaked figures to tell you that you are not worthy and then take your money. There is no inquisition to condemn you to death if you happen to disagree with someone else's metaphysical conclusions. There are no politics or heretics. No one is going to benefit from you financially or tell you how to think. No one is going to call you evil or demand that you be killed because you don't comply with his or her edict.

Shamanism is less of a belief system and more of a form of philosophy. Belief systems often claim to have every single correct answer in the universe, which can have a negative impact on society. If people believe there are no new intellectual frontiers, they will stop looking and stop questioning. When this happens, they are cutting themselves off from opportunities for further growth. Major human advancements result from individuals trying to expand the collective pool of knowledge — not from recycling the information handed down by authoritarians for centuries.

Our lives are a grand mystery, forever unraveling. Every time a question about our universe is answered, ten more surface in its place. Even if one were to live for a hundred years in daily research and meditation, he or she would still have questions. There would still be more left to uncover.

Every great teacher who has walked this earth has recognized the infinite mystery of life. This is the attitude that is necessary to investigate the spirit world through shamanism. This path will not give you a prepackaged set of ideals and convictions wrapped with a bow and carried by a savior. You will be forced to create your own beliefs that will change every day with every new situation you encounter. In truth, this way of life should not even have a name. The fact that we even call it "shamanism" is simply because we have to attach a term to the philosophy in order to articulate the idea. Spirituality is a personal experience that should be a respected mutual interest among all humanity instead of a barrier.

It is important to point out that not all shamanic traditions have been free and peaceful. As with all spiritual traditions, there have been individuals who have claimed to have a direct connection with the divine and have exacted authority over others. This has resulted in many brutal shamanic regimes where human sacrifice, war, and slavery were all common practices. These practices, which violate natural law through aggression, are considered, "dark shamanism."

This is a common theme you will notice throughout this whole book: spiritual belief can be used for great healing when an individual has a connection with the universe, God, or their deepest self. However, spiritual belief can also create unimaginable harm when individuals and organizations act as gatekeepers for that connection.

We want to take a moment to note two important terms when dealing with shamanism in the modern age. These are "plastic shamans" and "neoshamans."

A plastic shaman is as another term for a snake oil salesman, or someone who sells fraudulent products or promotes their work as something it is not. In this case, it applies to those who purport to be of indigenous descent or have learned native ways yet have no direct involvement.

Furthermore, a plastic shaman is someone who sells native knowledge or alleged teachings in exchange for profit. Selling sacred teachings is extremely frowned upon and disrespectful. Many Native communities in America see the modern world's appropriation of indigenous teachings as another form of colonialism. A plastic shaman will claim he or she can teach you a lifetime of understanding in a weekend—if you just pay the right price. A plastic shaman may have learned a thing or two from a native community to sell the lessons to the curious, unaware suburban folk. This is not only a detriment to the communities but also to the seekers themselves who learn false teachings and likely spread those false ideas to other inquisitive minds.

This appropriation of culture has caused several tribes and assemblies to declare war against plastic shamans. On June 10, 1993, Lakota, Dakota, and Nakota nations from the United States and Canada met at the Lakota Summit V. At this gathering, around 500 representatives from 40 different tribes and bands of Lakota unanimously passed the *"Declaration of War Against Exploiters of Lakota Spirituality."* The declaration contains the following statement:

"We assert a posture of zero tolerance for any 'white man's shaman' who rises from within our own communities to 'authorize' the expropriation of our ceremonial ways by non-Indians; all such 'plastic medicine men' are enemies of the Lakota, Dakota and Nakota people."

This statement from the *"Resolution of the 5th Annual Meeting of the Traditional Elders Circle,"* drafted by several nations at Camp Rosebud Creek, Montana, on October 5, 1980, amends this strong stance:

"We concern ourselves only with those people who use spiritual ceremonies with non-Indian people for profit. There are many things to be shared with the Four Colors of humanity in our common destiny as one with our Mother the Earth. It is this sharing that must be considered with great care by the Elders and the medicine people who carry the Sacred Trusts, so that no harm may come to people through ignorance and misuse of these powerful forces."

In this spirit of cooperation, we hope to learn from diverse Native cultures and evolve with respect to their ancient teachings while incorporating newly discovered forms of healing. This brings us to the topic of neoshamans. Neoshamanism describes modern interpretations of older forms of shamanism and traditional teachings. Neoshamanism is not a single set of beliefs but a variety of ways to attain altered states of mind and commune with the spirit world.

A neoshaman may be a non-native and have no connection to any past tribe. Rather, the neoshaman absorbs knowledge from many places and incorporates the individual pieces into a tapestry of spiritual awareness. With the advent of computers and rapidly expanding technologies, many students of shamanism have learned to alter their states of consciousness for the purposes of healing using computers, binaural beats, and other non-traditional methods. The terms "techno-shaman" and "crypto-shaman" have even come into use in recent years.

What is the difference between a plastic shaman and a neoshaman? This is a matter of great debate and opinion. We believe that encouraging people from around the world to share and learn from one another is a positive action that will propel humanity forward, not backward. However, we understand that many Native communities look back at the history of relations between themselves and outsiders and have little desire to invite the Western world into their sacred teachings. We respect these decisions and hope that non-Natives who are interested in learning native ways seek out Native teachers with tribe affiliation and a true understanding of the culture. We also hope those interested in spirituality and shamanism can learn from many sources and decide which path to God/Source/self-actualization resonates the strongest with them.

As long as we learn with an open mind and do not speak for tribes, peoples, and cultures in which we are not well versed, we can build bridges between these diverse worlds without destroying the individual cultures. In fact, the idea of keeping a powerful interpretation of God and the universe all to a small group of people rings of elitism. At the same time, it is up to each community and each individual to decide what teachings they share and with whom.

The fact that various people from different cultural backgrounds have attempted to stamp a copyright on spirituality is itself a complete sacrilege. Everyone should have their own religion that they ponder and share. If more people proclaimed their beliefs aloud, the better ideas would be more likely to surface and become more popular, while the bad ideas would dwindle off rather easily. The best ideas would be passed along to the next generation and molded based on whatever new information came in during that time. This shamanic worldview would be a constantly changing collective religion actually built by everyone in society. This would eliminate a lot of the spiritual segregation that is caused by modern religion because participants would be encouraged to learn from one another instead of looking down on one another.

If humanity chooses to discuss philosophical concepts and debates surrounding shamanism and belief itself, there is hope. If we come together and reach the spirit realm using meditation and psychedelics, we can achieve the same kind of breakthroughs that we have in the material realm, bringing us much closer to peace.

Chapter 12
Intersections of Christianity and Anarchism

There is no doubt that unimaginable suffering and division have been caused by the political organizations that formed around Christianity, Judaism, Islam, and the other religions of the world. However, as we intend to explore in the following chapters, there is ample evidence to suggest these religions all carry knowledge from similar ancient teachings. Sadly, the hierarchies of these organized religions perverted these teachings according to the politics of the time.

The biblical accounts of Jesus were not consolidated and printed until roughly 300 years after his death. At that time, his followers had caused a massive social upheaval, which threatened the established religious and state powers. Even in his time, Jesus was an enemy of the state and an enemy of the established religions for his radical views of peace, freedom, and equality. The established religious order of the time was the "state church" of the Roman government, and they were so threatened by his philosophy that they silenced him.

However, his death did not silence his message, and his ideas spread all over the empire. Fearful that this anti-establishment movement would break down their spiritual monopoly, the government developed a plan to corrupt the message of Christ and use his cult status as a banner for their religious institution.

The institution responsible for the death of Christ and the persecution of his followers was now planning to merge his popular image with their dogmatic tradition. In 325 A.D., the Roman Church held the Council of Nicaea, a meeting of ranking church figures. They discussed how they would deal with the explosion of the Christian philosophy in their society. The church knew that if they let things continue as they were, all of their subjects would convert to Christianity in a very short time. They had to find a way to subvert this trend and convert the Christians back to the traditional structure to maintain control.

To achieve this goal, the establishment decided to merge Christian teachings with their own in such a way that the radical message of peace and freedom was replaced with the hierarchy of the Roman church. The outcome of the Council of Nicaea stated that Jesus Christ was the son of God and that he was to be treated as a divine figure. This went against Christ's insistence that he was only a messenger and that people should follow his message, not worship him. There is a great deal of controversy surrounding the divinity of Christ, and many say that he didn't want organized churches in his name.

Christian followers, who mostly belonged to the working illiterate class, were deceived by the church into supporting the Council's changes, even celebrating the fact that the church had finally formally recognized their savior. Most Christians did not understand the true implications of the terms that their rulers laid out at the Council of Nicaea. The church then used "the divinity of Christ" as supporting evidence for all of their philosophies even though the issue of divinity had been decided at the conference.

With the image and following of Jesus now a part of their church, the establishment was able to neutralize the social movement of Christianity from within. Once the state molded the Christian ideologies to fit its own political agenda, it was also able to dictate an "official" but corrupted recording of history. The church focused only on their fabricated depictions of Christ's birth and death and gave very little mention of what he actually stood for and what he did throughout his life. Certain historical accounts of Jesus have been suppressed by the religious institutions because the reality of his political struggle would expose many of the primary falsehoods of our authoritarian society.

This is the way the establishment has "watered down" and misdirected the revolutionary message of Jesus. This is the most successful strategy of silencing and corrupting revolutionary movements, and it is the ruling class which it when they are backed up against a wall. They know attempts to fully eradicate a social movement only make that movement stronger and give it more credibility, so instead they corrupt the message and turn it into a tool of social control. Even in the accounts of Jesus that have not been destroyed by the church, we can see his apparent opposition towards the oppressive systems of government, banking, and organized religion. In all of the biblical depictions of Christ, he has a peaceful state of mind, except when he is dealing with "the money changers."

According to biblical writings, Jesus used physical force to throw the money changers out of a temple, which was the only account of him ever getting physical with anyone. The money changers were an ancient banking cartel that manipulated the ancient world by lending money to governments and applying interest. Just like today, the money changers of biblical times were deeply embedded with the government.

Behind the fabricated image of Jesus that the church has been perpetuating for centuries, there is most likely a revolutionary who vehemently opposed the ruling class and fought for the rights of the oppressed throughout his life. His whole life was a struggle for peace, equality, and human rights, yet the religions that have sprung up in his name distorted his message because it stands against blind obedience to authority. Whether or not Jesus Christ was a divine being, a human revolutionary, or a character of astrotheology is not for the authors of this book to decide.

That is a matter for people to decide based upon their own studies. Regardless, the message of compassion, non-aggression, and anti-authoritarianism behind the story of Jesus Christ remains the same.

Since Jesus's time, political organizations in the form of religions have carried on his image, but they have largely abandoned his message. That being said, there have been a number of Christian thinkers with very strong anti-authoritarian views and a number of Christian movements with very strong anarchist traits. Within just a few generations of the Council of Nicea, Saint Augustine was quick to point out that the teachings of Christ were in total opposition to the values of the Roman Empire and the Roman church. In present times, there are Christian churches spread throughout the United States that have recognized the same thing. Sadly, there are still many warmongering neoconservative churches, as well.

The Quakers are an entire sect of Christianity that is openly anti-authoritarian. The Quakers are also the group with the deepest history of both activism and anarchist philosophy. Sadly, in mainstream thought, Quakers are often confused with the Puritans, a sect of Christianity in colonial America that was known for being repressive and tyrannical.

The Quakers and the Puritans had two totally different schools of thought. The Puritans believed the bible granted religious organizations authority over human beings, while the Quakers believed each individual was capable of forming his or her own connection with God and that there was no need for an external authority. The only reason these groups are often confused is because they are both Christian sects that escaped England for the new world, but in all other respects, they could not be more different from one another. The Quakers do not recognize human authority. In fact, authority isn't even a part of their vocabulary. For example, Quakers will not refer to a person by a title, such as judge, officer, president, your Highness, your honor, your majesty, or any of the terms that groveling peasants are coerced into repeating. The Quakers also played an essential role in the abolition movement and the Underground Railroad, and many of the civil rights struggles that followed.

Another important thread in the history of Christian Anarchism is the ideas presented by author Leo Tolstoy. Tolstoy was living under the rule of the Russian Orthodox church which had merged with the Russian state and promoted a sanitized State-Christianity. He recognized the hypocrisy of a government claiming to embody the teachings of the rebellious Christ. Tolstoy outlined his thinking and the vision of a Christian Anarchism with his book, *The Kingdom of God Is Within You*. The book was banned in Russia because Tolstoy called for organizing society based on interpreting Christianity focused on preaching nonviolence, nonviolent resistance, and universal love for all beings.

The Kingdom of God is Within You derives its title from the Bible, specifically Luke 17:21 which states, *"nor will they say, 'See here!' or 'See there!' For* indeed, *the kingdom of God is within you.*" Tolstoy rejected the idea that the Church or the State could have a monopoly on the relationship with Christ. "*Nowhere nor in anything, except in the assertion of the Church, can we find that God or Christ founded anything like what churchmen understand by the Church,*" he wrote. Tolstoy also believed that when Christ told his disciples to turn the other cheek he was calling for the abolition of violence. "*How can you kill people, when it is written in God's commandment: 'Thou shalt not murder'?,*" Tolstoy asked. He believed Christians were called to love their enemies and reject the notion of revenge. He was adamantly against war and considered it a betrayal of Christian principles. He also deemed the State to be a monopoly of organized violence which demanded money under the false promise of safety. Because of the inherently violent nature of government, and the hypocrisy of a Christian-state, Tolstoy believed the Bible implied anarchism as necessary for Christians. Finally, he believed all Christians should seek to undermine the illegitimate moral authority of the State.

By studying the history of Jesus Christ and the traditions that arose following his death, it is clear that his message has become distorted and corrupted. Perhaps all that is needed is for followers of Christ to abandon the churches and leaders who claim to have the path to his teachings and instead cultivate their own personal conversation with him and individually interpret his message.

Chapter 13
Intersection of Judaism and Anarchism

Due to Judaism's unique history, it tends to mean different things to different people. For many people being a Jew describes their religious preferences, while for others it is a race, and for some it is a cultural identity. Throughout the history of radical philosophy, there have been a large number of Jewish anarchists who fought for freedom and helped to advance the philosophy. Often, these Jewish anarchists have been secular. For many of these anarchists, their Jewish identity was directly tied to their shared experience of oppression. Many of them became atheists and rejected religion entirely while still maintaining a connection to their heritage. Emma Goldman, for example, wrote extensively on atheism and was critical of Orthodox Judaism and Zionism. She still resonated with her cultural heritage in many ways, but did not openly identify as a Jewish anarchist. Goldman was a crucial link between the Yiddish-speaking Jewish anarchist movement and the U.S. anarchist movement before World War II. This immigrant anarchist movement was based in New York City and opposed capitalism, the state, and organized religion. Due to the mostly atheist leanings of this Jewish population, there were often conflicts with more traditional Jews.

While the Orthodox Jewish community is traditionally very strict and puritanical — much like their Christian and Muslim counterparts — there are some outliers who have a more anarchist interpretation of the philosophy. The Orthodox Kabbalist rabbi Yehuda Ashlag promoted a philosophy that he called altruist communism, which he developed through his interpretation of the Kabbalah. In his writings, Ashlag called for the establishment of self-ruled communities, and said that, *"there is nothing more humiliating and degrading for a person than being under the brute-force government."* There was also Yankev-Meyer Zalkind, a British Orthodox rabbi and anarcho-communist who believed that anarchism was prescribed in the ethics of the Talmud. Initially a Zionist, Zalkind was involved in setting up some of the original settlements in Israel before quickly becoming disenfranchised with the human rights consequences of colonization. Ultimately, Zalkind moved back to London to campaign against war and militarism. He later proposed the creation of an anarchist society in Palestine, where refugees from any nation or culture would be welcome. In the 21st century, as anarchism continues to evolve as a philosophy, there is an increasing number of people identifying as Jewish anarchists. This growth can be seen in Israel where Jewish youth are rejecting the apartheid military regime that has controlled the region for generations. However, many of these anarchists would also identify as secular. Still, there does seem to be a renewed interest in exploring Jewish anarchism and what it might mean for a Jewish person to filter their anarchist beliefs through their religion. As recently as January 2019, The YIVO Institute for Jewish Research organized a conference on Yiddish anarchism in New York City with attendance of nearly 500 people.

Chapter 14
Intersections of Islam and Anarchism

All modern religious organizations have been tainted with authoritarianism and fundamentalism, and institutions created in the name of the Islamic faith are no different. However, as with the other traditions mentioned in previous chapters, there are still many practitioners of the faith who have beliefs that align with anarchism. As with Judaism, there are only a few philosophers that make explicit attempts to join Islam with anarchism. Our friend, Davi Barker, a Muslim and scholar of Islamic history, wrote a book called *Voluntary Islam,* in which he highlights the overlaps that he has found with anarchism. We have selected two essays from the book that we believe provide some insight into where these two philosophies tie together. We strongly recommend checking out his book for a deeper understanding of this topic.

The following are two guest essays selected from Davi Barker's excellent book, Voluntary Islam.

Islam and the discovery of freedom

I read the entirety of *Islam and the Discovery of Freedom* by Rose Wilder Lane on a direct flight from San Francisco to New Hampshire. I literally cried as she chronicled the great liberty of the past being eclipsed by tyranny. In my heart I found a new love for my friend and teacher Imam Suhaib Webb, whose Islamic literacy class gave me the tools necessary to better grasp the meaning of the commentary by Dr. Imad-ad-Deen Ahmad. Born in 1886, Rose Wilder Lane is regarded as one of the founding mothers of the libertarian movement. Her book *The Discovery of Freedom: Man's Struggle Against Authority* is said to have been written from beginning to end in "a white heat" and consequently contains numerous historical (but not philosophical) errors. Dissatisfied, and perhaps embarrassed, by these errors, Lane withdrew it from publication, but in her wisdom, she devoted a chapter to Islam's contributions to the philosophy of liberty. Now that chapter is available with commentary provided by Dr. Imad-ad-Deen Ahmad of the Minaret of Freedom Institute. He corrects her minor historical and theological errors but further bolsters her thesis that the golden age of Islamic civilization was the product of its abundant liberty, and its downfall was the result of its decline into tyranny.

Lane begins by summarizing Abraham's message as, "*there is only one God, who has blessed mankind with freewill. They bear accountability for their righteous or evil actions. The pagan gods do not exist, and do not control the affairs of mankind.*"

She regards this as the first great attempt to liberate mankind from illegitimate authority and describes history as a struggle between this conviction that human beings are self-controlling and individually responsible and attempts by earthly authorities to make themselves into false gods over mankind. She regards Muhammad's message as the second great attempt to establish liberty on Earth. I found her description of the Prophet as a practical, humorous, friendly business executive to be utterly refreshing. In Muhammad's view, according to Lane, priests corrupted the pure message of Abraham, Moses, and Jesus when they assumed authority to control mankind. It was therefore incumbent upon mankind to establish a direct relationship to God without priests.

This recognition of mankind as individually volitional beings laid the foundation for what Lane calls the world's first scientific civilization in the modern sense. She writes, "*Whenever authority was weak, men opened schools of science*," because in the Islamic worldview there was no distinction between sacred and profane knowledge. All truth is from God. Lane describes the earliest Islamic universities as marketplaces of knowledge like the bazaars. Men of knowledge came to sell their instructions in an open forum, and students were free to wander about listening. When they decided upon a teacher, they met privately to establish a curriculum and agree upon fees. These universities were privately funded and virtually without state regulation. They were regulated by reputation. A teacher's success or failure hinged upon the market demand for the knowledge he sold. If the student was dissatisfied, he simply left to find another teacher, and when he'd had his fill of education, he left school to apply his knowledge.

Lane writes:

"*Europeans were not able to impose upon that university any tinge of the European belief that minds acquire knowledge, not by actively seeking to know, but by passively being taught whatever Authority decides that they should know.*"

The result was an explosion of human energy that led to advanced mathematics, medicine, chemistry, astronomy, cosmetics, hygiene, art, and philosophy that appeared like utter magic to medieval Europeans.

Beyond schools, there were also hospitals, libraries, paved roads, and whole water irrigation networks built and maintained by similar private foundations. All institutions and infrastructure that might characterize an advanced civilization were produced without state intervention. Even law was developed by scholars independent of government. Law was not legislated but discovered the same way that natural scientists discover the laws of physical, chemical, and biological systems. A judge, or qadi, was independent of the State. To keep his reputation for wisdom, he had to find ways to settle disputes that satisfied everyone's sense of justice. No single organization, religious, social, or political, extended over the whole civilization. No monopoly means no state by modern definitions. Lane makes the argument—quite effectively, in fact—that through Italy, the Muslims gave Europe the enlightenment, and through Spain the Muslims gave Europe the maps, the navigational tools, and the love for freedom that drove them to the New World.

In Muslim Spain, generations of European Christians and Jews experienced freedom of thought and conscience unprecedented anywhere else in Europe. In the century after Granada fell and Spain returned to Catholic rule, the Spaniards were less submissive to government than any other Europeans, and it was during that century that Spaniards explored and conquered the New World. Lane suggests it was the love of freedom learned from the Muslims that drove free-thinking Europeans away from tyranny and across the Atlantic Ocean. Most Muslims fled to Muslim lands, but those who stayed in Spain were forced to convert to Catholicism and came to be called Moriscos.

There was doubt about the sincerity of their conversion when they persisted in their Islamic customs such as reading … and bathing. The State responded by burning libraries and prohibiting the Moriscos from bathing secretly in their homes. The Spanish Inquisition began in large part to expose secret Muslims in Spain and uncover the *"Apostasies and Treasons of the Moriscos."* In 1602, among the charges against the Moriscos was that they *"commended nothing so much as that liberty of conscience in all matters of religion, which the Turks and all other Mohammedans suffer their subjects to enjoy."*

What the investigation found was that freedom of thought, skepticism of government, and passion for freedom had infected Spaniards who had never been Muslim. So, naturally, those Christians accustomed to this freedom, who could not abide such religious persecution, fled to the New World. According to Lane, Muslims "forgot the god of Abraham" sometime in the 16th century and rejected the personal responsibility of freedom. Islamic civilization began to resemble the rest of Europe as a static society of controlling authority. But the mantle of liberty had been passed to the Americans directly from the Muslims in Spain. Lane regards the American Revolution as the third and most current attempt to establish a free society on Earth, where political conditions would not hinder mankind's natural inclination toward scientific progress. Many Muslims will speak of the Islamic golden age as an invitation to non-Muslims to challenge their stereotypes of Islam. This is not my aim. I intend to look to this glorious past and imagine what progress we are capable of if only we demand the freedom from tyranny they had in those days.

Unfortunately, Lane offers virtually no explanation for why the Muslim world changed. But if we're ever to reclaim the liberty we have lost, it's important that we don't try to manage the symptoms and instead diagnose the disease. It's important that we acknowledge that the success of the past was not achieved by central authority but by living in conditions where human energy was free from control.

Ninth-Century Muslim Anarchists

I came across an article titled "Ninth-Century Muslim Anarchists" by Patricia Crone, scholar of early Islamic history at the Institute for Advanced Study, Princeton, that centers around a discussion that was taking place in Basra in southern Iraq in the 800s. There was a general consensus that the Abbasid Caliphate, which controlled a vast empire from Baghdad, had become corrupt and tyrannical. So the question among the scholars became how the community should respond to a leader who had become *"all too reminiscent of Pharaoh,"* as Crone puts it. This article was originally published in 2000 in the *Past & Present* journal.

But in light of the Arab Spring, I think it's valuable to pick up the discussion where they left off. The mainstream opinions are broadly categorized as activists and quietists by Crone. The activists held that when a leader lost legitimacy, it was obligatory to stage a violent revolution and install a new legitimate leader. The quietists held that civil war was worse than oppression and that it was obligatory to patiently persevere under tyranny. You had to obey the tyrant, or at the most, resist passively. For whatever reason, the quietist position has been and remains the dominant position, even though it contradicts the opinion of Muhammad's companion Abu Bakr, who said upon his inauguration, *"Obey me as long as I obey God and His Prophet. But if I disobey God's command or His Prophet, then no obedience is incumbent upon you."*

The quietist position undoubtedly has contributed to the current state of political affairs in Muslim-majority countries. Unfettered State power is and always will be expanding State power. There was a third category of solutions they were exploring that Crone calls "anarchist." Most of these were what Crone calls "reluctant anarchists," in that they believed the society could function without the Caliph.

For them, anarchism was not an ideal they hoped to achieve, but the acknowledgment that the ideal, the Medina Caliphate, was lost and could not be restored. They proposed a kind of evolutionary anarchism. They made no proposal to abolish private property except to say that the illegitimacy of the ruler spoiled the validity of titles to property, presumably those granted by the ruler. This may be similar to the way some modern libertarians view eminent domain, corporate title, and intellectual property as invalid. Predominantly, it was factions among the Mu'tazilites, the Kharijites, and the Sufis who proposed that if leaders kept turning into tyrants, perhaps they'd be better off without leaders at all.

Essentially, they argued that the Caliph must be agreed upon by the entire community, either unanimously or by consensus, and that without this, no legitimate Caliph could exist. It was widely accepted that God did not impose obligations that were impossible to fulfill, so it was reasoned that there was no obligation to establish a legitimate Caliph, although hardly any of them denied the possibility of one emerging in the future. But in the meantime, alternatives had to be explored. Some pointed out that the Bedouins had gotten along fine without rulers.

Crone writes that *"anarchists were clearly drawing on the tribal tradition which lies behind all early Islamic political thought of the type which may be loosely identified as libertarian."* Crone didn't specify this in the article, but this view of the Caliphate is consistent with the hadith in which the Prophet informed us that after him would be leaders who followed his example, then there would be kings, and then there would be tyrants. If you accept this hadith, it's clear that we have progressed from Caliphs to kings and hard to argue we haven't progressed from kings to tyrants.

Viewed this way, any attempt to re-establish the Caliphate by force could only result in further tyranny. Their specific reasons for arguing against the Caliphate are not particularly relevant to us today, as there has not been a Caliphate, legitimate or otherwise, since the collapse of the Ottoman Empire. The reality for us is that this is less an intellectual exercise than a practical necessity, especially in light of the tenuous grip the current tyrannies hold over their people.

Their proposed solutions of the "reluctant anarchists" ranged from a radical decentralization of public authority to a complete dissolution of public authority. A subset of proposals involved replacing the Caliph with elected officials, the argument being that if you polled enough people, you minimized the danger of bias and collusion that had become the signature of the Caliphate. These proposals could be called "minarchist" in modern parlance. They proposed that people could elect trustworthy and learned leaders within their local communities, arguing that there could never be unanimous agreement upon one leader of the Muslims, and one could not assess the quality of candidates at great distances.

These leaders could either be completely independent of one another, or they could be joined together in a federation, the reasoning being that independent leaders would forever be fighting with their neighbors. This is strikingly reminiscent of the federalist vs. anti-federalist debate that took place in the American colonies 1,000 years later. Some minarchists viewed these elected officials as temporary, only remaining in office when legal disputes arose or when an enemy invaded. When the problem was resolved, they would lose their positions, much as an imam does when he has finished leading prayer, and society could return to statelessness. This is very similar to the stateless judicial system in Somalia today, which we will discuss next. Admittedly, the minarchist proposals were not really anarchist. They advocated abolishing the form of government to which they had grown accustomed and replacing it with systems with far more public participation. Most of them were proposing new forms of government for which they had no historical precedent. But there were still some who were true anarchists in that they wanted a complete dissolution of public authority. Some argued that a sufficiently moral society would have no need for authority, while others argued that because society was not sufficiently moral, they couldn't have a legitimate authority. Either way, they believed that the welfare of society would be best if people were only left alone. The most prominent group calling for the complete abolition of the State was a minority sect called the Najdiyya. They argued that so long as there was not sufficient agreement to establish a legitimate Caliph, there could never be enough to establish law at all. Even the consensus of scholars could not be a source of law in a community where no unified consensus existed, anyway. To the Najdiyya, every individual was responsible for his own salvation and entitled to his own legal interpretations through independent reasoning (ijtihad). Indeed, any intellectual tradition must be built on this foundation because in order to persuade others to adopt it, you must first appeal to their independent reasoning.

The Najdiyya not only demanded political independence but also complete intellectual independence because believers were, as the Prophet said, "like the teeth of a comb," and therefore should have no master but God himself. Divine law could be conceived of as the natural law, available to all mankind like fingerprints in the clay of Adam. Crone calls this *"radical libertarianism,"* and as far as I can tell, it is one of the first appearances of it in history.

None of the anarchists or minarchists explained how to put their proposals into practice while the State still existed. They merely speculated, leaving it to future generations to implement their radical reform. We may be those generations. None of them proposed fomenting rebellion, happy to enjoy the comforts the State provided its intellectuals. Only the Sufis avoided material comforts, but their solution was simply to transcend politics and seek meaning in other pursuits, not to revolt. However, in 817 anarchy was foisted upon them when the government in Baghdad collapsed. A civil war had ousted the previous Caliph, and the influence of the new Caliph hadn't been established yet. Chaos ensued, and the public responded, as many would have predicted, by forming a vigilante group to protect private property, maintain commerce, and allow the meek to move freely through Baghdad. This is exactly the kind of spontaneous order we saw in Egypt when police in plainclothes picked fights and looted stores. Civilians self-organized into neighborhood watch programs to protect each other. We see now what they saw then: In the absence of public authority there is a natural emergence of order out of chaos without central planning. The Muslim anarchists of the ninth century concluded, as many have in the modern world, *that when people are forced to rely on themselves, they discover talents they did not know they had."*

Chapter 15
Intersections of Buddhism and Anarchism

This chapter will focus on the philosophy of Buddhism, specifically Zen, and anarchy, specifically agorism. Zen is the Japanese pronunciation for Chan or Dhyana, which translates roughly to "meditation." It is also the name for the School of Mahayana Buddhism that began in China and spread to the south and east around the 6th century of the current era.

Although certain sects of Buddhism have promoted obedience and been used as state religion, Zen Buddhism was actually a rejection of certain ritualized Buddhist practices and philosophy that had become more rigid since the death of the Buddha, Siddhartha Gautama.

Siddhartha is believed to have been born a prince in the subcontinent of India about five centuries before the current era. His parents did their best to shelter him. However, the story says that at age twenty-nine, Siddhartha made several trips outside of his pampered palace and witnessed human suffering for the first time in his life in the form of a sick elderly man and a dead body. Siddhartha decided to abandon his privileged life and begin a spiritual quest.

After trying out extremes of dedicated, deep meditation and fasting to the point of starvation, the former prince discovered the Middle Way, a path of balance and moderation. At age thirty-five, while meditating under the Bodhi tree, he achieved enlightenment as he touched the Earth, declaring his victory over Mara, a demon that represents temptation. From then until the time of his death in his eighties, the Buddha taught his philosophy of compassion, non-violence, meditation, and non-attachment.

Around twelve centuries after the Buddha's life, an Indian monk named Bodhidharma was credited with bringing Buddhism to China and popularizing the importance of Zazen, or sitting meditation. He taught that the path to enlightenment would not come from reciting the Buddha's words or lighting a certain number of candles but rather by doing what the Buddha was doing when he achieved enlightenment—meditating.

The Buddha's victory over Mara underneath the Bodhi tree is the reason Zen stresses the importance of Zazen. Through Zazen we better understand the nature of reality as we achieve self-realization by recognizing the truth that there is nothing but the present moment.

Zen and the Agora: Anarchy, Agora, Action, and Awareness

As noted earlier, agorism is the branch of anarchy that focuses on self-sufficiency, the idea of counter-economics, black and gray markets, and creating alternatives to state institutions. Our desire for anarchy comes from a desire for collective liberation. Our interest in agorism comes from a demand for actions that create solutions in this life in attempts to create a better world.

While agorism calls for action in the physical realm by creating alternative currencies, self-sufficiency, and barter networks, Zen calls for action in the mental realm. Zen is the action of the mind. In Zen, the greatest action you can take is to sit, still your mind, and be with yourself. You must silence the noise and detach. It is about connecting with your mind and recognizing the ultimate truth of reality and freedom beyond words.

Both of these philosophies call for action. One calls for action in the physical world, the other in the internal world, but both are about taking action.

Meditation is a completely personal and direct experience. It "requires" letting go of fears, insecurities, and ego. Whatever you find in your own mind, nobody can take that away from you. In terms of anarchy, we see meditation as our direct connection to being sovereign, free humans with no authority over us. We are not pretending that this (or anything in this book) is a one-size-fits-all solution. Obviously, those don't work. Rather, we are providing another option—what we believe is a further advancement of anarchism.

In the *New Libertarian Manifesto*, the first book to introduce agorism, Samuel Konkin III writes, "*[T]here is no one way, one straight line graph to liberty to be sure, but there is a family of graphs that will take the libertarian to his goal of a free society and that space can be described.*"

We believe another solution is having a sense of spirituality and an understanding of self-reflection coupled with a philosophical understanding of anarchy and the role of government. It is not enough to simply understand the nature of government and the immorality of force. If we do not learn about ourselves and conquer our inner demons and attempt to get to the root causes of statism, statism will live on. We may be able to beat the current government, but until we explore the root of the issue, a new type of statism will exist every couple hundred years or so.

Konkin continues:

"*[A] lot more than statism would need to be eliminated from individual consciousness for this society to exist. Most damaging of all to this perfectly free society is its lack of a mechanism of correction. All it takes is a handful of practitioners of coercion who enjoy their ill-gotten plunder in enough company to sustain them—and freedom is dead. Even if all are living free, one 'bite of the apple,' one throwback, reading old history or rediscovering evil on his own, will 'unfree' the perfect society.*"[1]

It will take more than the elimination of statism to create a free society. We can spread the ideas of liberty, anarchy, self-rule, and an understanding of the

1. p. 25.

immorality of force and the like, but until we as individuals deeply examine our own inconsistencies, we are doomed to repeat the same mistakes and create a new form of statism. Humanity must pursue an understanding of the self and the motivation behind violence, theft, and fear. If free people continue to be bound by fear, we will keep creating the same situation.

In Buddhism, the endless cycle of life and death, which students of the Middle Path seek to end, is known as Samsara. Until you gain a level of balance and tacit awareness through meditation, chanting, prayer, or ritual (depending on the sect of Buddhism) you will continue the cycle of Samsara. As a species, we find ourselves stuck in State Samsara, an endless cycle of attempting to fix the world and manage humanity's problems by allowing a small group to maintain a monopoly on force and violence. It doesn't work. We will continue this cycle until every individual makes a choice to go within and stop feeding the state.

When Konkin introduced agorism, he also introduced the three "A's." These include the agora, anarchy and action. "Agora" means the marketplace, or the exchange—humans interacting freely without interference. "Anarchy" amounts to self-rule, and "action" is what's needed to move these things forward. Equally powerful as the three A's are the Buddhist sentiments of wisdom, compassion ,and action.

If you have wisdom, you possess knowledge and know how to use it. You have a solid understanding of the physical world around you. With wisdom but no compassion for your fellow human being, you are all mind and no heart. However, if you are all compassion, being led solely by your heart and possessing no wisdom, you might find yourself being taken advantage of and led astray. Even if you have wisdom and compassion for yourself and the community around you, nothing gets done without action. It is with this in mind that we propose a fourth A for the spiritual agorist.

We believe that "awareness" should be a part of the Agorist path—awareness of self so you can better know "rule" yourself. How can we know what freedom means to us if we do not know ourselves? This is also considered mindful awareness or mindfulness—mindfulness with our interactions with the community, in the market, and in our actions.

When we apply the same understanding and awareness to our individual paths and our place in the universe, we are furthering our understanding of what it truly means to be free. It is time for us to slow down, to be conscious, and to become more aware of our own thoughts, words, and actions. From this balanced standpoint, we can begin to build alternative institutions that will rival the state and allow freedom to flourish.

Consistency From Samuel Konkin III to Siddhartha Gautama

Throughout our lives, we encounter individuals who profess certain ideas or principles, whether political or otherwise, yet display behavior quite the opposite of their words. After repeatedly witnessing such hypocrisy, one learns not to trust the words of such a person. If we cannot be held accountable for our actions and words, why bother taking anyone seriously?

In the "*New Libertarian Manifesto*," Samuel Konkin III speaks of the importance of consistency. He writes:

"*The basic principle which leads a libertarian from statism to his free society is the same which the founders of libertarianism used to discover the theory itself. That principle is consistency. Thus, the consistent application of the theory of libertarianism to every action the individual libertarian takes creates the libertarian society.*

"*Many thinkers have expressed the need for consistency between means and ends and not all were libertarians. Ironically, many statists have claimed inconsistency between laudable ends and contemptible means; yet when their true ends of greater power and oppression were understood, their means are found to be quite consistent. It is part of the statist mystique to confuse the necessity of ends-means consistency; it is thus the most crucial activity of the libertarian theorist to expose inconsistencies.*"[1]

Konkin understood the importance of consistency when it comes to libertarian/anarchist philosophy, and we can take it even further. If we move the strictly libertarian mindset from the sentences, we see they remain applicable to any individual regardless of their political or philosophical association.

"*The application of consistency to every action the individual takes creates a more consistent society.*"

Obviously, as Konkin states, statists are quite inconsistent, as well. They may claim to stand for certain principles, yet their actions show their true nature and intentions. One can assume the statists in power are either completely unaware of their actions, or are, in fact, total and complete liars.

Siddhartha Gautama also spoke about the importance of consistency: The Buddha believed mindfulness and self-awareness were the two keys to eliminating suffering. He believed one could attain a new understanding of self and move past the dualistic understanding of reality by turning the focus inward and meditating.

With a consistent application of compassion and self-reflection, the Buddhist sees a way to free the people from themselves and thus create a freer society. We see the importance of consistency in this quote attributed to the Buddha:

"*Mind precedes all mental states. Mind is their chief; they are all mind-wrought. If with a pure mind, a person speaks or acts happiness follows him like his never-departing shadow.*"[2]

---

1. p. 23.
2. *The Pairs*, Dhammapada.

What you create in thought form becomes your words. After repeatedly listening to your words, your actions begin to reflect your thinking. So if you are of the statist mindset, you speak from a statist perspective and, your actions and character reflect your statist position. On the other hand, if you are pursuing ideas of compassion, the non-aggression principle, self-rule, and reflection, it follows that your thoughts, words, and actions will reflect the same.

This is in line with voluntaryist philosophy. Author Albert Jay Nock said it best in his book *Memoirs of a Superfluous Man*:

"The only thing that the psychically human being can do to improve society is to present society with one improved unit. In a word, ages of experience testify that the only way society can be improved is by the individualist method which Jesus apparently regarded as the only one whereby the Kingdom of Heaven can be established as a going concern; that is, the method of each one doing his very best to improve one."[1]

Once again, the ideas of introspection and self-governance align. We see great value in a path that includes an autonomous, sovereign practice of Zen meditation, compassion, and non-violence that also respects the principles of self-governance and self-determination.

---

1. p. 308.

Chapter 16
Intersections of Taoism and Anarchism

Taoism is an ancient Chinese tradition that emphasizes living in harmony with what is referred to as Tao. The term Tao means "way," "path," or "principle." It is a concept found in Chinese philosophies and religions. However, in Taoism, the Tao is believed to be both the source and the force behind everything that exists.

Although Taoism drew its cosmological philosophy from the School of Yin Yang, the *Tao Te Ching* by early Chinese philosopher Lao-Tzu is considered by many to be its primary source. *Tao Te Ching* roughly translates to *The Book of The Natural Way and of Natural Virtues*.

Written around 600 years before the current era, the *Tao Te Ching* presents a model of Wu wei, action without action, or non-action. Wu wei is not the promotion of absence of action, but the state of being in harmony with the nature of things, or Tao. Lao-Tzu has been recognized as one of the earliest-known anti-authoritarian thinkers. He espoused a very individualist philosophy that saw social institutions as a hindrance to rather than a benefit for human beings. Lao-Tzu's writings explored the errors of prohibitions and government regulation many centuries before anyone else was challenging these concepts.

In Chapter 57 of the *Tao Te Ching*, Lao-Tzu writes:

"If you want to be a great leader, you must learn to follow the Tao. Stop trying to control.

"Let go of fixed plans and concepts, and the world will govern itself. The more prohibitions you have, the less virtuous people will be. The more weapons you have, the less secure people will be. The more subsidies you have, the less self-reliant people will be. Therefore the Master says:

"I let go of the law, and people become honest. I let go of economics, and people become prosperous. I let go of religion, and people become serene. I let go of all desire for the common good, and the good becomes common as grass."

In Chapter 75, Lao-Tzu comments on the importance of self-governance:

"When taxes are too high, people go hungry. When government is too intrusive, people lose their spirit. Act for the peoples benefit. Trust them; leave them alone."

In Chapter 31, Lao-Tzu references the principles of non-aggression and non-violence.

"Weapons are the tools of violence; all decent men detest them. Weapons are the tools of fear; a decent man will avoid them except in the direst necessity and, if com-

pelled, will use them only with the utmost restraint. Peace is his highest value. If the peace has been shattered, how can he be content? His enemies are not demons, but human beings like himself. He doesn't wish them personal harm. Nor does he rejoice in victory. How could he rejoice in victory and delight in the slaughter of men?"

Two centuries after Lao-Tzu came philosopher Chuang Tzu, who took the teachings of his predecessor a step further. His writings became so popular that his intellectual services were sought far and wide, even among the aristocracy and monarchy. Eventually, Chuang Tzu received an offer from King Wei of the Ch'u kingdom to serve as his chief minister of state.

Chuang Tzu passionately refused his offer. Chuang Tzu put forward many bold anti-state positions in his writings, including the following statements, sourced by Murray Rothbard in his work *Concepts of the Role of Intellectuals in Social Change Toward Laissez Faire*:

"There has never been such a thing as letting mankind alone; there has never been such a thing as governing mankind with success. Letting alone springs from fear lest men's natural dispositions be perverted and their virtue left aside. But if their natural dispositions be not perverted nor their virtue laid aside, what room is there left for government?"

He has also been quoted as saying that the world *"does not need governing; in fact, it should not be governed."*

In the nineteenth and twentieth centuries, philosophers like Proudhon and Hayek were pioneering the concept of *"spontaneous order,"* but even earlier, the Taoist teachings of Lao-Tzu and Chuang-tzu taught that *"Good order results spontaneously when things are let alone."* This balanced perspective of self-reflection and self-governance is a key aspect of both anarchism and Taoism. Despite criticism from some scholars who believe Taoism was a tool for the elite to pacify the peasant class, the philosophy is completely consistent with the ideas of withdrawing from the State and working with the natural flow of the world. Rather than solely fighting external battles against state powers, the lesson is to follow the Tao, the natural way. This natural state of humanity is, of course, a path that lacks force and coercion as imposed by state institutions.

In his book, *Demanding the Impossible: A History of Anarchism*, Peter Marshall writes:

"It is impossible to appreciate the ethics and politics of Taoism without an understanding of its philosophy of nature. The Tao Te Ching celebrates the Tao, or way, of nature and describes how the wise person should follow it. The Taoist conception of nature is based on the ancient Chinese principles of yin and yang, two opposite but complementary forces in the cosmos which constitute ch'i (matter energy) of which all beings and phenomena are formed. Yin is the supreme feminine power, characterized by darkness, cold, and receptivity and associated with the moon; yang is the

masculine counterpart of brightness, warmth, and activity, and is identified with the sun. Both forces are at work within men and women as well as in all things."[1]

Taoism teaches that individuals who pursue balance with nature will be happy, free people who do not wish to be oppressed or oppress others. Instead, students of the Tao find themselves content to walk their own path in harmony with the external world and to spread the gospel of the Tao.

(All quotations from the Tao Te Ching are reprinted from Stephen Mitchell's translation.)

---

1. p. 54.

Chapter 17
Intersections of Anarchism and Confucianism

In this essay we will explore potential connections between anarchist thought and the Confucian worldview. Confucianism is a school of thought described as a philosophy, a humanist religion, a doctrine, a tradition, or a system of governance, based on the teachings of the Chinese philosopher and politician Confucius (alternatively known as Kongfuzi or K'ung-fu-tz). Confucianism emphasizes the importance of the family unit, methods for creating harmony in social relationships, government morality, justice, and kindness. Confucius is also said to have espoused a version of the Golden Rule, *"Do not do unto others what you do not want done to yourself."* Confucianism developed between the 6th to the 2nd century BC, in the period known as the Hundred Schools of Thoughts. After experiencing periods of popularity in China Confucianism was eventually suppressed by the Legalist movement and Qin dynasty. Following the collapse of the Qin dynasty Confucianism gained official support from the new government. The teachings of Confucius have continued to evolve and are sometimes known as Neo-Confucianism or New Confucianism.

As explored in the previous chapter, Taoism has typically been associated with anarchism rather than the often rigid Confucianism. With the history of Confucianism, we see a pattern emerge as it has in nearly every religious or spiritual teaching: the original teaching is relatively liberty minded or even anti-authoritarian while later manifestations are supportive of the State or used by the state to encourage obedience.

Despite this pattern there does appear to be a period of Confucian history which supports some Anarchist principles (or at the least, libertarian values of small government). In his essay, *Austro-Libertarian Themes in Early Confucianism* (later a book, *Rituals of Freedom: Libertarian Themes in Early Confucianism*), Professor Roderick Long makes the argument that Confucius and his student Mencius (aka Mengzi or Meng-tzu) were actually some of the first libertarians. *"While no school of early Chinese thought is consistently libertarian, the Confucians score higher than any of their rivals, offering many intriguing anticipations of contemporary libertarian ideas,"* Long writes. He notes that Confucius recognized that the natural universe maintains order without the need for commands and a wise ruler should do the same. Obviously, the notion of a ruler at all generally goes against anarchist principles yet Confucianism does not advocate blindly following the State.

Instead, Confucian writings are *"characterized by unrelenting hostility to governmental abuse of power."* Long notes that Confucian sage Sima Qian complains that the builders of the Great Wall of China were *"no different from a bunch of bandits"* because the wall was *"made free with the strength of the common people."* Mencius is also seen condemning the seizure of private property for government use and "imperialist expansionism." Additionally, Confucian scholar Jia Yi counseled Emperor Wen to abolish the act of punishing an entire family for the actions of one individual, abolish mutilation as a punishment, and abolish taxes on agriculture. Wen also abolished laws regarding "criticism and evil talk," noting that if an emperor does not allow his officials to express their feelings in full, he *"has no way to learn of his errors."* Professor Long calls this *"one of the earliest instances of the epistemological argument for free speech."* Confucianism proposed that all relationships should be beneficial and have its own logical reason for being. *"Ruler must justify his position by acting benevolently before he can expect reciprocation from the people. In this view, a King is like a steward,"* Long writes. Confucius's student Mencius took a more radical approach than his teacher when it came to rulers who ignore the needs of the people and the rules which are supposed to guide society. Mencius believed that it was acceptable for the people to overthrow or kill a ruler if they ignore the people and thus are no longer a "true ruler." For Long, this was Mencius "clarifying the proper hierarchy of human society," namely that a king is *"actually subordinate to the masses of people and the resources of society."*

In Herbert Fingarette's *Confucius: The Secular as Sacred,* Fingarette argues that the consistent Confucian must be *"a kind of anarchist in the respect that he is radically opposed to the use of force, compulsion, coercion, or punishments in government or in human affairs generally."* However, Author Henry Rosemont and Fingarette argue that any connections between Confucianism and Anarchism are strictly of the anarcho-communist variety rather than an individualist interpretation. Long disagrees with this assessment, writing, *"if Confucianism truly has greater affinity with Kropotkin than with capitalism, how are we to explain the fact that Confucian thinkers consistently rejected the Kropotkin-style autarky and collectivist primitivism of the Taoists in favor of a global network of commerce and trade?".* While it's clear that Confucianism is not a purely anarchist school of thought we do appreciate the insights gleaned by Long and others. It appears, at the least, that Confucius and his students were interested in promoting a philosophy which could encourage a moral and just life, while also attempting to hold rulers responsible for their actions. This interpretation leans more towards minarchism—a situation where the State is greatly reduced and limited by the people—rather than our preferred anarchism. However, it is clear there were some Confucian teachers who maintained a belief in the values of anti-authoritarianism and equity.

Chapter 18
The Art of Not Being Governed

Throughout this book we have suggested that people of various cultures, ethnicities, religions, and philosophical backgrounds can share the same geography in relative peace without a government for long periods of time. This is no fairy tale or utopian pipe dream but a documented historical fact.

Until recently, a mountainous region of Southeast Asia the size of Europe was completely stateless. In fact, the area was almost entirely inhabited by anarchists who had fled into the mountains to escape the reaches of various governments. Naturally, there was no official name or flag for this area, but it has been thoroughly studied, and in 2002, European historian Willem Van Schendel of the University of Amsterdam named the region *Zomia*. In 2009, Yale Professor James C. Scott expanded on the study of the region with his book *The Art of Not Being Governed: An Anarchist History of Upland Southeast Asia*.

Zomia was an area of around 2.5 million square kilometers, spanning from the central highlands of Vietnam to northeastern India and covering five Southeast nations including Vietnam, Cambodia, Laos, Thailand, and Burma. The area contained around one hundred million minority peoples. It was not an actual state but a collection of many peoples and regions mainly living in the hills and mountainous regions that were largely unwanted or inaccessible to the State.

Scott's argument is that these widely varied peoples came together to trade among each other and developed customs and practices that were inherently anti-state. As evidenced by their agriculture, politics, and spirituality, they sought to live in ways that were not congruent with statism. In the preface to *The Art of Not Being Governed*, Scott writes, "*these people's livelihoods, social organization, ideologies and oral cultures can be read as strategic positionings designed to keep the state at arm's length.*"

Rather than seeing humanity as having evolved towards the conveniences of the modern state, he argues that until recently, humans organized through self-governing kinship units that would cooperate in hunting, fighting, trading, and peacemaking. "*In other words, living in the absence of state structures has been the standard of the human condition,*" (*The Art of Not Being Governed*, page 3). Instead, he argues, we should recognize that many people in the past have purposefully lived and operated outside of the state for as long as possible. He goes on:

"*Their subsistence routines, their social organization, their physical dispersal, and many elements of their culture, far from being the archaic traits of a people left behind, are purposefully crafted both to thwart incorporations into nearby states and to minimize the likelihood that state-like concentrations of power will arise among them. State evasion and state prevention permeate their experiences and, often, their ideology as well,"[1]*

The establishment of villages allowed the state to encourage the peasantry to remain sedentary and thus able to be taxed and brought into the fold of state control and influence. In Zomia, attempts to assimilate non-state communities were less about development and economic progress than they were about ensuring that economic activity in these communities was taxable and confiscable if needed. This highlights the importance of building counter-institutions through agorism. As Scott mentions, *"The main, long-run threat of the ungoverned periphery, however, was that it represented a constant temptation, a constant alternative to life within the state."[2]*

Once free communities are established and thriving outside of the State, those living under state rule will be quick to consider the alternative. Scott also notes that the myth of state powers being able to save peasants from the clutches of barbarians is largely false. He argues that refugees of the State were quite common as people recognized that life under a State might mean taxes, conscription in wars, forced labor, and servitude. This cycle of state-making and state-unmaking created zones of refuge, or "shatter zones," where those escaping the clutches of the State came together to form complex groupings of various ethnicities and family units. This complexity, along with "relative geographical inaccessibility," were common characteristics of these shatter zones. Groups seeking to escape the State would form partnerships and reside in areas that growing government influence could not reach.

When discussing the differences between the valleys of the state and the mountainous regions that make up Zomia, Scott remarks: *"The hills, unlike the valleys, have paid neither taxes to monarchs nor regular tithes to a permanent religious establishment. They have constituted a relatively free, stateless population of foragers and hill farmers."[3]*

Zomia has been the site of indigenous struggles, secessionist movements, and armed opposition movements. The spiritual beliefs of Zomia often leaned towards animism, a rather decentralized viewpoint that sees God in all objects rather than exclusively in spiritual traditions and religions that have been used to centralize the people, such as Theravada Buddhism. In the same way Native Americans saw their belief systems threatened or completely extinguished by Christian missionaries, residents of Zomia faced similar threats from the

1. p. 8.

2. p. 6.

3. p. 19.

Buddhist orthodoxy that sought to ban local deities and practices. Scott believes the animist practices and other forms of belief outside the accepted canon *"represent zones of resistant difference, dissent, and, at the very least, failures of incorporation and domestication by state-promoted religion."*[1]

Zomia was not the only stateless region throughout history. From 1918 to 1921, an experiment in an anarchist society took place in what was known as The Free Territory of Ukraine or Makhnovia, after Ukrainian anarchist Nestor Makhno. The time was extremely chaotic in Ukraine and Russia as the Bolshevik government attempted to establish dominance in Russia and maintain a momentary peace with the Central Powers of World War I. In March 1918, the Bolsheviks ceded large territories to the Central Powers, including Ukraine, which was facing internal turmoil and an increasingly divided population. Some of Ukraine's peasant population defected to the Bolsheviks, some followed various forms of socialism, and still others waved the black flag of Anarchism under the leadership of Nestor Makhno.

Makhno has been viewed as a bandit, a criminal, a leader, a soldier, and a brilliant strategist. Some accounts of his early life describe him as a Robin Hood type character who is committing robberies to distribute money to the people. Eventually, Makhno was arrested and spent time in a Russia prison. When the February 1917 revolution overthrew the tsar, political prisoners were liberated from prisons in Moscow. In October 2017 the Bolsheviks launched a second revolution and in the process installed the "dictatorship of the proletariat." When civil war broke out, Makhno and other prisoners were released from prison. At the end of World War I, Russia was divided between the Communist Bolshevik Red Army and the Tsar loyalist, nationalist White Army. As an anarchist, Makhno disagreed with the authoritarian practices of the Bolsheviks, specifically their targeting of anarchists. He also opposed the nationalist supporters of the tsar. Additionally, he opposed foreign military occupation of Ukraine. In response, Makhno organized a small group of supporters and launched guerrilla attacks against the German and Austrian troops occupying Ukraine. Makhno also fought the red and white armies, while partnering with the Reds out of necessity on occasion. His forces came to be known as the "Black Army," or the Revolutionary Insurrectionist Army of Ukraine. Mahkno started with about 15,000 armed troops and saw his numbers grow to nearly 100,000 soldiers who oversaw much of eastern Ukraine and a population of several million people. The Makhnovist military strength reached its peak in late 1919 with 83,000 infantry, 20,100 cavalry, 1,400 machine guns, 110 artillery guns, seven armored trains and several armored cars.

Makhno was the primary strategist and planner of this army. His goal was to retake as many areas of Ukraine as he could from what he viewed as in-

---

1. p. 300.

vading forces and threats to liberty for all Ukrainians. The army consisted of peasants, Jews, anarchists, and recruits from foreign nations. The Black Army even gained support from Red soldiers who had lost faith in the Bolsheviks after witnessing their utopian dream turn authoritarian.

In November 1920, the Black Army temporarily aligned with the Bolshevik army to defeat White Army forces. Immediately after, the Bolsheviks turned their focus on Makhno and the anarchists. Several of Makhno's associates were arrested and executed. Makhno managed to escape as the authoritarian Bolsheviks targeted anarchists around the country. Ultimately, in August 1921, Makhno and more than 70 of his men were wounded and barely escaped to Romania after an attack by the Red Army. This was essentially the end of the Army, but some historical accounts record activity by the Black Army as far as late 1922.

Setting aside debates about Makhno's strategic moves or if anarchists need or should want military forces, we can learn from this fascinating piece of history. Makhno's Anarchist Army was intended to be the defense force for the Free Territory of Ukraine. Their goal was never to conquer the land or the people, but to return it to the people so they may freely organize without fear of tyrants or statists. When entering a town in which they had just defeated the Red or White army, the Black Army would post notices on the wall stating: *"To all the workers of the city and its environs! Workers, your city is for the present occupied by the Revolutionary Insurrectionary (Makhnovist) Army. This army does not serve any political party, any power, any dictatorship. On the contrary, it seeks to free the region of all political power, of all dictatorship. It strives to protect the freedom of action, the free life of the workers, against all exploitation and domination."*

The bulletins invited the people to attend a meeting where the Black Army would share their views in detail. They encouraged all the towns to respect freedom and organize without authority or exploitation. Clearly, not everyone who lived in the areas liberated by the Black Army were anarchists. However, the Army was providing protection and the opportunity for the people to self-organize in the absence of a monarchy or state-Communism. The Army also protected the right to freedom of speech, press, assembly, and political affiliation. They also repealed all restrictions on press and political organizations. Every political party and group was allowed representation, even the Bolsheviks who had silenced all opposition in their territories.

In some of the territories under the watch of the Black Army, the people did radically rethink the way they organized their lives. Communities organized in decentralized councils or soviets and focused on rebuilding schools which had been abandoned during the war. These schools took inspiration from the free-school movement of Francisco Ferrer. They offered classes for illiterate adults and helped them read and learn history, sociology, and political theory. Some communities also adopted the economic principles espoused by Anarchist Peter Kropotkin.

This experiment in Anarchism was not perfect by any means. Makhno and the Black Army were accused of maintaining their own counter-intelligence forces. The Kontrrazvedka intelligence service was viewed by some anarchists as entirely inconsistent with anarchist principles of economic free association, mutual aid and non-coercion. Critics also claim Black Army used conscription in some instances. However, other sources discount this theory, pointing to the presence of Red soldiers who volunteered to join the Black Army.

The flaws of Nestor Makhno and the Black Army should not be seen as a reason to completely discount the efforts and lessons. Rather, we should recognize that political theories often look very different when they make the jump from paper to the real world.

Another, more recent, example of communities operating in the absence of centralized authority comes from the Mexican state of Michoacán. In the last decade community protection groups known as autodefensas have gained significant numbers as communities sought to defend against dangerous drug cartels. Beginning in 2014, all autodefensas were given the option of disarming and joining a newly formed rural police force or be considered criminals with illegal weapons. The federal government attempted to convert these rural militias into official police forces with the backing of the government. The vast majority decided to remain independent and the Mexican Ministry of the Interior stated that it lacked the resources to maintain a federal police presence in Michoacán. One community in Michoacán which said they will continue to operate their own community defense force is the town of Cherán, in the Purhépecha region of Michoacán. In early 2011 residents of Cherán created armed militias to fight off illegal logging in their community. The community kicked out politicians and police accused of ties to the drug cartels. When the uprising began, you might see elderly women with sticks defending the community. These days the community guard is mostly young men and women with professional weapons.

The people of Cherán began a new system of governance based on traditional Purhépecha indigenous law enforcement and accountability. One of the ways this is done is by maintaining a volunteer-run community guard that defends the community and answers to the town assembly. The neighborhood assemblies and the larger general assembly are examples of traditional forms of self-governance that were practiced in Cherán 40 years earlier. However, over time political parties and external forms of governance were forced on the people. While the community guards and assemblies are by no means perfect institutions, they do offer benefits to the locals that were not available under the police or cartels. The community guard is accountable to the town assembly and chosen by the people. Also, local business owners are no longer forced to pay several hundred dollars a month to criminals.

As of this writing, Cherán has been a recognized autonomous region for 8 years. They have successfully kept political parties, Mexican police, and cartels from retaking their town. However, Cherán is not without problems. There have been reports that the community is beginning to see political fracturing even without the presence of the national political parties and they do receive state and federal funding. Even with the inevitable growing pains of birthing a new concept of governance we take much hope and inspiration from the people of Cherán.

We would also be remiss if we didn't at least make a note on the Zapatista Army of National Liberation, EZLN, or simply the Zapatistas, who occupy an autonomous region in Chiapas, a state in the south of Mexico. The Zapatistas have been fighting a physical and ideological battle with the Mexican government since 1983. The movement is made up of mostly indigenous Mayans and supporters from urban areas. The Zapatistas eschew any attempt to categorizing their ideology and philosophy, but it has been classified as libertarian socialism by historians. While the struggle between the Mexican government and the Zapatistas is mostly at a stalemate in recent years, the Zapatistas have been able to successfully expand the territory under their control in the last 30 years. We do not have the space to undertake a full exposition of the history and work of the people of Cheran or Chiapas, we highly recommend the reader dive into this rich history.

In a country where civilian gun ownership is highly restricted and the government seems incapable of defending average citizens, it makes sense that at some point the people would come together in search of solutions. In the United States, however, the idea of community defense is not necessarily one many people want to entertain. Corruption and crime exist but there is enough of a semblance of "law and order" that, for most people, taking up arms in defense of the community is not high on their list of priorities. By understanding indigenous community models for defense, we may be able to apply the same concepts to other cities where a future economic downturn may require such action.

Before the advent of modern travel and technology, cultures around the world found freedom living in a wide variety of decentralized anarchist societies that were outside the city walls and outside the reaches of the empires. It has been written in history books that these people were savages and primitives who had no knowledge or contact with the so-called civilized world. However, in the case of Zomia and other breakaway cultures, we see that these societies were well aware of the empires and wanted nothing to do with them.

The struggles of American Indians best exemplify this concept. Far from the fairy tale Thanksgiving, the history of the relations between the United States government and the Indigenous peoples of North America has been filled with violence and war. American Indians recognized that the colonizers were not after cooperation and partnership but were more interested in taking what they wanted from whomever they wanted. For five hundred years, governments of the world have failed to recognize the sovereignty and autonomy of indigenous communities.

George E. Tinker, a professor of American Indian cultures and religious traditions at Iliff School of Theology and a member of the Osage Nation, believes it is this failure that has caused severe harm to indigenous peoples who do not wish to assimilate. In his book *Spirit and Resistance: Political Theology and American Indian Liberation*, Tinker writes:

"Namely, the political and economic bias in the international discourse is to recognize only states as the fundamental actors in the international political discourse. As such, the natural national identities that make up indigenous peoples' communities are seen today as merely ethnic minorities within state structures, who may have individual rights but do not have any distinct set of community or cultural right as an independent people."[1]

Tinker believes the growing state could not accept Indians living among themselves; it needed them to join the impending status quo. The colonizers had a burning desire to "civilize" the natives. *"The result was the consistent imposition of European cultural values, norms, societal structures, and technologies on peoples who had lived remarkably well with their own values, norms, structures, and technologies for some thousands of years,"* Tinker explains.[2]

This trend continues today in the form of "sustainable development" projects that only further colonize and damage indigenous communities. Whether we are speaking of those indigenous to the North American landmass, Ukraine, Mexico, or Zomia, there is a consistent history of oppression by states and their refusal to accept the autonomy of these groups (*for further reading on indigenous communities that operated in an essentially stateless fashion read Pierre Clastres' Society Against the State.*) However, indigenous communities are not the only populations oppressed by the state.

The lessons learned from Zomia, Ukraine, Mexico, and indigenous communities reiterate our central thesis: attempts at overcoming violence and authoritarianism must be accompanied by the call for healing and trauma. Despite the appearance of normalcy and convenience of living under the control of a state, there is a much freer world waiting outside the imagined boundaries of state institutions. Learning that freedom truly begins within is a huge lesson

1. p. 7.
2. p. 10.

we hope to impart. We believe that once we work to know ourselves more deeply and begin the process of healing on an individual level, the concept of living in cooperative, autonomous panarchist communities—built around the ideas of mutual aid, non-aggression, voluntaryism, and mindfulness—will have far greater appeal.

In fact, as these ideas grow, they appear so obvious that it makes us wonder—*what has taken humanity so long?* As usual, all things happen in the time and space they are supposed to. We see much hope in the growing interest in liberation, self-ownership, self-reflection, and cooperation. Together we are creating a paradigm shift that will allow our planet to heal and evolve toward a more peaceful, free, awakened state of being. We thank you for being a part of this journey.

Remember, if you can see this, you *are* The Conscious Resistance.

BOOK II

•••

FINDING FREEDOM IN AN AGE OF CONFUSION

A Message From the Authors

After releasing Reflections on Anarchy and Spirituality, we realized the philosophy and ideas behind our perspective need to be elaborated even further. The first book in this trilogy laid the foundation for our ideas and now we want to share more detail on our worldview. For many of us, being an activist—especially an anarchist one—can be a difficult road. Most of us encounter the same struggles in our path, but these struggles are rarely ever talked about. When someone "wakes up" and realizes that our society is not free, it can sometimes lead to depression, confusion, or alienation from family and friends. This is what happens when the whole world is crazy and you are seeing clearly for the first time.

To help make this difficult transition easier, we decided to tackle these very personal issues and offer solutions to overcome these obstacles. In the following pages, you will find essays on overcoming the depression, confusion, and fear that can come with the realization that much of the world still lives in slavery.

If the first book in the series was the body of our philosophy, consider this book the heart. We aim to show the human struggle of the search for freedom. Book 3 will examine real world applications of the ideas presented in both books and could be considered the mind of our philosophy. We have tried our best to find the beauty and positivity that surrounds us on this path and have actually found plenty of reasons to be optimistic. Both of us have also made more than a handful of mistakes and wasted much time worrying about fears that may never manifest in our everyday reality.

All of these experiences, both good and bad, have resulted in the essays contained in this book. These are our suggestions on how to navigate this crazy, beautiful world. We hope our words encourage and inspire you to continue down the path of physical, mental, and spiritual liberation.

John Vibes & Derrick Broze
April 2016—August 2020

Chapter 1
You are a Pioneer of Peace

Every single one of us was born into a chaotic world. We collectively inherited a complicated web of problems that have been plaguing humanity for millennia. Violence and subjugation have been accepted as facts of life for so long that they appear impossible to change. Understandably, this culture of acceptance can leave any sane person seeking to change the world feeling hopeless. Often, we feel defeated before we have even begun to actively work to heal the planet.

Coming to terms with the harsh realities of our existence can be a deeply confusing or even traumatic process because the truth is so different from what we were taught to believe by the "mainstream" culture. Most people react with horrified aversion when they are approached with information that contradicts the ideas that they have built their lives around.

When it comes to the violence of the state and the corrupt nature of the social institutions that surround us, it is rare to see anyone absorb, reflect, and accept the information without having to rethink their worldview, so most people refuse to look.

For those who do have the courage to venture outside of the mainstream worldview, the path dedicated to creating a more peaceful and free existence is incredibly difficult and frightening. It may even seem like a futile suicide mission. This is an obstacle that prevents most people from attempting to change or criticize the society that "raised" them. If creating a free society and a world without war was easy, then you can guarantee that overnight millions of people would instantly be condemning the state and the immorality of the violence carried out by politicians and their corporate partners.

Since creating freedom where there is now slavery is a fragile and painstaking process without an instruction manual, it is a very daunting task. However, humanity is capable of incredible feats—ideas that were once seen as impossible and unthinkable are now benign and commonplace. We live in a world with tools and capabilities that would appear to be magic to our ancestors, yet we still have been unable to escape the animalistic, primitive traditions that have held humanity back for generations. We can instantly speak to people all over the world, travel to space, and store entire libraries of information on tiny thumb drives, but sadly many people still live their day-to-day lives in confusion and fear just as so many generations before us.

The current era is an extremely pivotal time in the human story. We have reached that long-awaited moment where humanity has become advanced enough to destroy this planet and everything on it. This massive responsibility, a responsibility that can only be met with a radical elevation in consciousness, is one which will allow our species to finally become civilized beings. No self-respecting individual wants to look at themselves or the society that they identify with as being barbaric or uncivilized. However, when a species is killing each other by the millions, enslaving one another, and taking part in the culturally justified violence that we see today, it becomes apparent that there is much work to be done before we can honestly say that humanity is "civilized."

As radical Native activist John Trudell stated, "*The Great Lie is that it is 'civilization.' It's not civilized, it has been literally the most bloodthirsty brutalizing system ever imposed upon this planet. That is not civilization, that's "the great lie." The great lie is that it represents 'CIVILIZATION.' Or if it does represent civilization and it's truly what civilization is; then the great lie is that civilization is good for us.*"

To do what we can during our lives to leave the world and the human consciousness in better condition than when we arrived is a gravely important task but one we should not shy away from. No matter the obstacles, the goal is worth the effort. One could even argue that this is the meaning of life! It is not an easy path to take and there is no guarantee that you will see the fruits of your labor in your own lifetime, but the potential of any new frontier is always shrouded in uncertainty, danger, and controversy.

The creation of the world's first free society in recorded history is simply the most recent field of exploration in the realm of human consciousness, just as space is the most recent field of exploration in the physical realm. Only 100 years ago if you told someone you were going to build a rocket to fly people into outer space you may have run the risk of being committed to a mental hospital. Yet, despite popular opinion, the human imagination has once again defied our previous conception of reality by exploring new frontiers and pushing beyond the boundaries of what was previously thought to be possible.

If you are reading these words, then you are without a doubt in the midst of the expanding frontier that is human consciousness and thought. You have found yourself in a fight for freedom and a search for peace. You are a pioneer who has the courage to journey into uncharted territory and be your own mapmaker. Along with millions of others worldwide who are beginning to find their purpose, you have the ability to change the world for the better in your lifetime, no matter what background you come from or where you call home. You have found yourself on a rewarding but arduous and sometimes lonely path. We know this because we have been walking this path for the better part of our lives and some years ago we passed the point of no return and we now call this path "home." Once you decide to educate yourself about the lies we are taught, there is no turning back.

Chapter 2
Reclaiming Your Self-Esteem

The current societal model we live in has a way of making people feel insignificant. We are faced with many forms of stress and pressures in our lives that seem designed to make us feel like nothing we do will ever be enough. We live in a world where humans are ranked and categorized and the overwhelming majority of us are placed in the bottom tier. These circumstances are enough to make any caring person feel depressed and worthless, especially if we buy into all of the cultural conditioning that tells us that our position in society is our own fault. Of course, we each have some level of control over our well-being, and that is why self-empowerment is so important. However, there are also systemic obstacles and conditions of our society that are intentionally designed to keep the vast majority of us in poverty (or very close) and in constant servitude. Our value in society is measured by our usefulness to the system and our willingness to obey authority, which is why some people take pride in being "taxpaying, law-abiding citizens."

The social, legal and financial pressures of our society push the populace down a path of uniformity so we are much easier for the "powers that wish they were" to manage. In reality this path is like a never-ending treadmill where most of us remain in the same place no matter how hard we run. Far too many of the world's people feel inadequate and insignificant because they do not match up with the unrealistic and insane expectations that are set by the mainstream culture. If we must be judged, it should be according to our actions and how we treat those around us, not the superficial standards imposed by a society that is just using us as a resource.

Using arbitrary traits like wealth, status, and appearance as social measurements degrade human beings and set false ideals of self-worth. Unfortunately, this is the world we are living in. So, for now, we need to learn ways to contend with these routine assaults on our self-esteem. First, it is important to realize that we have been conditioned for self-loathing, and that we need to question many of the expectations that our culture has thrust upon us. Some of these expectations are impossible to escape, and many are impossible to fulfill—especially the legal and financial ones. However, once we see these manufactured barriers our mind seeks to find a solution to overcome and succeed. Beyond the structural obstacles that we face, much of our cultural programming is intended to work against us, making us our worst enemies.

Coming to terms with these internal issues will make us more prepared and better equipped to fight the collective battles that need to happen in the political, economic, and cultural realms. However, the modern world does not make this easy. In an effort to keep up with friends, hobbies and opportunities, we choose to be plugged into a constant stream of information that is often sending the message that we're not good enough. This was already a problem in the age of traditional media with its unrealistic beauty standards and emphasis on celebrities, but now, with the advent of social media, we are given the false impression that everyone is living much better lives than we are.

Many social commentators have pointed out that when we are on social media we are comparing our "bloopers" with everyone else's "highlights." Many of us present our best faces online and do our best to keep our pain, flaws and insecurities secret. This creates a constant feedback loop where everyone is putting out an unrealistic version of themselves to the world. This in turn leads many to be increasingly insecure because they are trying to live up to the impossible standards which are perpetuated by the false personas of others. We have been conditioned to compare ourselves to our peers and interpret their wins as our losses, but this mindset is no longer serving humanity. It's likely that this mentality never benefited humanity in the first place.

There is a brilliant metaphor that is frequently used in American Hip-hop which does an excellent job at depicting the current mentality that many people have in their relationships as well as their business and political ventures. This is the idea that humans behave like crabs trapped in a bucket, looking at the world as a zero-sum game, where there is no such thing as a mutually beneficial exchange. Every situation has winners and losers with this worldview, and everyone is out to make someone else a loser. In reality, there are solutions that people can come to without getting hostile with one another and that lead to an outcome where everyone involved is better off than they were before.

The phrase describes a way of thinking that is along the same lines of, "if I can't have it, neither can you." The metaphor refers to a pot of crabs, each of which could easily escape from the pot individually, but instead, they grab at each other in a useless "king of the hill" competition which prevents any from escaping and ensures their collective demise. The analogy in human behavior is that members of a group will attempt to "pull down" (negate or diminish the importance of) any member who achieves success beyond the others. This mentality is probably relevant to many of our lives, as we can see it all around us. If we continue to operate in this fashion, none of us will ever truly be happy or fulfilled. Instead of obsessing about climbing the social ladder and surpassing those on top of you, think about taking a look at those below you and finding ways to lift them up. This approach to life will much better serve your mental health and your personal goals in the long run. As Gandhi reportedly said, *"The best way to find yourself is to lose yourself in the service of others."*

When we learn to reclaim our sovereignty and self-ownership, we are taking steps to reclaim our self-esteem. When we know for certain that we are in charge of our own path we take personal responsibility for our emotional state. We come to recognize that the only power others have over our mental state is the power we give them. We strive to see the beauty and strength in ourselves so that we may have the will to help empower others who are also dealing with the same struggles. For the good of the world, we should all take time to focus on our own healing and self-love.

Chapter 3
You Are Divine

The mainstream view of history which most state-educated children are familiar with has been handed down through the generations by the victors of past conquests. The oppressor's perspective presents the idea that great things will only be accomplished by mythical heroes who have all of the right things to say, know all of the right things to do, and who are completely devoid of fear, doubt, regret, or any other feelings of vulnerability which are part of the great spectrum of human emotion. For the better part of history, kings and priests have created a social atmosphere in which they were these heroes. However, in reality, this ruling class is nothing like the image they put on display.

In American culture the politicians are often presented in this mythical context where they are said to have the superhuman ability to know what is best for millions of other people at all times, just as the kings and priests before them. Often during times of social upheaval revolutionary changes are credited to figureheads and "authorities." This happens in part because of the personality cult that is traditionally inherited by those in positions of power. However, this view of history relies too heavily on the individuals who have waged wars and signed declarations.

We live in a world where different classes of people have different rules and different rights according to their relationship with those in power, or their ability to use force and commit fraud upon others. Despite the predominant view that humans have equality in some form or another, the division of classes and power happens without much condemnation from the masses. The truth is that we are equal as free, self-governing humans, but we live in societies where we are not treated as equals because small groups of sophists have established cultural norms which ensure that they are the rulers of everyone else, instead of their equals. We call them the Predator Class. This was obvious during the times of the monarchy and open slavery, but now the rulers hide behind democracy and communism, both ideas that claim to put the power in the hands of the people, but often end up creating the illusion of power, while strengthening the state and the ruling class.

While recognizing the limits and failures of the State's view of history, we should also remember that our current situation is only temporary and does not have to be the future of humanity. While it may be true that there are people who think they have authority over you and will probably use force to maintain that power—this does not mean that this false authority actually exists. This authority is nothing more than an illusion. The fact that the majority of the population

Derrick **Broze** • John **Vibes**

believes in the illusion does not make this undue authority and power an objective fact. Simply put, we should not live our lives like second class "citizens" just because we are treated as such.

As beautiful, free, powerful, autonomous human beings, we can choose to be free at a moment's notice. Every one of us has the right to think and act as we wish, as long as we bring no harm to anyone else. In other words—you are your own king, queen, priest, authority, etc. This does not mean that we believe everyone is a "special snowflake" and should be granted certain privileges by the State in an attempt to establish equality. Rather, we believe you own yourself, regardless of how many politicians come along and claim ownership over you. You are the master of your own domain and the creator of your future. We should not live our lives as if the State is the master of our fate. Sure, we are living in a situation where our possibilities are limited and we are forced to conform in certain ways when "the powers that wish they were" are looking, but none of that changes reality, so it should not change the way we perceive our own power.

When you accept the worldview of those who oppress you and act as if it were objective truth, you are disempowering yourself and giving your abuser the upper hand. This is what happens when we attempt to conform with standards that we know are unjust, and then proceed to emotionally attack ourselves when we inevitably fall short. It would seem that our ancestors were unable to come to terms with these facts and were never able to achieve true freedom by resisting the establishment of the control systems that exist today. However, the generations born in the late 20th century and the beginning of the 21st century have tools at their disposal that their predecessors could not fathom. We have the capability and the power to turn things around and create a world where every living being has autonomy. One of the first steps towards individual and collective liberation is to claim your power, be your own master, and to make efforts to advance and spread the philosophy of self-ownership.

Chapter 4
Trust Yourself, Vacate the State

For many free minds learning to trust another human being can be a monumental task. The fears and doubts we pick up along our journeys might lead some to believe that trust is an unworthy venture. Navigating the jungle of life can be quite difficult and learning to trust—to trust yourself, let alone another human being—may seem like a far-fetched idea, but it is essential for our development as free, conscious human beings in the pursuit of liberty. We are pursuing liberation, not only in the physical world but of the mind. This means that at some point we will also need to confront our internal tyrants. We must learn to overcome our fears and trust our judgments and choices. We must learn to value and appreciate ourselves. From there, we can assess which individuals are worthy of certain levels of our trust. This could be anything from trusting someone to pay their share of the rent, watch your dog, build a community garden, or learning to trust someone with your love. Regardless of the situation, we can see value in learning to trust other human beings.

We can also see the consequences of a lack of trust within community relationships. The State not only thrives off a populace that is low in self-esteem and self-worth, but also a population that views each other with mistrust. State programs like COINTELPRO are perfect examples of the government spreading lies and disinformation in order to breed mistrust among allies. This underscores the importance of having a tight-knit group of people that you can trust enough to organize community initiatives. We call this group a Freedom Cell, an idea which we will elaborate upon in book 3 of this series.

So, how do we avoid this? How do we avoid becoming full of doubt, mistrust and unfounded fears? Our minds can be our greatest enemies when it comes to trust. We have powerful minds and imaginations capable of dreaming up our most surreal fantasies and our worst nightmares. Many of us are still healing from deep scars created from misplaced trust. These scars can last a whole lifetime if we choose to allow it. We can exercise caution while still allowing ourselves to face the pain of being deceived or disappointed, and choose to heal from those experiences. We can choose to see ourselves for the powerful, beautiful, free human beings we are, and recognize that we deserve to be happy. We deserve to have relationships that are filled with trust, and honesty rather than fear and doubt. As Anarchists, we recognize that the State only offers a one-sided relationship that does not require trust because the authorities will impose their will regardless.

In order to build empowered, self-reliant, and sustainable communities, we are going to need to trust other people in a variety of ways. Trust is essential to carving the path to a free world. As we work to trust and love ourselves and our place in this journey, we can encourage the same behavior in others. This will only make creating communities based on non-aggression, voluntary association, personal responsibility, mutual aid and empowerment, that much easier. In order to help the world continue to evolve, we need to start at home. That means starting with ourselves and our interpersonal relationships. If the goal is the evolution of hearts and minds, it only makes sense to start with your own.

Chapter 5
You Are Not Alone

The process of self-discovery and learning to question the commonly accepted beliefs that most of our society holds as infallible, is not always an easy or especially fun journey. For many of us, the process can be quite scary as you feel like your whole life has been turned upside down. Both of us have vivid memories of many nights spent researching the nature of government, and the nature of reality itself. Sleepless nights often lead to hopeless days and depression.

When you "wake up" and challenge dogmas related to government, health, relationships, authority, and history, you may experience a journey similar to those who are grieving the loss of a loved one. In her 1969 book, On Death and Dying, Swiss psychiatrist Elisabeth Kübler-Ross discussed what came to be known as the Kübler-Ross model of grief. This included five different stages—denial, anger, bargaining, depression and acceptance.

This was not meant to be seen as a specific set of stages every individual will experience, or a specific order in which they may occur. Some individuals may grieve for long periods of time and experience all the stages while others may not. Still, the model offers some insight into what one may experience after challenging everything they have ever been taught or told by parents, teachers, priests, and politicians.

These feelings of anger and depression can often lead to feeling alone in a world of insanity. For far too long, people who have cared about freedom and imagined a better world for our species, have felt alone in their interests, and have been forced into the fringes of society. However, as the philosophy of freedom and non-aggression is beginning to seep into the mainstream culture, the times are changing. In past generations, those who rejected authority in their hearts might never cross paths with another anti-authoritarian, liberation-minded individual. Today the world is much smaller and there is now a wealth of information available to more people than ever. Our digital world allows free thinkers to cross paths with regularity, which is helping to push along the philosophical renaissance predicted in Reflections on Anarchy and Spirituality.

With that said, there is still a great deal of work to be done. Unfortunately, we are fighting an uphill battle where our opponent was given a head start. The vast majority of people alive today in the Western world were molded by the state in public schools and entertained by propaganda. Many of these people have been taught a deep love and support for the status quo. Still, despite the propaganda, the human spirit is so resistant to the irrational and unnatural concept of authority that even after 12 years of indoctrination and constant manipulation, we can still overcome and free our minds.

Despite the growing awakening, you may have experienced uncomfortable situations when you try to talk about your concerns in public. This creates a situation where no one feels comfortable sharing their opinions in public and thus, none of us truly know how many rebels exist. In reality there are a lot more rebels out there than most people think, but many go unnoticed because human beings want to fit in and often we will avoid speaking about uncomfortable truths or ideas to avoid being ostracized.

This is why it is important for you to start making as much noise as possible. We must let the other rebels know they are not alone and encourage them to come out of hiding. Deep down we are all rebels, and the more people who step forward to admit it, the closer we will be to achieving freedom. We are all born rebels—that is our natural state. It is only after a lifetime of being beaten down by an insane culture that we come to embrace insanity for the sake of convenience. Could it be possible that everyone out there is just pretending to go along with the status quo? It appears even those who wholeheartedly embrace the status quo are still forced to use watered down language and euphemisms to describe the world around them because the cold hard truth is simply too difficult to acknowledge.

As the State's failed policies and unsustainable practices become more obvious, the status quo will become less of a convenience for people and they will begin to open to new ideas more than ever. The rebels will come out of hiding. These like-minded people are already all around you, and the more open you are about your own beliefs, the more open-minded people you will attract. This does not mean that it is a good idea to get in everyone's faces about your beliefs and create awkward situations for yourself. However, it would be wise to begin testing the waters with subtle hints about your newfound beliefs to see if anyone picks up. Discover who may be receptive to your ideas and who refuses to listen. If someone is genuinely not interested do not force your views as this will only create tension in your personal life.

It is important to remember not to be resentful and hateful towards those who cannot or will not research the information that is hiding behind the curtain. Words like "sheeple" and "statist" quickly turn from descriptors of an ignorant person, to a way to dismiss anyone who may not agree with your opinion or theory. We have to learn to accept people where they are and help those we can. The goal is collective liberation through individual empowerment, so ultimately it is up to each individual to carve their own path to freedom. Sometimes all you can do is plant seeds. Surely, we are not the only ones who have noticed that even the "freedom movement" is quickly becoming as polarized and divided as the mainstream political circles. While it is crucial to remain true to your principles, it may not be the most productive action to immediately disregard anyone who does not see the world exactly as you see it.

The truth is, we all have blind spots in our thinking and we all have things to learn from other people. It is possible to have a friendly conversation with someone who sees the world completely different from you without sacrificing your beliefs, and without expecting them to sacrifice theirs. That is not to say that there are no right or wrong answers—often there are things which can be verified and proven. But standing on opposing ends of an issue and shoving ideas down one another's throats is how the republicrats communicate. It is not how free people should communicate with each other.

For those of us standing outside of the left/right political paradigm, we see the stagnation and inefficiency that is caused by this sort of divisive approach to communication and problem solving. Debates in political circles are typically centered around attacking your opponent and showing off, instead of being focused on actually solving the problems at hand. This is one of the many reasons why the solutions to the world's problems will not come from governments as we know them today.

We must recognize that a growing number of people throughout the world are becoming disgusted with the violence and subjugation that has become commonplace in society. We all come from different backgrounds, environments, and experiences. The information that has shaped our worlds differs from individual to individual. We have entered this "movement" with different preconceived notions about why we are in this mess and how to get out. This may seem like a dangerous and volatile situation to someone used to seeing people with different opinions tear each other apart, but in reality this is a beautiful gift that we should all embrace as we attempt to learn from each other. If we think of the global situation as a giant puzzle, we can describe all of these different people with different viewpoints as a unique piece in that puzzle that is essential for its completion.

Some of us may be conservative on certain issues and are liberal on others. We may call ourselves voluntaryists or libertarians, constitutionalists or anarchists. We may be socialists or futurists, communists or individualists. We may disagree on a range of ideas, but the bottom line is that we have a great deal to learn from one another. There is no way we are going to fight the Predator Class that stands before us if we don't respect one another's opinion and banish the idea that someone with a different opinion may actually have something valid to teach.

As free thinkers we should celebrate the moment that we learn new information, even if that information may cause us to change our minds and feel differently about certain things. ESPECIALLY if that information causes us to change our minds. The ability to overcome one's own ego and humbly change your mind when presented with new information is one of the fundamental characteristics of a "free thinker."

Again, we want to be clear that this does not mean that you should go around agreeing with what everyone says, or that you cannot be firm in your convictions. But it is just as important to remember that we are in this fight to solve problems and reduce the level of accepted violence. We are not here to break each other down and further divide our world. We are here to teach, learn, and build a better world. Engaging in debates with people who are deeply entrenched in their own worldview may have some importance and value, but you will be disappointed if you expect to find like-minded people through this process. The more often we interact and connect with our brothers and sisters of similar worldview and goals, the more we contribute to a paradigm shift of hearts and minds.

A paradigm shift is a process in which individuals gain new knowledge which completely alters and evolves their understanding of the world. We believe we are currently experiencing a paradigm shift that has been taking place for generations with increasing awareness in the last decades of the 20th century. By educating yourself about the hidden truths of the world and seeking solutions that empower each of us, you are contributing to this paradigm shift. As the State continues its death march and eventual collapse, it will become increasingly important to build communities in the digital and physical worlds. Together, we can educate each other and create solutions which put an end to systematic oppression, and allow the human spirit to flourish.

Chapter 6
Learn From Everyone, But Be Your Own Teacher

It is important to exercise your ability to learn from every person and situation that we experience. Never allow yourself to limit your knowledge by ignoring information that may be contrary to your viewpoints. Even after reading our work, we urge each of you to continue your research so you can form your own unique opinions about what is going on in the world. No single source of information should be the foundation of your worldview. This dependency is equivalent to giving another person the power of thinking for you.

Much of the western world has been taught to look at society in a very polarized way. When certain issues are presented to us through mainstream circles, they are typically oversimplified to the point where all concepts are presented as black or white—as if there are always clear "good guys" and "bad guys." The reality of the situation is that life is often more complicated than that. There are usually many different ways of looking at things and many different sides to every story.

This is especially true in the study of philosophy where terms are constantly being redefined and ideas constantly reexamined with every new generation of philosophers. When it comes to the idea of governance, the situation is more complex than simply picking a political party or social clique and subscribing yourself to a whole system of beliefs based on other people's ideas. Unfortunately, this is the approach that is generally embraced worldwide. Largely because this is how we have been taught to think. It is a lot easier to have someone thinks for you than to do all of the rigorous research and contemplation necessary to get to the bottom of important social issues.

Especially today, with the incredible amount of contradictory information that is available on the internet, people are becoming increasingly overwhelmed when trying to separate facts from fiction. Sifting through all of this information and cross-referencing sources is time-consuming and not easy for some, but it is a necessary part of achieving any certainty in your research. This is the difference between coming to your own conclusions and adopting the conclusions of others. There are many people out there with great ideas, and there is nothing wrong with having trusted researchers that you regularly look to for reliable information, but do not take anyone's word at face value and do not disregard information purely based on the source. Always confirm the accuracy of new information for yourself.

There are some researchers who are wise in some respects, while still uninformed and off base in many other areas on which they comment. This is why we should critically assess all of the information we come across, and search for alternative

Derrick **Broze** • John **Vibes**

views to get a well-rounded perspective. There are researchers who are brilliant in terms of analyzing foreign policy, but who have terribly misguided views on economics, and vice versa. No one is perfect and we should all be aware of our strong and weak positions so we may continue to learn and grow. This is why it is important to look up everything for ourselves, and check the source documentation to confirm that the information we are receiving is accurate. No one has all the right answers all the time, and if someone pretends to, you might want to proceed with extra caution.

For far too long, learning has been a top-down process in our culture. It is up to each of us to use the tools available to our generations to educate ourselves and our communities so that we may continue to mine one of the most vital resources on the planet—the human imagination.

Chapter 7
Understanding Family and Friends

As we move from examining our internal relationships to the world at large, we want to take a moment to discuss the difficulties that often come from explaining your views and opinions to your closest family and friends. One of the main roadblocks preventing us from actually achieving peace and freedom, is the simple fact that many people who actually are unhappy with the status quo are too afraid to speak out for fear of what their parents, friends, or even complete strangers will think of them. Whether you believe the world is being corrupted by a cabal of government officials, banking institutions, military interests, reptilian aliens, or some mix, we generally understand that there are rebellious minds out there that question official proclamations made by government agents, police officers, and media pundits. Whether we come to the same conclusions or solutions does not yet matter. We appreciate all those who choose to peek behind the veil of statism and authority. Personally, we both believe the State, as an institution, is immoral, and the majority of the world's government are corrupt pawns for various interests that operate in the shadows.

Perhaps your view is not as extreme, but chances are if you are reading this book, your views could be classified as outside the "mainstream." There is also a good chance you have spent some nights researching on the internet, watching documentaries, and rearranging your worldview. You have likely attempted to share this information via social networks, internet forums, and casual conversations with friends and family. Perhaps you are now comfortable proclaiming to your loved ones that you have "woken up" and have begun to chastise them for not taking action and joining the revolution! Unless you're one of the lucky ones, you were, unfortunately, probably met with silence or straight up mockery. This silence and rejection may lead to feelings of anger and resentment that can cause real damage to important relationships. For those of us who feel like we have discovered long hidden truths, it can be extremely disheartening to have our close friends and family turn a blind eye, with our words falling on deaf ears. Remember, sometimes your job is only to plant seeds, not to attempt to constantly "convert" people to your perspective.

We understand that tumbling down certain rabbit holes can lead to life-altering revelations—new values, new principles, and a new understanding of the world—which leads to a reassessment of the types of relationships you keep. Some individuals will choose to disown family members and friends over differences that are deemed to be too great to continue the relationship. While we do not believe free individuals should be obligated to maintain any relationship which is counterproductive or destructive (whether blood relative or not), we also think this decision should not be taken lightly. Simply appreciating an individual for where they are on their path can also be of value. We are all at different points in our journey. This does not mean you should abandon your values, but remember that everyone is learning. Have compassion for those who do not see what you have come to see. Lead by example and others will be encouraged to begin their own search for answers.

Chapter 8
The Rabbit Hole Trap

Many of us who find ourselves in this struggle for freedom were first tipped off to the fact that something was wrong with the world by reading a book, watching a documentary or perhaps a conversation about some type of conspiracy. That was the case for the authors of this book, and both of us look back on these discoveries as transformational events in our lives.

As we grow up, it is often the case that the media, the education system, and our families teach us that the government has our best interest in mind, that they are here to protect us, and would do nothing to hurt us. Clearly, this is very far from the truth. History is filled with examples of governments committing genocide both at home and abroad, conducting experiments on people, and lying about a wide range of atrocities. There is an abundance of documented evidence which confirms these crimes of state.

Whether we talk about the CIA shipping drugs and weapons, funding terrorists, infiltrating activist groups or protecting pedophile networks, there are cases on record which illustrate a pattern of behavior. This pattern of behavior naturally arouses suspicion in the populace and leads many to speculate about what else the government could be up to. We begin looking for the true source of power and wonder if their hidden hand is guiding the headlines of the day.

It is entirely healthy to have these thoughts, but it is important to draw a very clear line in our minds between what we are speculating about and what we know to be true. Unfortunately, many people have a hard time with this because we instinctively search out information to prove the things we want to believe. This inclination is even more prevalent when we are sifting through evidence about an enemy that we know has already lied about so much. Still, the task of exposing their crimes is an important one, and it is not to be taken lightly. Any assumption that we make in our research will come back later to haunt and discredit us if they are incorrect. It is essential that we are thorough in our research, and obvious about when we are speculating if we discuss these topics in public.

It is also necessary to look into the mainstream angles as well, see what the "normies" and so-called experts are saying about the subject, It's a mistake to exclusively focus on the conspiracy angle. For example, there are many people who know very little about cryptocurrency, but are convinced that the technology is a "New World Order" plot to shift everyone onto a digital currency. This widespread assumption among some activists comes from concerns about a "cashless society"—concerns which we share. However, in the discussion about cryptocurrency, many of these suspicious activists are failing to understand the nuance involved in the crypto-discussion.

The early developers and adopters of cryptocurrency were actually also very concerned about the specter of a cashless society, and this is actually one of the primary reasons they worked to create a type of "cash" for the digital world. In fact, most cryptocurrencies were built to be the exact opposite of a central bank. They aim to be deflationary, decentralized and transparent while also private. However, after years of hearing predictions about a coming cashless society, some activists are convinced that all cryptocurrencies are contributing to a cashless society and thus a NWO. The only problem is that the attacks on crypto ignore the fact that in its most decentralized, anonymous, and private version it has the potential to be a solution to their fears.

Both of us have worked as freelance independent journalists over the last decade and in that time we have witnessed some of the most passionate, hard-working reporters fill the gaps left by the corporate media. We have also seen internet personalities spread absolute garbage, straight up lies, and uncorroborated rumors. While some internet journalists actually hit the ground and talk to people or try to confirm their reporting, this is not always the case. Some social media talking heads simply put their own spin on mainstream events and expect the reader to trust them on blind faith.

We have also seen how the viewing audience almost expects content creators to make predictions and offer insight into the state of our world that may not be available in the mainstream. This has caused some less-than-credible journalists to become obsessed with attempting to make predictions about what's right around the corner. There are also social and financial incentives for journalists or activists to "connect the dots" in a way that confirms their own bias, and tells their followers what they want to hear. Often, these predictions are coupled with an invite to sign up for the special newsletter that will make you rich, or the secret club that has all the hidden truths. Be skeptical of these types of charlatans.

Of course, not all people are motivated by money, some are simply in it for their ego and their desire to appear to be the smartest person in the room. Some actually believe the lies they peddle. It is up to you to be discerning and practice critical thinking.

It's also vital to understand that conspiracy theories are no longer the domain of your "crazy" friend. In the age of the internet politicians all over the world have learned how to harness the psychological appeal of conspiracy-themed propaganda to gain support for their often authoritarian policies. In recent years, government agencies, politicians and nationalistic domestic terror organizations have learned how to weaponize conspiracy theories to push establishment agendas and discredit activists. In American politics, Democrats have been hooked on conspiracy theories about Russia since the 2016 election, seeing Russian boogeymen in every opposition to their policies or candidates. Meanwhile, Republicans and right-wing extremists appear to have mastered the art of using conspiracy theories to vilify foreigners or to promote nationalism and traditionalism.

In the very early days of video hosting on the internet, an explosion of conspiracy documentaries about 9/11 and the banking system created a diverse grassroots movement of anarchists, anti-war activists, new agers, sovereign citizens, UFO hunters, left-wing revolutionaries, and right-wing patriots—all of whom opposed both political parties and wanted to create a free world where individual rights were protected. We were very much a part of this movement, and for a short period of time, there was hope that we really were changing the world.

Indeed, that moment of magic did create a million sparks that each went off on their own journeys to make a change, but the cohesive movement where many of us began has deteriorated, and is no longer centered around the ideas that originally drew such diverse rebels together. Despite our different backgrounds and philosophical views, we were able to rally together against the military industrial complex, the police state, government surveillance, monopolized central banking and other genuine and provable conspiracies that are major factors in the ongoing destruction of our world. Sadly, over time, these issues have all taken a back seat to the more sensational click-fetching rabbit holes like flat earth and suspicious celebrity deaths, or topics that appeal to the mainstream voting population, such as Q-Anon.

The online communities that once organized around issues relating to government corruption, have now deviated into partisan politics, and there has been a renewed focus on the right/left paradigm. To our dismay, this division is common even among anarchists, who appear prepared to kill one another over economic theory. The constant baseless speculating, partisan division, calling every event and person fake, and using real conspiracies to spin off fantasies has poisoned the well of the conspiracy research community. It has become so toxic that we now recognize that some of the criticisms of "conspiracy theorists" are based in reality. Of course, the corporate media uses the term as an attack, but the reality is that some people do genuinely see conspiracies everywhere, even when evidence is lacking.

The most detrimental trap of conspiracy culture is the tendency towards defeatist attitudes and hopelessness. As mentioned above, many people believe that all cryptocurrency is a part of the Predator Class plan so they reject all uses of the technology despite the benefits. We have seen theorists complain that if you go to the streets and protest you are feeding into the elitists plan for martial law. We have also heard defeatists discourage others from buying land, forming an intentional community, or going off grid because the authorities will pull a Waco on your community. These examples are endless and every time it seems as if the person complaining has no solutions of their own and has accepted defeat. They assume that "they" are too omniscient and omnipotent for us poor plebs to succeed in our quest for a better world. We reject these notions wholeheartedly.

We both still enjoy tumbling down the rabbit hole from time to time. However, these days we do so with the knowledge that there is not a single one of us who know the complete truth about what is happening behind the curtain. The pursuit of truth is not for the faint of heart. If you are truly curious to understand the inner workings of power, the institutions and people who pull the levers of the machine, and the plethora of dark secrets in our world, you have to learn to separate the lies from the truth. You need to develop a sense for *bullsh*t* and a consistent commitment to find the truth and chase it wherever it goes — especially if it conflicts with your assumptions. This is the only way we will ever find the elusive bottom to the many rabbit holes in the conspiracy realm.

Chapter 9
The State is Not Invincible, It's Just a Bad Idea

Throughout humanity's history, war after war has been waged against various forms of authority, only to lead to further subjugation. This happens because the people are often mesmerized by yet another "savior" promising hope and change, while truly chasing after "power." To understand this drive for power and control we must understand power itself. The traditional definition of power is "the ability to control people or things" or "political control of a country or area." Power, like any tool, can be used to create positive or negative outcomes depending on one's perspective. There are also different types of power. There is power over another person and there is also power that is diffused or shared among a group of people. Political power could be seen as the exercise of constraints on people's action.

On Thanksgiving Day 1980, radical American Indian activist and poet John Trudell spoke about the illusion of power:

"We have to re-establish our identity. We have to understand who we are and where we fit in the natural order of the world, because our oppressor deals in illusions. They tell us that it is power, but it is not power. They may have all the guns, and they may have all the racist laws and judges, and they may control all the money, but that is not power. These are only imitations of power, and they are only power because in our minds we allow it to be power. But it's all an imitation.

"Racism and violence, racism and guns, economics—the brutality of the American Corporate State way of life is nothing more than violence and oppression and it doesn't have anything to do with power. It is brutality. It's a lack of a sane balance. The people who have created this system, and who perpetuate this system, they are out of balance. They have made us out of balance. They have come into our minds and they have come into our hearts and they've programmed us. Because we live in this society, and it has put us out of balance. And because we are out of balance we no longer have the power to deal with them.

"They have conquered us as a natural power. We are power. They deal in violence and repression, we are power. We are a part of the natural world. All of the things in the natural world are a natural part of the creation and feed off the energy of our sacred mother, Earth. We are power. But they have separated us from our spiritual connection to the Earth, so people feel powerless. We look at the oppressor and we look at the enemy because they have the most guns and the most lies and the most money.

"People start to feel powerless... They want us to believe that we are powerless. We are a natural part of the earth, we are an extension of that natural energy. The natural

energy which is spirit, and which is power. Power. A blizzard is power. An earthquake is power. A tornado is power. These are all things of power that no oppressor, no machine age, can put these things of power in a prison. No machine age can make these things of power submit to the machine age. That is natural power. And just as it takes millions and billions of elements to make a blizzard happen, or to make the earthquake, to make the earth move, then it's going to take millions and billions of us. We are power. We have that power. We have the potential for that power."

As Trudell points out, power is more than just the physical mechanisms of the State, more than politicians who can be voted out or even imprisoned. There have been countless battles to overthrow the established powers, but none of them have resulted in freedom for humanity in the long term. This is because all of these struggles were being fought on the wrong battlefield.

Obviously, dealing with the physical manifestations of oppression will be a part of any evolutionary movement, but we must recognize the fight that exists beyond the physical realm. That is, the internal struggle between your desire for freedom, and your internal tyrants desire to bend your will to authority. The oppressed have always thought we were fighting against people when we are truly engaged in a war of ideas. Without a doubt, slavery and physical abuse exist and have resulted in a great deal of damage and destruction. But let's imagine that all the slave masters, policy-makers, and bureaucrats who approved of "legal" slavery and abuses, were suddenly removed from the equation. Would that end slavery and the inherent injustices of the State? No. The ideas and the widespread acceptance of such ideas which allowed them to commit their crimes without consequence, would still remain. This leaves the door open for future authoritarians to repeat the process.

As long as someone holds a desire to wield organized power for their own means (whether benevolent or not), there is a risk of the State being recreated and inevitably growing beyond the control of the people. Yet when we look around at our world today, it is obvious that this concept is still not understood by the majority of the population, who have the understandable (but misguided) tendency to think that violence is going to solve their problems. For far too long, our species has used violence as a tool to achieve our goals. Violence has been at the very basis of social organization and problem solving for the better part of history. This may be why some people are so quick to resort to violence in any conflict—they have learned it from the State!

Perhaps we have become desensitized to the use of violence after a lifetime of witnessing government and their corporate partners employ violence in the form of war, taxation, ecological destruction, and outright slavery. We must unlearn the narrative that has been provided and rewrite our understanding of the nature of government and human relations in general. One of Albert Einstein's most famous quotes is, "*Problems cannot be solved by the same level of thinking that created them.*" This applies perfectly to the situation we are discussing and sheds light onto why the violent revolutions of the past were never able to achieve their goal of setting the human race free from authority.

Since birth, the establishment has fed us perpetual lies and, unfortunately, even when someone discovers the violent nature of that establishment, they are still met with the task of determining what is true and what is not. When the unlearning does not take place, it is common for people to get caught up in the vengeful mentality that comes along with learning about one's own enslavement. When lies about "human nature" or the capabilities of our species are still not recognized and addressed, then it is difficult for people to wrap their minds around nonviolent and apolitical solutions to the problems we see in the world today.

The State and all of its predatory appendage, like the corporate and military industrial complexes, are not simply groups of people with weapons that need to be overthrown; they are just bad ideas that can very easily be rendered obsolete with the right combination of good ideas. The first battlefield that the revolution needs to be won on is the mind. To destroy the problems that were created with violence, the most effective weapons are good ideas and nonviolent solutions—not continued violence and failed politics.

Chapter 10
The Golden Age is Now

Every generation that has walked the earth was unable to imagine or comprehend what tomorrow would bring. This inability to anticipate coming changes causes many to believe their moment in history, and what they see in their day-to-day life, is humanity's maximum level of advancement and understanding of the world. Generation after generation has been proven wrong as we continue to advance in both our understanding of the world and our ability to impact society at large.

Still, there are many who live their lives as if humanity has stopped evolving. Those living with this mentality often espouse an intense nostalgia for an era they were not around to see, but which has been idealized by older generations in the stories that have been handed down through the ages. When politicians and leaders make mistakes and things go wrong, as they often do, the population does not know where to look for inspiration, and instead dwells on the image of the "good old days" which has been imprinted in their mind since childhood. If only the people were to look for inspiration within their own hearts, minds, and communities, the ruling class would surely tremble in their ivory towers.

While every nation and people may have their own Golden Age myth, in America children are indoctrinated with a love of the founding fathers and the myth of limited constitutional government. It is a deeply ingrained idea that goes something like this: *"While things may be a bit screwed up now, once upon a time there were these heroic and selfless aristocrats called the founding fathers who birthed a nation, helping make the people free and prosperous."* We are also told that generally everyone loved them and was happy. This is the cartoonish version of events that plays out in our history books and the cultural myths that are so present in our everyday lives. However, this nationalistic folklore has nothing to do with reality and completely ignores the history of oppression and violence unleashed on the thousands of tribes and nations who were already living in what came to be known as the United States of America.

America's founding fathers may have expressed brilliant ideas and helped spread the general idea of freedom, but they are not perfect. There are some core philosophical principles they did a great job enshrining for future generations (at least in theory; in reality these principles only applied to rich, white men). However, many of these people were still quite oppressive both in their personal and political lives. Many of these men owned slaves, and were racist, classist, and sexist. They were also not as popular in their own times as the history books describe either.

Many of the hallowed politicians of the past were just as unpopular as politicians of our time. The founding fathers were no different. There were constant rebellions among the general population in the generation surrounding the Declaration of Independence because many people rightly saw their local colonial government just as oppressive as the British Empire. These rebellions were often met with brutal force by the aristocrats who are idealized in American history books.

Nevertheless, people took up arms and risked their lives fighting against the government, as we saw in Shay's Rebellion and the Whiskey Rebellion. In some ways, people living during this time were probably significantly freer than your average person today, as they had to deal with fairly little government intervention in comparison to us. However, this was still a rough time and place to live because the political structure was responsible for an extremely low standard of living among the general population. It is safe to say that America's founding should not be looked at as a golden age worthy of repetition.

Humanity's history has been one of constant but slow progression towards a freer society. Slowly but surely, one by one, generation by generation, we shed the insane and irrational political ideas that previously held our ancestors captive. When history is approached from this angle, it may be counterproductive to reach into the past to find a path towards a free society. There are lessons that can be learned from studying history, yet we should seek to combine the best of yesterday with the ever-evolving present reality and accumulated knowledge.

One of the great mysteries of the world is the repetitious cycle of history and how our species continues to make the same mistakes over and over again. This cycle likely has many different causes, but the cultural myth of the golden age is without a doubt a contributor. In past generations republics and democracies were seen as the ideal ways to organize society, but time and experience have shown that these systems of government breed corruption just like any system of coercive social control inevitably does. This corruption resulted in an economic and cultural collapse that was spread out across the whole civilized world and lasted many generations.

With the democratic and republican systems of government a proven failure, our ancestors had an opportunity to create a free society in its ashes. Unfortunately, this did not happen. This is due, in part, to the fact that the minds of the masses were still trapped in the paradigm of domination. So, while they may have escaped their physical chains, they failed to overcome these ideas on a philosophical level. Putting an end to tyranny is not accomplished by simply overthrowing a tyrant. There is no treaty that can be signed to prevent other tyrants from rising in their place. The prevalence of violence and oppression on a mass scale is only able to continue as long as the general population is conned into believing the status quo is the best possible outcome. The "powers that wish they were" would like you to believe that their money, military, media, and "authority" has achieved as close to a utopia as humanity can come.

However, when the masses decide the violence of the ruling class is immoral and socially unacceptable, it will be impossible for tyrants to convince anyone to take part in their madness. This is what is meant by "philosophically overcoming" violent ideas, rather than changing the person sitting on the throne or signing new documents.

At the fall of the Roman Empire the paradigm was not changed, there was no philosophical advancement. In fact, there was actually a regression to long-term feudalism. Perhaps this came as a result of the collective fear of pursuing the unknown (freedom) and the comfort of the past (slavery). This is just one prominent example that relates to today's political climate, but history is rife with examples of people making the same mistakes over and over again by embracing the same bad ideas of the previous regime. Today we find ourselves in another time of great change. From our perspective, the established powers are on shaky ground and the general population is starting to realize the way of life that has been hoisted upon them is unsustainable and a new path is necessary. This regularly happens every few generations, but unfortunately, every single time there has been a revolution or social upheaval, the worldview has remained the same and the cycle was not broken.

The pain, depression and confusion that can come from admitting the twisted nature of our day-to-day existence, is too much for most people to cope with. With that being the case, they create extremely complex justifications and rationalizations for the violence and insanity taking place around them. This is how our species has gotten to where it is today, with numerous brutal empires stretching across the entire globe to the point where there is no longer an option to escape to the promised land. With the general population in a constant state of denial for many generations, the people and organizations that controlled the world's land and resources have been able to consolidate their power with minimal resistance. This is a process that has been taking place since the dawn of civilization. The battle between freedom and enslavement has been raging for centuries, and has played out like a relay race where each generation passes the mission along to the next. The only problem is that those on the side of freedom have not had the ability to participate in this process. For the better part of history, the general population was illiterate and poorly educated, making it that much more difficult to immortalize their side of the story and their ideas for future generations.

Meanwhile, those who sought to enslave humanity were very familiar with planning beyond their own time, as it often took many generations to complete large projects, such as palaces, bridges and monuments. Military conquests were known to take several generations as well. The ruling class has grown accustomed to long-term plans and goals that outlasted their own lifetimes. With most of humanity simply surviving (as opposed to thriving) for the better part of history, it has been hard for people to see past their next meal, so the idea of planning for future lifetimes was probably not prevalent.

However, we do see an example of thinking of future generations in the Constitution of the Iroquois Nations. The Constitution of the Iroquois Nation has helped popularize this idea, often known as the principle of seven generations, or simply considering the impact of your actions on the unborn. The Constitution reads:

Cast not over your shoulder behind you the warnings of the nephews and nieces should they chide you for any error or wrong you may do, but return to the way of the Great Law which is just and right. Look and listen for the welfare of the whole people and have always in view not only the present but also the coming generations, even those whose faces are yet beneath the surface of the ground—the unborn of the future nation.

Under the current paradigm of sophisticated mental conditioning via the media and government schools people have been trained to live as if they were the last generation on earth. Many people continue to pass along the mentality of their oppressors onto their children as their ancestors did to them. Luckily, thanks to the widespread decentralization of information that has been made possible by the internet, there are now more people than ever who are starting to question the nature of society and political power.

This is a great victory in the struggle for freedom, but unfortunately many people become depressed and discouraged when coming to the reality of their existence.

A world of peace and rationality seems like such a total stretch of the imagination, because it is drastically different from what we experience today—but this does not mean a better world is impossible. With every generation, there are drastic paradigm shifts that radically alter the way the people interact with each other. Taking a long view of history, it could be said that these shifts are contributing to a slow upward progression towards a more peaceful world. Unfortunately, tragedies like mass murder, slavery, and subjugation still take place, but they are getting harder and harder to justify because our species is in the process of evolving beyond the type of mentalities that trigger such behavior. When approached from this perspective, it becomes obvious that freedom and peace are inevitable for our species. This does not mean that you should just sit back and wait for it to happen. No, we need you to be actively engaged, using your intellect and energy towards outgrowing the violent social systems that we were all born into. Together we can make the shift happen.

By noting that the revolution will be won over many generations, we are not claiming the current generation cannot make great progress and lay a solid foundation for a free society. We are simply stating that although it may seem like this moment in time is the climax of the human story, every person who is alive right now was born into an age-old revolution that will eventually be carried on by future generations. We all have the potential to discover, develop, and share new ideas which will help lay the foundation for the first truly free society that has ever existed.

Chapter 11
The Sky is Falling, But It's Only a Storm

As more people become aware that something just isn't quite right in the world, the police state has gone into overdrive to counteract this growing resistance to the status quo. We will be the first to admit that the growing police and surveillance states are only one facet of the many serious issues that must be faced by our species. However, despite the overwhelming nature of our predicament, we also see many reasons to feel optimistic about the future of humanity. The more aware the populace becomes, the more frantic the media, government, and corporate partners become. Their whole scam is dependent upon their control over the human consciousness and that control is beginning to unravel. This is the equivalent to someone in a debate screaming ad hominem attacks when faced with an argument superior to their own. When a thief or liar is exposed, you often see them act out in verbal or even physical aggression. It is not unusual for guilty parties to act outraged about accusations against them and play the victim. This is exactly what has been playing out in the macrocosm of geopolitics, as more and more people are becoming aware of their enslavement. As the leaders and authorities are exposed as illegitimate, the establishment is lashing out with all their might.

There is no doubt that we are in the midst of a storm that has been raging for centuries and the intensity of that storm is growing by the minute. If the people of today are willing to work together and cooperatively face adversity, they may be able to weather any potential storm and emerge stronger than before. History is full of societies and empires collapsing and rebuilding. We should make any preparations that we deem necessary, but we should not be consumed by fear to the point where we are considering violence or nihilism.

One reason there is so much fear surrounding the downfall of the state is because people have grown detached from their communities and have lost their ability to be self-sufficient. With that being the case, the first step towards overcoming that fear and preparing for the oncoming storm is to get more familiar with your community and start thinking about ways in which you can expand your skills and knowledge. Growing food, getting to know your neighbors, establishing community study groups, and learning about off the grid solutions are just a few ways to strengthen your family and your community, as living standards continue to deteriorate. (In part 3 we elaborate on ideas for building off the grid community solutions.)

There is an ongoing fascination with talking about "the end of America" or the end of the world. It's as if some people believe everyone alive today would somehow forget all we have learned as a species and return to pre-industrial living conditions simply because the government and their fiat currency failed. This is completely false and ignores the ingenuity of the human mind. While we are still dealing with the dictatorship of the State, we must remain vigilant and not become overwhelmed with what they throw at us because this is exactly what they are trying to provoke.

We can and must recognize the injustices taking place in our world today. We can and must identify the mechanisms and people behind these injustices. We must not be scared into thinking that the status quo is our only option, or that we are fighting a losing battle. Defeatist attitudes will prevent us from making any real progress. While we should remain aware of the dangers posed by the oppressors, we should not fear them. If we combine education with action and work to dismantle the lies, violence, and fear we can regain control of our own lives and liberate ourselves from this matrix.

Chapter 12
The Illusion of Race

Every human being is a unique individual. We each have different thoughts, different inspirations, and different physical features. These differences should be embraced as it shows that everyone is bringing a unique and enlightening perspective to the table for humanity. Sadly, throughout much of history, our "rulers" have conditioned us to be frightened and hostile towards those who are not under their rule. As part of this "othering" process, the rulers often overemphasized differences in physical features and culture to create a sense of separateness.

That is because people in control of large societies have always depended on slavery, subjugation, and conquest to maintain their power, and the lives of luxury that came with it. In order to orchestrate this type of human subjugation, it is necessary for authorities to convince a significant portion of the population that there are different classes of people, and that some lives are worth more than others. These class structures can be defined in different ways, but they are often centered around race, religion and financial inheritance. These class separations were very obvious and explicit in the old world and they have not fade with time. In fact, they are still directing society today even though they exist on a different scale and in different forms than they did during the time of our ancestors.

In the past there were no attempts to hide racial or gender discrimination, royal dynasties, holy wars and slave states because these things all fit into the cultural mythology of the time. As the fight for civil rights has evolved over the years, this mythology was forced to change to accommodate the newfound semblance of freedom. However, despite politicians paying lip service to lofty ideas about equality and social justice in speeches and legislation, the power imbalances in society still remain. The systems that control our lives were built with precise intentions in mind and regardless of how much we attempt to modify these systems to keep up with the changing times, they will still continue to operate as they were intended.

In the United States it is a controversial but provable fact that the United States was founded by white supremacists, who believed in male superiority and the genetic superiority of the ruling class. The system that we live under today was built to protect the culture of racial subjugation that made their conquest of the country possible in the first place. Americans look back on the 1960s civil rights movement and feel good about the country's history because there is far less explicit racism today than there was in the 1950s, but the implicit racism in the system and in many of our minds is rarely discussed. This topic has recently exploded in popularity among the youth in America, but it is still taboo to discuss modern day systemic racism in most mainstream circles. Sometimes it is often viewed as a radical or divisive topic because people like to imagine that we are living in a post-racial, "colorblind" world. It is often suggested that racism is a thing of the past because it is less socially acceptable to be blatantly racist in public and there are more black people in leadership positions. In truth, the racial oppression in American society goes much deeper than these superficial examples.

Many of the laws and government agencies that are seen as pillars of our society today were actually created with the intention of enforcing racial subjugation. The first police forces in the United States were developed in the South as slave-catching patrols. Likewise, gun control laws and drug prohibitions were put into place to criminalize people of color and political dissidents, and these laws are still disproportionately policed in low-income communities of color. There are also prejudicial hiring practices, permit requirements and other obstacles that make it more difficult for people from these communities to make progress in the economy. Of course, these barriers are often invisible for people who don't have to contend with them, but for those who do, it can be a major source of stress in their life.

While it is true that race is nothing more than a social construct, bigotry is deeply woven into the social and political fabric of our world. Solving it is much more complex than just advocating tolerance and changing the color of leadership; our entire culture and political system needs to be reconsidered. While the issue might be largely invisible to those who are not directly affected by it, the existence of institutional racism is one of the main reasons many modern institutions need to be replaced.

In the development of artificial intelligence, engineers are learning that bias viewpoints they didn't even know they had are being hard-wired into their AI programs. For example, it turns out that self-driving cars are more likely to hit people with darker skin when they are forced to avoid accidents or obstacles in the road. Many of these programmers are well intentioned and would probably consider themselves anti-racist, and yet the nature of the culture they grew up in has created blind spots and caused them to see "white" as a default, which has manifested in flaws programmed into the system they created.

This implicit bias in the programming of self-driving cars was revealed in a study conducted by researchers at the Georgia Institute of Technology. The researchers found that many of the image processing systems used in self-driving cars were 5% less accurate at detecting dark-skinned pedestrians, even when the researchers controlled for variables like shade and time of day. It is not clear what is causing this discrepancy, but many experts believe that there were fewer images showing faces with darker skin in the file that was used to train the machine. Facial recognition software has also been shown to identify people of color as criminals falsely. As a result many of the companies currently developing this technology have promised to stop selling their products to law enforcement until this biased programming is removed.

If an AI system in an industry that claims to be anti-racist and "colorblind" is unwittingly programmed to undervalue the lives of people with darker skin, just think about the specific bias that would be hard-wired into a system of government that was created by people who owned slaves and intended to protect their position of dominance. It is not only our political system either. In many ways, white supremacy is hard-wired into American culture. Much of this holdover from previous generations has been brought into question as the country comes to terms with its racist heritage.

The bias in AI technology shows how easily the unconscious bias of a system's creator can affect the integrity of a system. This flaw in the development of artificial intelligence is a vital example of implicit racism, a topic which many people are having a difficult time communicating about at this time in history. This is a more subtle racism that exists in our culture and political systems which are often hard for those of European descent to recognize. On the other hand, this subtle bigotry is easier for people of color to see because they are ones who have to constantly navigate the challenges that come along with having dark skin in a white supremacist society. How many of these blind spots exist in our technology, culture, and political system? More than likely, far more than any of us realize.

While much of the discussion on bigotry focuses on racism—the act of judging another person for their race—we believe there is an even more vital element to this discussion which is often ignored. As we noted above, race is largely a social construct, something that society has bought into over time. However, this does not mean that bigots and primitive judgments of other people do not exist. But, if race is a social construct, then what is it that people are judging each other over?

You might not realize it but much of the way we relate to each other has to do with the color of our skin. For example, many people use "white" to describe lighter skinned people whose ancestors originate from various parts of Western Europe. Some say those who originate from Africa are black and those from South America or indigenous to their homelands are brown. This practice has been normalized for generations around the world.

If we take the term "white supremacist" with its literal meanings then it is someone who believes in the supremacy of "white" people. Of course, there is no "white" nation because white is a color, it is not a nationality or ethnicity. Regardless, the term has meaning. We have come to believe there is a more specific ideology behind this judgment and bigotry—colorism. Colorism is defined as "*prejudice or discrimination especially within a racial or ethnic group favoring people with lighter skin over those with darker skin."*

Colorism describes the discrimination that can take place by someone because of the literal color of their skin, often by people within their own ethnic groups or families. When we speak of a white supremacist society or culture, we mean a society in which some people attempt to lighten or bleach their skin to gain a lighter complexion because they feel it will help them "fit in" or receive less judgment. We have also seen that in many countries the media and television personalities are more likely to be lighter-skinned.

However, colorism is not exclusively a preference for light skin. In some situations, a person of a certain ethnicity might be deemed "too light" or even "too white" by their peers. This can lead to teasing, bigotry, exclusion, or even violence. On the other end of the spectrum, there are also those with brown or black skin who are deemed too dark. In this instance they are maligned for being born a shade that some other person has decided is not an acceptable pigment. All of this judgment leads to beautiful humans living their days feeling like they are not wanted, or that their natural looks are something to be rejected. Clearly, this is not a healthy mentality to live with and has resulted in negative self-images for many people.

The point is whether you are speaking of racism or colorism, this is a primitive low vibrational mentality which breaks complex human beings into a single designation of a color or a constructed racial identity. The only way to heal the human species is to individually and collectively process the intergenerational trauma caused by centuries of discrimination. We should always judge ever person as an individual and to see past race and color. However, we should not erase anyone's experience of racial and colorist discrimination. We can work together to heal these wounds and contribute to a future where every single person celebrates their unique beauty.

Chapter 13
Another Look at the Doomsday Myth

With the constant barrage of news headlines and media pundits warning of the impending doom of our civilization, some have begun to prepare for the possibility of a period with fewer modern conveniences than we have today. Some would call these people prudent or wise, others might even call them paranoid, but these days the mainstream media has branded these people as "Doomsday Preppers." This title not only works to discredit people who seek to be independent and get off the grid, but also perpetuates the myth that doomsday is even coming.

It is true that something is coming, the signs are all around us—a deteriorating economy, rampant global war, destruction of ecosystems, and an overall unsustainable system of governance. So if it's not doomsday, then what is everyone preparing for, and where is all this madness leading us? If doomsday means the possible downfall of "civilization" perhaps we need to start viewing this event in a new light. The end of the status quo could be the greatest thing to ever happen to humanity. This could be the final fall of "Babylon."

Think of it this way: millions of people feel helpless because they see the madness in our world and search for the root causes, but cannot conceive of a way to make change that does not include working within the current system. Meanwhile, this system is overthrowing itself right in front of us. Many of us wish that the government could be overthrown, yet we fear it's inevitable collapse when we should be embracing it. If the U.S. government (and other western nations) continues on their current path, a significant reduction in quality of life and geopolitical influence are inevitable. In the United States, the Federal Reserve System props up the economy with more debt and fake money. Without the Fed performing this act of economic magic, the average American would likely be more aware of the theft and loss of value taking place right in front of their eyes. The Ruling Class would have no method for hiding the miserable state of affairs, and the masses would be spurred to action. Either way, the charade is going to end eventually. They can only play this game for so long before hyperinflation takes effect and topples their already fragile house of cards.

This presents an incredible opportunity for the human race. If we are adequately prepared in terms of getting our physical needs met, as well as developing the mental and philosophical maturity that is required for the establishment of a free society, we can create a network of autonomous, individually sovereign communities. While the world seems to be descending into insanity all around us, it is important for us as individuals to assess the kinds of goods and services that may be needed after an economic collapse and devise peaceful, sustainable methods by which we can provide these values to our families and communities.

The Ruling Class and the complex of the military, government, banking, media, and corporate entities are not blindly pushing towards destruction without a plan in mind. When the opportunity presents itself, this cabal will seek to create order out of chaos and implement their own sadistic plans for the human race. However, they will only be able to create their authoritarian slave farm if the slaves themselves ask for this and assist in creating it. The slaves (the general population to varying degrees) will only ask for this deeper enslavement if they are unaware of its consequences and see no possible alternatives.

This is why it is important for each us to develop solutions to meet our needs—and the needs of our neighbors, without depending on the initiation of the use of force. The use of outright violence or the use of systems predicated on violence is a method of doing business which has destroyed civilizations repeatedly. Likewise, it is equally important for us to advance a proper understanding of philosophy and of our current situation so the population is socially mature enough to be their own masters. We need to prepare the people for the new and unusual nonviolent solutions that will be presented to them by intelligent people like yourself.

Chapter 14
There is Nothing Positive About Willful Ignorance

If you find yourself dissatisfied with the status quo, you may begin to research ways to improve the world. Once you find a few ideas or issues that resonate with you, you might have tried to discuss these feelings with your closest friends and/or family. Chances are, at one time or another you were told things like "stop being so negative," or "can't you just focus on the more positive things in life?"

We can all probably think back on at least one of those frustrating moments where our peers have expected us to share in their blissful ignorance, as they choose to evade reality. Unfortunately, the longer that we ignore the problems that face our species, the worse our predicament becomes. At first glimpse these issues may seem overwhelming and insurmountable but acknowledging the problem is the first step towards freeing your mind and creating a better world for all of us.

In this book we have focused on more positive discussions, but we cannot deny the unpleasant realities of the world that we have to live in. If you had a debilitating illness that could be cured, would you not want to get a diagnosis and immediately start doing what was needed in order to begin healing yourself? Alternatively, would you rather do nothing and ignore the disease because it was "negative"? Sadly, we have been led to believe that ignorance is bliss, while it is actually the reason for the majority of the suffering that has taken place throughout history.

If we are not fully aware of the problem, then there is no way that we can improve the quality of life on this Earth. There is simply no excuse for ignoring legitimate problems that need to be fixed, and we certainly should not allow crimes to be committed before our very eyes. Would you allow an attacker to commit murder in front of you without (at the least) calling for help? Would you stand by and wait for someone else to offer their assistance or would you take control of your own life and do what needed to be done? This is the same situation we find ourselves in. Except in this situation the attacker is the institutionalized violence and theft that is the result of statism. The State does a great job of compartmentalizing the theft and violence so that the average person is unaware that it is even taking place. However, once you become aware of injustice, the greatest mistake you can make is to stand by and do nothing.

Except for a few new radicals with every generation, the majority of the human species has remained unwilling, or unable to stand up and challenge the status quo. For centuries, the buck has been passed down the line, and our species has continued to ride this roller coaster of confusion and oppression. In many ways we have come so far and learned so much.

While much of modern civilization still unquestionably accepts slavery, racism, war, and authoritarianism as simple facts of life, many of us are finally beginning to shed some of these neuroses and are starting to consider the fact that a better path may exist. By considering new ideas for governance and law, we can help break ourselves from chains of past dogma. We must now push further into learning, understanding, and teaching these concepts, and then move towards actually building communities that are living examples of these philosophies.

The fact that questioning the status quo is looked at as socially unacceptable allows the population to go on thinking that they are alone in their dissatisfaction. This isolation can lead to feeling weak and powerless. After being discouraged from pursuing change, some people will create justifications for what's going on around them, telling themselves this is the only world that's possible. They may even come to ridicule anyone who challenges their unconsciously created facade. Simply put, the fear of alienation from peers can lead to accepting standards which do not meet our needs or represent our values. Push on, do not be discouraged by people who cannot handle reality.

Have compassion and remember that many people are just afraid and are not ready to come to terms with the truth. Like a battered child who cries when being taken away from the "safety" of their abusive parents, you may feel comfort in unacceptable situations simply because you are familiar with them. Much like the child, we need to break free from the familiar confines of our abuse and oppression. This condition is known as "Stockholm syndrome."

Stockholm syndrome is typically used to describe hostages who develop positive feelings for their kidnapper because they are dependent upon them for sustenance. When we apply this concept to the macrocosm of our civilization, we find that people living under a system of authoritarianism exhibit these same characteristics. This concept has been illustrated many times in the past, such as the allegory of the cave from Plato's Republic. There is nothing positive about running away from freedom and putting off peace. One of the most important steps you can take is to learn as much as you can about how to fix the problems that you see taking place in our world. Sheltering ourselves from the harshness of our reality will only foster a more toxic and oppressive world for future generations. Embrace the opportunity to create a better vision for tomorrow by changing your thoughts and actions today.

TOOLS FOR ACTION:
NVC, MEDITATION, AND POSITIVE AFFIRMATIONS

In the first book of The Conscious Resistance trilogy, we briefly explored the idea of "conscious healing," using various tools and exercises to provoke deep introspection and reflection. We discussed meditation, psychedelics, flotation tanks, yoga, conscious language, and positive affirmations. Our goal was to inspire the reader to delve deeper into these various modalities and decide what, if any, practices promoted personal and spiritual growth.

For this book, we decided to expand upon a few of these practices to provide a better understanding of how to incorporate mindfulness into your daily life. We will be exploring Non-Violent Communication (NVC), meditation, and positive affirmations. If you are interested in these topics, please pursue further research for individual healing.

Chapter 15
What is Meditation and how do I meditate?

As we outline in Reflections on Anarchy and Spirituality, meditation is a beneficial practice as old as human life. As long as human beings have been conscious, we have come to nature for quiet contemplation and reflection. So what exactly is meditation?

The dictionary definition of meditation is, *"an act or practice that brings you to a place of contemplation, a state of relaxation."*

The consistent application of bringing one's attention to the present moment is key to any form of meditation. This means that nearly any experience can be meditative. A bike ride, a walk under the stars, writing poetry, or any practice that offers individual quiet time within your own heart and mind can be considered a form of meditation. Over time, various teachers organized their specific meditation practices into cohesive styles and philosophies, each with its own instructions and insights. Around the 5th and 6th centuries BCE, Confucian and Taoist meditations appear in China, and Hindu, Jain, and Buddhist meditations developed in India.

These various schools of meditation taught different methods for remaining in the present moment, some involving the counting of breaths, contemplative thought, or repeating sacred words and sounds known as Mantras. There are also different types of meditation positions. Some schools practice sitting cross-legged ("lotus" or "half lotus"), walking, or lying down meditation. You also may have noticed that certain traditions will feature symbolic hand gestures and positions during their meditation. These are known as mudras and are found in Hindu and Buddhist practices. People also meditate for different reasons. Most people would say that meditation can be a religious or spiritual experience, while others find it to be a helpful relaxation and anger management tool. For example, if you are dealing with stress and looking for answers, you may choose to focus on finding the source of your stress, or attempt to clear your mind of all distractions. Different situations require different solutions.

For those interested in learning different types of meditations, we recommend Transcendental Meditation, Zen Buddhism, Mindfulness Meditation, and Contemplative Prayer. We would like to offer a couple methods that we have found to be helpful for general meditation.

First, think of a time that you can meditate on a daily, or weekly basis. The more consistent you are with meditation, the more mindful you will become in your everyday life. Once you have worked out your schedule, decide if you would like to focus on sitting meditation or lying down. Finally, for those who say they cannot meditate, we say, be patient! You cannot expect to go from bombarding yourself with stimuli and distractions to a perfectly still mind overnight. Keep at it and you can push past the static. Try the following four exercises to get you started.

Clearing the Mind

If your goal is to clear your mind, begin by sitting cross-legged with a straight, firm back. Position your shoulders above your hips and place your hands open on top of your knees. You can keep your eyes open and stare softly about four or five feet in front of you, or close your eyes. Take slow, deep breaths. Focus on your breath. As you breathe deep in through your nose count "one." Exhale and repeat to yourself, "one." Continue this process as long as you can. You will find yourself lost in thought within a couple of numbers. This is perfectly normal and not a reason to be discouraged. Your mind wants to think, to fill the quiet, dull spaces with chatter. When you realize that you stopped counting after 3 and began thinking about your next blog post, take a deep breath and start over.

Think of these thoughts like passing clouds, acknowledge them, give thanks for them, and then return your attention to counting. In a 5-minute session, you might not make it past 5, but that's not the goal. You are not attempting to suffocate or ignore your thoughts, but simply focusing on being present. The goal is to simply "be" in that moment, without stress or concern. However, if a situation or person continues to appear in your meditations it may be a sign that you need to focus and work to find clarity.

Finding Clarity

For this meditation, you can set up exactly the same as you are when clearing your mind. The difference here, is that instead of clearing the mind, you will relax and focus on a specific situation or person that needs your attention. This could be a relationship that you are uncertain of, or a friend that you want to celebrate. Whether for clarity or to affirm the positive, you want to sit and take a deep breath as you focus. If you are looking for answers, take the time to imagine the ideal outcome and consider the situation from the perspective of everyone involved.

If you are giving thanks for a new opportunity or friendship, focus your mind on expressing gratitude and appreciation. Taking time for reflection during uncertain times helps one develop a predisposition for mindfulness over impulsiveness.

Connecting to the Earth

This exercise can be done lying down or sitting. Either way, you want to begin with slow, deep breaths. Imagine that you are connected to the Earth physically and energetically.

All the power of the planet is flowing up from the ground in the form of a white light. Imagine this white light coming up from the Earth into the base of your body. The light runs up through your feet, into your waist, connecting to your heart, and out through the crown of your head.

As the light flows through each piece of your body, imagine you are being cleansed. You feel this white light removing the stresses from each piece of you. As the light flows out the top of your head, it goes up into the sky and back down into the Earth to start all over again. Continue imagining and feeling this light for at least 15 minutes.

Thanking Your Body

This meditation is meant to be done lying down with your arms at your side. Beginning with your toes, you are going to slowly move and become aware of each piece of your body. Imagine that your awareness is within your toes, and gives thanks to them. Think of all the work your toes and feet do to ensure you can live your life. Take your time slowly going from your toes, to your feet, to your ankles, your shins, etc., and give thanks to each individual piece of your body. Recognize the power of each piece of you.

Chapter 16
Non-Violent Communication

Language is, without a doubt, one of the most important and profound developments in human history. It has allowed us to describe the world we live in and express ourselves to one another. Language lays the foundation for our belief systems and also our idiosyncrasies. Our view of the universe is also shaped by the words that we use to describe what we see and experience. The written language is especially important because it immortalizes information and makes it possible for humans to record a meticulous history. In order to surpass the systemic violence we see in much of our world, we must expand the limits of our vocabulary. Advancing our communication skills is an essential step towards achieving world peace. All of us can contribute to the positive expansion of our different culture's vocabulary, and tear down the linguistic barriers set by those who keep us mentally enslaved.

One man who has worked tirelessly on communication is psychologist Marshall Rosenberg. Rosenberg is responsible for developing a new way of speaking which he calls Non-Violent Communication (NVC) or Compassionate Communication. This method of communication is simple and has had profound success all over the world, from feuding tribes of the southern hemisphere to the broken homes of modern America. Marshall recognized that all human language is filled with traps that inevitably lead to conflict. These traps are trigger words which he referred to as "jackal language." Jackal language consists of words that imply guilt, humiliation, shame, blame, coercion, or threats. Marshall believes that this kind of language and interaction is not a natural process, but a byproduct of the "culture of domination" that he believes has consumed our species for thousands of years. We agree with his assertion. To resolve conflicts, it is necessary for us to avoid using jackal language, and learn to be empathetic when working out our problems.

According to NVC, conflict arises between two or more people when someone in the equation has needs which aren't being met. This is the root cause for humans acting out and the reason why some people are oftentimes unhappy with the actions of others. In most conflicts, these issues are never addressed. Instead of identifying everyone's feelings and needs in order to work towards a solution, the two parties begin a battle of blaming, which neither side can ever truly win. Nonviolent communication is a very easy method to explain, but it can be difficult to master. One of the most difficult parts of the process to grasp is the very first step actually—observation. In times of conflict, many of us are quick to confuse judgments with observations.

An observation would be *"Our project is due next week."* In this case you are only stating the facts of the situation, you are not making any judgments. A judgment relating to this observation would be *"Our project is due next week and you haven't done a damn thing, I have done all of the work, you are lazy."* This is an example of the kinds of judgments that cause a lot of arguments and miscommunication. It is very common for conflicts to be filled with judgments and labels that only push the conversation into a more negative direction. Don't get discouraged with yourself if you find it difficult to speak without passing judgments or using jackal language, as these are both things that are fundamentally woven into our language and seem natural to most people.

Once an observation is made, it's time for the parties involved to express their feelings on the subject to establish a mutual understanding. For example, one could say, *"Our project is due next week, and I'm very worried about our grade, what can we do to make sure we pass?"*

In situations of conflict, it is an unmet need that is causing discontent, so the objective of the conversation is to identify the needs which are causing the feelings. Once everyone's needs are on the table, it becomes very easy to see a possible solution in which everyone's needs are met and the conflict can be resolved.

This was a very quick and basic introduction to nonviolent communication but there are many books written by Marshall Rosenberg that discuss his theories in greater detail. There are also local NVC groups around the world where you can learn the techniques. Marshall Rosenberg is just one great mind in a sea of millions, and it is very likely that others will improve upon his method, or develop an entirely different communication method. In fact, it is probably necessary for each generation to be working to improve our language constantly, so it can be a tool of expression, rather than a tool of oppression.

Chapter 17
Affirming the Positive and Manifesting Reality

I n our first book, we discussed the connection between Creative Visualization, Positive Affirmation, and Manifestation. When you exercise your imagination and visualize that which you hope to create or achieve, you attach a powerful symbol to your vision. By creating "vision boards" with words and images that represent our desired goals, or by simply meditating on what we would like to see in our lives, we remind ourselves of the steps we must take to achieve those goals. By sitting in quiet reflection and allowing our minds to clear of distraction, we can achieve all we desire. Through visualization, we can see, smell, taste, hear, and touch the ideal situation we are trying to manifest, and work through the difficult problems we may be facing. Once you are comfortable with visualizing your path, it is important to affirm the path. This is where positive affirmation comes into play.

Positive affirmation is a highly effective method of programming oneself. We face external programming every day through the corporate media, the government, and those we communicate with. One way or another, whether by our own doing or some external force, we will be programmed. The mind is much like a computer that can be loaded with a variety of programs. Many of us buy into cultural and environmental programming that does not empower us as individuals, but rather teaches us to doubt our potential and capabilities. We must take steps to deprogram ourselves from such destructive thinking. With daily affirmations, we can create a positive, compassionate view of ourselves and of the world around us. By using affirming statements, such as "I AM...," we allow our minds to let go of negative habits and begin to rewrite the pathways our thoughts take.

For example—perhaps your insecurities are a constant prison, a paralysis that limits your social life as much as your internal world. By changing your internal self-talk that says you are incapable of certain tasks or that other humans view you in a negative light, and affirming, "*I am capable, I am deserving of love and compassion,*" you can overcome a lifetime of unnecessary insecurities and doubts. Over time this reprogramming of your mind becomes habit. Rather than buying into the limiting thoughts when they appear, you are able to say, "*No, Thank you, I no longer need you!*" and instead tell yourself, "*I am capable, I am loved, I am becoming stronger every day in every way.*"

This simple act can have long-lasting, life-changing effects. Through creative visualization and daily affirmations, we are not only changing our state of mind and the way we look at our world, but we are energetically altering the course of our lives. Manifestation is the power of watching an idea go from a seed in your mind, to a daily focus, to a physical reality. Manifestation is the culmination of an empowered individual understanding what they want, making a conscious choice to pursue that goal, calling out to the universe for assistance, and taking steps in the physical world to bring that idea into reality. These tools are not simply a method of praying or wishing away the problems we face. We must remember that the power of the mind is assisted by actions taken by the physical body. Through personal responsibility, determination, and a focused work ethic we can produce the results we seek and have everything we desire.

We would like to offer the following six affirmations to help you get started. Our experience has shown that repeating these aloud in the morning (before you get distracted by work, school, etc.) is a great way to start the day with mindfulness. Before you start, find a quiet place to relax. You can do this in front of a mirror, or meditating while repeating the affirmations. Once you have found your spot, take a deep breath, fill up your lungs with as much air as possible, and then slowly release your breath through your nostrils. Do this a few times until you are completely relaxed and then begin your affirmations. Feel free to adjust the words and themes to suit your specific situation. Wherever and whenever you decide to do your affirmations, remember to be consistent. Doing these on a daily basis, as often as needed, will promote gratitude and empowerment.

Choosing Self-Control

This one is beneficial for when you are having a rough day. It will help to remind you to be thankful. When you find yourself getting agitated, or angry, slow down and repeat these words:

Today I give thanks to the Great Spirit that flows in all life. I am filled with gratitude for another day, another set of moments that allow me to create the world of my own choosing.

I am indebted to my friends and family for being constant reflections of the lessons that I need to see. Today, in this moment, I am getting stronger in every way. My ability to take on difficult situations and to see the lessons is constantly growing. I no longer need self-pity, grudges, or anger. I choose to see all that comes my way as motivation for my future endeavors.

I am powerful. I am free. I am powerful. I am free. I am the only person who can dictate my emotions and actions. I choose to let my thoughts, my words, and actions from this moment on flow from a place of love. I choose to let my thoughts, my words, and actions from this moment on flow from a place of love.

Choosing Self Forgiveness

It's important for us to remember to forgive and love ourselves. The sooner we heal and love ourselves, the sooner we can amplify and emanate that energy out into the world.

Today, in this moment, I am filled with gratitude for my path and the lessons presented to me. I choose to see any and all hardships as temporary, and as opportunities for growth.

I forgive myself for my past mistakes and flaws. With each passing moment I am becoming better, stronger, and more compassionate. I understand that life is a constant learning experience. I see any bumps in the road as possibilities for alternative outcomes.

I remain committed to my path as a beautiful, free, independent human being. I choose to remain open to the lessons that manifest on my path. I remember that I am the master of my own life and the creator of my destiny.

Today I choose (what do you want to manifest today?)

Being Present Today I give thanks for the present moment, the endless, repeatless NOW. I give thanks for endless "NOW's" to manifest my highest good. I am completely present in this time and space. I choose to "be here now" in whatever I am doing. In this moment I choose to be the best secretary, the best artist, the best musician, the best chef, the best mechanic, the best husband, wife, and the best human I can be. I choose to let the distractions of my active mind float past my awareness like passing clouds. I choose to embrace my present circumstances and to "be the Buddha" in this moment.

Letting Go

Today, in this moment, I choose to reflect on any and all situations that might not be contributing to my highest good. I choose to examine the conflict, external and internal, and decide whether I can rectify the situation. I choose to come from a place of love and compassion, and make a decision that will be best for all involved. If, upon examining the situation, I find no solution, I choose to let go. I choose to see the positive, the lessons gained from the experience and let go for my health and sanity. I give thanks for these experiences and the lessons they have provided. I choose to be in control of my life and my experiences. I choose to remain open to new lessons and open to letting go when necessary.

Finding Balance

Today, in this moment, I am thankful for my strength and my success. I am grateful for the perceived failures that are lessons for me on my path. In this moment, I choose balance. I choose to release that which is weighing me down or keeping me in the clouds. I strive for an acceptance of all my emotions, good, bad, and everything in between. I accept and own all my emotions. I choose to listen to my body, mind and spirit, and move in a direction that stabilizes me and promotes balance. I choose to remember that balance must start with my thoughts, move to my words and then my actions. Only then will the balance be long lasting and genuine. I recognize that this is a continuous process and allow myself to stumble so I may pick myself up stronger than ever.

BOOK III

•••

MANIFESTO OF THE FREE HUMANS

A Note From Derrick & John

Thank you for taking the time to conclude the journey that we began in 2015 with the release of Reflections on Anarchy and Spirituality. By examining the intersection of spiritual practices predating organized religion and the political philosophy known as Anarchism, we believe we successfully carved out a new path for those who reject authority in their spiritual and political beliefs. Reflections laid the foundation for what we believe can help create a more balanced, and free world. It could be considered the "body" of our philosophy.

The second book, Finding Freedom in an Age of Confusion, could also be considered the "heart" of our ideas. In a series of essays, we explored the human struggle for freedom. We talked about how to overcome the depression, confusion, and fear that often comes along with understanding the harsh realities of our world. For this final installment in our series, we will explore various corners of anarchist philosophy and provide workable solutions for creating a free society. This book could be considered the "mind" of our philosophy. Our goal is to provide our brothers and sisters with a "how to" guide for individual healing and empowerment, community building, and ultimately, for breaking away from the State to form new communities.

In Reflections we briefly explored the history of the anarchist philosophy and the American libertarian movement. By providing the history of the thinkers and ideas we are drawing from, we hoped to illustrate the evolution of the concepts that have come to be known as The Conscious Resistance. Our focus has been the libertarian and anarchist movements because they have historically contained the most radical activism and propaganda. Although the term "libertarian" may have varied meanings around the world, it is a term that is rooted in an antiauthoritarian, anti-statist philosophy. In America, this libertarian philosophy can be traced back to Josiah Warren, America's first individualist anarchist.

Warren was born in the late 18th century and helped to expound the doctrine of individualist anarchism. He was responsible for launching several intentional communities (Utopia, Ohio; Modern Times, NY) that operated under his "Sovereignty of the Individual" ethic, which we explore in the 3rd part of this book. Warren would go on to work with and inspire Lysander Spooner, Benjamin Tucker,

Voltairine de Cleyre, and other American Anarchists, many of whom became known as The Boston Anarchists. (For more information we recommend reading Men Against the State.) The work of these men and women would influence Austrian economist Murray Rothbard and other young freedom minded Americans during the 1960s. Rothbard would borrow ideas and inspiration from the Boston Anarchists, and add Austrian economics and subjective value theory to craft his philosophy of Anarcho-Capitalism. Soon after, Samuel Konkin applied Austrian economics to a more class-conscious and less political philosophy that he coined as Agorism. We perceive our work as a continuation and expansion of the Individualist Anarchist tradition that predates the many modern Anarchist divisions, such as Anarcho-Communism and Anarcho-Capitalism. We also hope to expand upon and continue Konkin's Agorist philosophy.

Readers should note that use of the term "libertarian" refers to the philosophy that includes self-ownership, anti-authoritarianism, and individual sovereignty, not the American Libertarian Party, which we see as contradictory to libertarian and anarchist values. We do not intend to propose a one-size-fits-all model of anarchism, but instead seek to establish a world where people are free to move in and out of competing economic and political systems. This is commonly referred to as "panarchy" or "panarchism," a concept that we will explore in depth later in the book. This would allow individuals the freedom to vacate the state in favor of self-governance, or, if they choose, stay under the rule of the unsustainable state. However, we believe that people will freely choose self-governance because the inevitable and ongoing consciousness shift will erase the notion that authoritarianism has any place in our world.

Finally, please do not forget that each of you are powerful, beautiful, and free. The future depends entirely on the actions we choose to take today. We hope the following essays provide inspiration for those seeking to join the fight for a freer world.

PART 1—A STRATEGY FOR DEFEATING THE STATE

Chapter 1
Overcoming the Fear of Freedom

A narchy! It might be the most feared and propagandized term in existence. The public has an extremely distorted perception of the word and most seem to be terrified of removing authority from their lives and allowing for self-organization. In fact, it is actually extremely rare for serious discussions on this topic to happen due to the knee-jerk reactions that are provoked when individuals are presented with the possibility of a world without authority. However, once one is able to find the courage to step beyond social convention and question the control systems they were born into, they will find that real anarchy is actually nothing like the doomsday fiction presented by mainstream culture.

When looking deep enough into this situation, it becomes clear that the serious problems facing our species, such as war, poverty, and environmental destruction, are all exacerbated, if not created, by the legalized monopoly on force made possible by government. Ironically, these problems are always cited as reasons to keep the state intact, when in reality, it is the state that is creating the problems in the first place. For centuries, those who reap benefits from the concept of authority have worked tirelessly to keep this idea alive. The parasite class has fought against the rising tide of human ingenuity which has been progressively tearing away from the destructive traditions and control mechanisms of the past. Unfortunately, every time humanity has managed to overcome one oppressive tradition, the ruling class has been able to modify their propaganda to form a more convincing case for their authority.

In the case of racial slavery in the American south, many slaves who were bred into a life of servitude actually held the belief that slavery was not only a necessary price to pay for "civilization" but was also in their best interest. When reading *"The Narrative of the Life of Frederick Douglass,"* one cannot help but notice the similarities between the brainwashing that he saw among the slaves in his time and the perspectives held by much of the modern American public, although the slaves obviously had much more serious physical threats to contend with. In his autobiography, Douglass points out that slaves would often argue about who had the better and wealthier master. He also described how many slaves came to equate slavery with wealth, and many slaves, Douglass included, believed that in the absence of slavery there would be no wealth, much in the same way that citizens today believe that there would be no peace or prosperity without government. The book details how Douglass had to first remove the chains of mental slavery before he could escape his physical bondage. One of the most profound passages describes the moment when he finally experienced life in the northern states firsthand and learned that wealth could be achieved without slavery.

Douglass wrote that, "*I had very strangely supposed, while in slavery, that few of the comforts, and scarcely any of the luxuries, of life were enjoyed at the north, compared with what was enjoyed by the slaveholders of the south. I probably came to this conclusion from the fact that northern people owned no slaves. I supposed that they were about upon a level with the non-slaveholding population of the south. I knew they were exceedingly poor, and I had been accustomed to regard their poverty as the necessary consequence of their being non-slaveholders. I had somehow imbibed the opinion that, in the absence of slaves, there could be no wealth, and very little refinement. And upon coming to the north, I expected to meet with a rough, hard-handed, and uncultivated population, living in the most Spartan-like simplicity, knowing nothing of the ease, luxury, pomp, and grandeur of southern slaveholders. Such being my conjectures, any one acquainted with the appearance of New Bedford may very readily infer how palpably I must have seen my mistake.*"

In humanity's dark history, there were periods where gangs of men could own the lives of millions by claiming to be given that right by a supernatural being. Once that excuse fell out of favor, the power-hungry authoritarians were forced to create new justifications for their authority. This desire for elite groups of individuals to rule over large areas of land and conquer the inhabitants within is what gave rise to our current political paradigm. The popular myth states that "the people" created things like governments and militaries as a compromise, to create a mostly peaceful world. In reality, these organizations were all created by sophists and aristocrats, specifically intending to enslave entire populations. As the general public has become more intelligent, increasingly complex rationalizations for authoritarian powers have become necessary to keep the herds in line.

Ideas like the social contract, the national interest, common good, majority rule and representative government have replaced the divine right of kings and the privilege of the aristocracy. In today's more sophisticated culture, it is necessary to make people believe they rule themselves in order to rule over them effectively. This is why the rhetoric of the social control systems that we live under is riddled with euphemisms that hide the oppressive and violent nature of their existence. The mass murder of innocent people is called defense, strong-arm robbery is called taxation, kidnap and extortion is called justice and gangs of people who claim dominion over specific geographic locations are called governments.

"Government" is itself another one of the words that mean different things to different people, but when examined objectively, it becomes apparent that organizations known as government always maintain a monopoly on the use of force over a given territory. Considering that this is the primary characteristic shared by all governments throughout history, to describe the entity as anything other than a monopoly of violence is euphemistic and dishonest.

We are surrounded by a false definition of the word "government" just as we are surrounded by a false definition of the word "anarchy." We have been told that the word "government" is simply the inevitable form civilized society takes, but this may be one of the most deceptive linguistic tricks used since the Dark Ages, as it implies that structure and organization will cease to exist in the absence of institutionalized violence and central planners. Since all governments share the common characteristic of establishing and promoting institutionalized violence, we can safely say that a lack of government would increase the opportunity for peace. In other words, when there is peaceful, spontaneous order in a society, there is anarchy, but when a society is organized around the constant threat of institutionalized violence, there is government. This is not to say that violence would never occur in a society without government, but it would not be justified and celebrated, nor would it be as widespread or powerful.

Despite the obvious violence inherent in the institution of government, many people have a difficult time considering the possibility of a world without such a monopoly. When someone suggests that we simply do away with this unjust and unnecessary organization they are typically met with negative reactions. This conversation often ends very quickly because both sides have completely different ideas of what the word "government" actually means. If we attempt to examine government from an outsider's perspective, we would see a world where people are grouped into two different categories—those in government and those not. At face value we can see that these two groups of people have completely different standards and expectations, even though they are the same species and have the same basic needs. Looking closer, we can see that these different standards and laws are not neutral, and in fact, they are very much benefiting those in government at the expense of those who are not. The most important discrepancy to mention here is the fact that many government employees and agents of the state have the "legal" authority to steal, cage, or kill you.

However, if you ask any random person on the street to define "government" for you they will likely repeat the propaganda taught in government school. You know, the tale about how government is the backbone of civilization and the means by which people in the community come together for mutually beneficial projects. This may sound good, but it isn't at all true, because the government does not produce anything and would not be able to provide any "services" if it wasn't for the resources forcibly extracted from the rest of society. Therefore, it is safe to say that all functions that are currently being carried out by the organization known as "government" could actually be better served by individuals in the community working together for common goals, without the middleman, since all the resources and labor is coming from them to begin with. Voluntary trade, charity, and other peaceful methods of interacting would create a far better society than the one that we see today.

The most common argument against having a stateless society is the notion that we are all stupid, worthless savages who would not be able to figure out how to build something as simple as a road if there wasn't someone with a gun in our face every step of the way, telling us how, when, and where to do it. But if people are stupid savages, and politicians are people, then isn't the government made up of a bunch of stupid savages who should not be trusted with a license to kill? If we are all equal and supposedly incapable of governing ourselves, why should we trust other incompetent people to rule over us?

Of course, we know this to be propaganda spread by the powers that wish they were. There is nothing that a government can do that you and a large group of focused individuals cannot also accomplish. The government doesn't provide services, they simply take money from everyone and use a small portion to sell back "services" to the people. Looked at in these terms, it becomes apparent that the government is nothing more than a violent middleman who forces their way into nearly every interaction that takes place between each of its so-called citizens. Everything that the government does is an attack on people who don't belong to that organization.

If you think about it, every single action the government takes is some kind of punitive measure against people who are not part of the club. Even when the government claims to do something for the goodwill of all people, they are doing so with resources collected by using threats and violence. There is no such thing as a virtuous act of government. This organization is not here to protect our rights. In fact, when the government steps in and gives itself the responsibility to protect your rights, it is simultaneously stripping you of your ability to defend yourself. When you are dependent upon the whims and capabilities of another human being to protect your rights, you are literally handing your rights over to them and opening yourself to slavery.

Although there are only a few examples of stateless societies and communities throughout history that we know of, this should not be seen as a failure of anarchist philosophy. The lack of examples says more about the primitive condition of the human race thus far, than it does about the possibility of a stateless society. Humanity is constantly accomplishing feats and smashing paradigms previously believed to be impossible. So to say that a society without institutionalized violence is impossible because there are not many historical examples, is to say that our current state of affairs is the pinnacle of human achievement. This is obviously a naive, arrogant and blatantly false worldview, which has been projected onto the entire planet through the institutions and conventions established by those who claim ownership over other free human beings.

These institutions and conventions are the very reason why many people have such a distorted view of words like "government" and "anarchy." Our cultural norms have been handed down from those in power, so it is only natural that these norms reflect the needs and interests of the power structure rather than the needs of the people. Therefore, the perceptions of government and anarchy that many of us have adopted are not accurate descriptions of reality, but simply a description of the world as seen through the eyes of our rulers. In a system of government, our rulers have infinite power and control. In the absence of government, they are forced to live by the same rules and standards as everyone else. The ill-informed will make the mistake of believing that anarchy means without rules, but what it truly means is without centralized authority ruling over others.

In the eyes of a tyrant, a world without complete dominion over the lives of others is a life of lawlessness, chaos, and disorder. This perspective does not reflect reality, but instead reflects the deranged worldview that drives the parasitic state and corporate classes. This is why a peaceful term like anarchy has such a negative social stigma, while a word like government is seen as a benign and unquestionable construct of nature. We have adopted the language and worldview of our oppressors. It's time for the free hearts and minds of the world to overcome the fear of freedom, reject the authoritarians and statists, and begin governing ourselves.

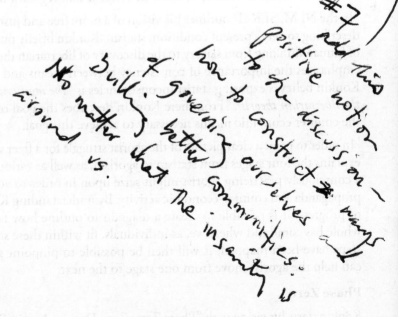

Chapter 2
What is Agorism?

In the late 1970s, anarchist, activist, and writer Samuel E. Konkin III (SEK III) released *The New Libertarian Manifesto*, presenting his case for a new strain of libertarianism that he called "New Libertarianism." The philosophy behind the New Libertarian Movement was agorism, named after the "agora," the Greek word for marketplace.

"An agorist is one who acts consistently for freedom and in freedom," SEK III wrote.

Essentially, agorism is a radical libertarian philosophy that seeks to create a society free of coercion and force by using black and gray markets in the underground or "illegal" economy to siphon power away from the state. Konkin termed this strategy "counter-economics," which he considered to be all peaceful economic activity that takes place outside the purview and control of the state. This includes competing currencies, community gardening schemes, tax resistance and operating a business without licenses. Agorism also extends to the creation of alternative education programs, free schools or skill shares, and independent media ventures that counter the establishment narratives. Also essential to the growth of agorism is the public's support of entrepreneurs who actively do business outside of the state's license and regulations.

In the NLM, SEK III outlines his vision of a more free and just world by first describing society's present condition: statism. Konkin briefly outlines the path of human thinking from slavery to the discovery of libertarian thought and also emphasizes the importance of consistency between means and ends. Indeed, Konkin believes exposing statist inconsistencies is *"the most crucial activity of the libertarian theorist."* From here Konkin describes the goal of agorism and the counter economic means necessary to achieve this goal.

In order to paint a clear picture of the agorist struggle for a freer world, Konkin explains the four stages from statism to agorism, as well as various actions that a consciously practicing agorist might seize upon in order to advance agorist propaganda and counter-economic activity. By understanding Konkin's vision of progress, it is possible to create a diagram to outline how far society as a whole has come and where we, as individuals, fit within these steps. After the steps have been mapped, it will then be possible to pinpoint strategies that can help the agorist move from one stage to the next.

Phase Zero

Konkin starts his vision with "Phase Zero: Zero-Density Agorist Society." Phase zero is the time when no agorists existed and libertarian thought was scattered and unorganized, which Konkin says has been "most of human history." Once libertarians became aware of the philosophy of agorism, counter-economic activity began and we moved into *"Phase 1: LowDensity Agorist Society."* In this phase the first counter-economic libertarians appear. Konkin believed that this was a dangerous time for activists who would be tempted by *"Get-Liberty-quick"* schemes. Konkin also reminds agorists not to be tempted by political campaigns. *"All will fail if for no other reason than Liberty grows individual by individual. Mass conversion is impossible,"* he wrote.

Phase 1

Phase 1 is presented as a time when the few existing practicing counter-economists' main goal is recruitment and creation of "*'radical caucuses,' ginger groups, or as a 'Libertarian Left' faction in general*" (More on the "Libertarian Left" in chapter 5). Konkin also notes that the majority of society is acting *"with little understanding of any theory but who are induced by material gain to evade, avoid, or defy the State. Surely they are a hopeful potential?"*

In order to achieve the free society, Konkin again emphasizes the need for education and *"consciousness-raising of counter-economists to libertarian understanding and mutual supportiveness."* SEK III also called for the creation of a movement of the libertarian left which may grow strong enough in influence and numbers in the latter stages of phase 1 to be able to "*block marginal actions by the state.*" The ability to block actions by the state has absolutely increased in recent years with the explosion of decentralized, peer-to-peer networks via the internet that allow for rapid sharing of information and calls to organize. There are a growing number of internet videos showing communities banding together to oppose unjust arrests by agents of the State.

For example, the websites and apps FreedomCells.org, and NextDoor.com offer tools that can be used to strengthen our communities, grow the counter-economy, and push back against the state. Using the Freedom Cell Network one can locate other freedom-minded individuals within their city, state, or country with the specific goal of organizing in the real world and bypassing the need for government. In 2016 we launched the site as an online platform for building mutual aid groups known as Freedom Cells, which we will explore in detail in the next chapter. NextDoor also allows the user to connect with the local community, both digitally and in the real world. The app has the added benefit of being focused on your specific neighborhood. This allows individuals to post important safety information, lost and found items, or counter-economic business opportunities, directly to those that live near them. Of course, the fact the NextDoor is a public forum which is monitored by the police means that all users should exercise caution and common sense when promoting their cell activities.

Phase 2

Each of these tools is a part of the technology of the counter-economy that has the potential to render government intervention and regulation completely useless. If we seize the moment, we can grow the black and gray markets using these emerging peer-to-peer platforms. This is exactly what Konkin believed would help society progress from phase 1 to phase 2. As we move to *"Phase 2: Mid-Density, Small Condensation Agorist Society,"* the statists take notice of agorism. Is it in this phase that Konkin believes the counter-economy will grow and agorists will begin to represent "an ever-larger agorist sub-society embedded in the statist society." Although the majority of agorists are still living within the state's claimed territories, we begin to see a *"spectrum of the degree of agorism in most individuals."* This includes benefactors of the State who are "highly statist" and "a few fully conscious of the agorist alternative," however, the majority of society is still engaged in the statist economy.

From here, Konkin suggests that agorists may want to start condensing into districts, ghettos, islands, or space colonies. We are, in fact, beginning to see the creation of Agorist minded communities, seasteaders, ecovillages, co-ops, and underground spaces which emphasize counter-economic activity and the creation of counter-institutions to the state. Konkin believed these agorist communities might be able to count on the sympathy of mainstream society to prevent an attack from the state. This is the moment where the question of community protection and defense comes into play. We have seen the creation of community protection alternatives to the police state monopoly (see *Threat Management Center in Detroit* and the *Autodefensas* in Mexico) but thus far, nothing completely agorist has come into existence. It is the creation of these syndicates of community protection which will ultimately allow the agora to flourish. However, in order for this to happen *"The entire society has been contaminated by agorism to a degree,"* leading to the possible creation of an above or underground movement which Konkin called the New Libertarian Alliance. The NLA simply acts as the spokesperson for the agora and uses, *"every chance to publicize the superiority of agorist living to statist inhabiting and perhaps argue for tolerance of those with 'different ways.'"*

Phase 3

This brings us to *"Phase 3: High-Density, Large Condensation, Agorist Society,"* which is described as the point when the state has moved into a terminal crisis period due, in part, to *"the sapping of the State's resources and corrosion of its authority by the growth of the Counter-Economy."* As the agora grows in influence, the state's stranglehold is also dissipating as a result of unsustainable economic practices. Konkin again warns that the statists will attempt to win over new libertarians with "anti-principles" and calls for maintaining *"vigilance and purity of thought."* Highly motivated new libertarians move into R&D to help create the first agorist protection and arbitration agencies that will compete with the state. At this point, government exists in pockets with the state mostly concentrated in one geographic territory. Those living under statism are very aware of the freedom being experienced by their agorist counterparts. The state has become weak enough that "large syndicates of market protection agencies" are able to contain the state and defend new libertarians who sign up for protection insurance. This, Konkin believed, was "the final step before the achievement of a libertarian society." Society is divided between the larger agorist areas and the isolated statist centers.

The transition from phase 3 to phase 4 brings about *"the last unleashing of violence by the ruling class of the state."* Konkin said that once the state's intellectuals recognize that their authority is no longer respected they will choose to attack. Defense against the state will be managed once the counter-economy has generated the syndicates of protection agencies large enough to defend against the remaining statists. The NLA should work to prevent the state from recognizing their weakness until the agorist movement has completely infected the statist society. Once the agorist communities have successfully resisted the state's attack, the Agorist revolution will be complete. As we move from Phase 3 to 4, Konkin notes that the first three changes "are actually rather artificial divisions; no abrupt change occurs from first to second to third." However, he envisions the change from the third to fourth step to be "quite sudden."

Phase 4: Agorist Society With Statist Impurities

Once the State has gasped its dying breath, the counter-economy becomes the freed market where exchanges are free of coercion. Konkin predicts that *"division of labor and self-respect of each worker-capitalist-entrepreneur will probably eliminate the traditional business organization—especially the corporate hierarchy, an imitation of the State and not the Market."* He imagines companies as associations of independent contractors, consultants and entrepreneurs. After the remnants of the state are apprehended and brought to justice, freedom becomes the basis of ordinary life and *"we tackle the other problems facing mankind."*

Whether the totality of Konkin's vision becomes realized, the world has, at the least, made some slight progress through the phases predicted in the NLM. All signs point to the counter-economy and consciously practicing agorist movement to be somewhere at the tail end of phase 1 and merging into phase 2. As mentioned above, the internet (and technology as a whole) has greatly increased the chances for success of the Konkian revolution. While mankind is being exposed to the value of a life free of coercion, they have not yet been properly exposed to the tools with which to create such a world. If the agorist movement and counter-economy continue to expand in equal rates to the violence and theft of the state, it will only be a matter of time before we see protection agencies with the capacity to defend the people. Konkin believed that once the people recognize the state is weakened and in decline they would naturally gravitate towards the counter-economy, leading his agorist vision to become reality.

To understand the potential for agorism to provide a solution to our current unsustainable, destructive system we must look to the real world. Political theories are fine on paper, but if the ideas don't reflect what we see in the physical world they serve as nothing more than mental masturbation. As Konkin wrote in the introduction to An Agorist Primer, *"Always remember that agorism integrates theory and practice. Theory without practice is game-playing; taken seriously, it leads to withdrawal from reality, mysticism, and insanity... Agorists believe that any theory which does not describe reality is either useless or a deliberate attempt by intellectuals to defraud non-specialists."* So then, are there real-world examples of counter-economics in practice? And if so, is there evidence that the practice leads to more freedom and prosperity?

To find an answer to these questions, let's look to the "informal sector" of Peru during the 1980s and 90s. The informal sector was made up of individuals who operated outside government laws and regulations. The activities of the informal sector are conducted outside the legal system without regard to government regulations. Collectively, the activities represent the informal economy. In his 1989 book, *The Other Path*, Hernando De Soto provides a detailed study of the emergence and operation of the Peruvian informal economy. De Soto argued that government regulations on housing, transportation, and trade should be removed to allow the dynamics of the informal economy to take over. Unfortunately, De Soto and *The Other Path* seem to equate capitalism with the free market, going as far as promoting "market-oriented reforms" which will allow the informal economy to become the new statist economy. Rather than promoting total liberation through the use of the informal economy and a truly freed market, De Soto and his Institute for Liberty and Democracy believe that a capitalist system of government will liberate the people. Despite these shortcomings, *The Other Path* is recommended for any student of counter-economic activity.

Another important point on Peru's informal economy is the fact that these black-market entrepreneurs were investing in and creating informal businesses as a direct attempt to escape the regulations of the state, and the violence of the Maoist-terror group, "The Shining Path." When *The Other Path* was released, it was designed to counteract the Marxist propaganda of The Shining Path, who had been teaching the peasant class the market was something to despise rather than a tool for liberation. The book would become a best-seller and help the growing informal economists recognize the power of unfettered trade and market action. Unfortunately, in the absence of a truly informed and organized agorist movement, the informal economy seems to have been absorbed by the Peruvian statist economy.

Still, during the rise of Peru's informal economy, the Institute for Liberty and Democracy reported that "extralegal entrepreneurs" and their extended families accounted for around 60 to 80% of the nation's population and operated 56% of all businesses. In the 2002 update to *The Other Path*, De Soto writes that the underground economies of Russia and Ukraine accounted for 50% of Gross Domestic Product, while 85% of all jobs in Latin America and the Caribbean were created in this informal or counter-economy. Obviously, the informal or counter-economy has become as important as Samuel Konkin predicted.

The Other Path not only highlights the importance of the counter-economy, but also illustrates how the state's restrictive and intrusive regulation of voluntary exchange directly lead to the growth of the underground markets. According to case studies conducted by the ILD, the average person attempting to launch a retail market in Peru during the 1980s would face 13 years of legal and administrative hurdles. In addition, it would take 26 months to get authorization to operate a new bus route, and almost a year, working 6 hours a day, to gain the necessary licenses to legally operate a sewing machine for commercial purposes.

"There is class warfare in Peru, to be sure. But the main line bisecting Peruvian society today is not a horizontal one dividing entrepreneurs from workers. The principal dividing line is a vertical frontier, to the right of which are politicians, bureaucrats, and businessmen who profit and live off the government's favor and to the left of which are legal and extralegal producers who are excluded from favor," De Soto wrote in 2002.

Faced with ongoing violence and the Maoist rhetoric of The Shining Path on one side, and statist regulation and theft on the other, the people of Peru chose to travel to the countryside and create informal marketplaces for trading, ridesharing, and housing. This is what free thinking people will do when faced with the constant threat of theft and bureaucracy. Eventually, the people tire of having every aspect of their lives invaded by the state, so they will seek outside solutions. This may include reformist schemes like electoral politics and voting, or possibly violent revolt. Counter-economics and agorism offer a third path towards liberty. A path that is peaceful, consistent and reflects the realities we see unfolding in the world today.

There are also numerous documented examples of this counter-economic reality in China, North Korea, Cuba, and throughout Africa. Radical propaganda and Western media are smuggled into North Korea via USB drives while street vendors around the world operate without paying any mind to the state's permission slips. According to Kenya's National Bureau of Statistics, the informal sector created 713,000 new jobs in 2015, constituting a total of 84.8% of all new jobs created *"outside small-scale agriculture sector and pastoralist activities."* Further, in the book *Stealth of Nations: The Rise of the Global*

Informal Economy, Robert Neuwirth documents the global reach of the counter-economy, or, as he calls it, *System D*. Neuwirth reaches the same conclusion that we have: People will organize outside of the state as a necessity, and, in many cases, with a preference for the untaxed, unregulated counter-economy.

It is clear that the workers of the world have a desire to exchange their goods and services without oppressive, elitist barriers to entry in the marketplace. The people desire to voluntarily associate and exchange without interference or intervention. This desire will always lead to the creation of counter-economic activity in the black and gray markets as long as the "mainstream" statist economy is subject to the whims of the current puppets in control. However, seeking to escape the state's regulation is not the only goal to our agorist and counter-economic strategy. The endgame is a stateless society where free people are not bound by the force and coercion of the parasitic state and corporate class.

Though it is rarely discussed in public schools or mainstream media, there are several examples of stateless societies and communities existing throughout history. For those interested in studying past stateless societies we recommend examining medieval Iceland, James Scott's *The Art of Not Being Governed: An Anarchist History of Upland Southeast Asia*, and Pierre Clastres' *Society Against the State*. We should also stress that those who believe a stateless society cannot exist because they do not see an abundance of examples, are only limiting themselves by setting preconceived barriers and assumptions regarding the potential of the human experience. If the hearts and minds of the world seize the opportunity and put agorist theory into action, we will see the rise of the counter-economy. As we will explore in the next chapter, all it takes is a self-aware, organized agorist movement to seize the potential of the counter-economy and truly weaken the state.

Chapter 3
Vertical and Horizontal Agorism

*"As more people reject the State's mystifications—nationalism, pseudo-Economics, false threats, and betrayed political promises—**the Counter—Economy grows both vertically and horizontally**. Horizontally, it involves more and more people who turn more and more of their activities toward the counter-economic; vertically, it means new structures (businesses and services) grow specifically to serve the Counter-Economy (safe communication links, arbitrators, insurance for specifically "illegal" activities, early forms of protection technology, and even guards and protectors). Eventually, the "underground" breaks into the overground where most people are agorists, few are statists, and the nearest state enforcement cannot effectively crush them."*

— SEK III, Applied Agorism, An Agorist Primer

We are going to take a look at two different types of counter-economic action which are applicable to a variety of individuals in a range of living situations. We refer to these strategies as vertical and horizontal agorism. We are working with two complementary definitions of horizontal and vertical which further explain the "how" of agorist philosophy. These definitions are taken from the above quote from Samuel Konkin III and from Swedish Austrian economist Per Bylund and his 2006 essay *"A Strategy for Forcing the State Back."* Let's compare the definitions and see how they can provide a path for the eager agorist.

Konkin starts by describing the counter-economy as growing horizontally in the sense of an increasing amount of the mainstream population turning their activities towards the non-statist economy. Vertical growth, in the Konkian sense, involves the actual creation of counter-institutions to the statist counterparts. This means building alternatives not only to the economic power centers via alternative currencies, but alternatives to the dead stream corporate media, the corporatized food production systems, the compliant academic centers, and the growing non-profit industrial complex. (*Side note: the industry formerly known as the mainstream media is correctly referred to as the dead stream media because everything produced by this industry leads to misinformation, faulty decision-making, and eventually, death. The corporate media is a constant stream of lies and decay.*)

Per Bylund describes his vision of vertical agorism as the "introvert" strategy based on the work and ideas of radical libertarian Karl Hess. Hess was an extremely eloquent speaker and speechwriter who grew from conservative to libertarian anarchist to a more left-leaning community organizer and activist. During the 1960s, he was heavily involved in organizing on campus during the rise of the new left and anti-war student movements. Hess worked with Murray Rothbard, Konkin, Carl Ogelsby of the Students for a Democratic Society, and several others, attempting alliances between the emerging new left and libertarian movements. He was also one of the few people to have 100% of his wages stolen by the IRS for challenging the income tax.

In the 1970s, Hess shifted the focus of his activism to experiment in community building within the low-income neighborhood of Adams Morgan in Washington, D.C. In his books, *Community Technology and Neighborhood Power*, Hess outlines how he worked with the local neighborhood to build an empowered community focused on sustainability, or what they termed "appropriate technology." Hess describes a neighborhood with aquaponic gardening in basements, rooftop gardens, and community services meant to replace the state option. He was adamant that tools and technology directly contribute to freedom. By being able to share tools with your community members, you are able to share access to the means of production and encourage entrepreneurship. It is this focus on community empowerment that Per Bylund refers to as the vertical or introvert strategy. These actions can be considered agorist in the sense that they are aimed at building self and community reliance rather than dependence on external forces, but they are not explicitly counter-economic because they do not involve black and gray markets. Still, these vertical actions are extremely valuable and necessary.

Vertical agorism would include participating in and creating community exchange networks, urban farming, backyard gardening, farmers' market, supporting alternatives to the police, and supporting peer-to-peer decentralized technologies. While these vertical steps could potentially involve the use of the state's currency (*and therefore not completely counter-economic*) they are still significant for challenging the dependency on the state and corporate classes. Other vertical steps may not directly involve exchanging currency but still work against dependency. This could include moral support and promotion of technologies that disrupt the status quo and foster stronger relationships among community members.

One very pronounced example of vertical agorism is seen in the growing alternative media, which has been made possible by the internet. Less than one generation ago, the mainstream media, owned by megacorporations and tightly regulated by government, controlled all of the information that filtered down to society. The distribution of information in society came from the top down, making it very easy to brainwash and propagandize the population. However, with the rise of the internet, activists and freedom-seeking individuals discovered that they could use this new medium to create their own media, become journalists themselves, and fight back against the propaganda of the state. In just a few short years, the independent media quickly upset the monopoly of the mainstream media, taking up large portions of their once exclusive market share. The surge of independent media provides an excellent example in our study of how alternative systems and institutions can be created to compete with existing state monopolies.

Our goal is to question and challenge the mechanisms of power that seek to influence and rule over our lives. This includes the state, as well as other institutions that attempt to exert control and influence. For example, by choosing to grow your own food or support local farmers you are taking a vertical step away from the biotechnology corporations that promote the heavy use of pesticides and a potentially hazardous technology. You also are not supporting the transportation of food products from thousands of miles away. Instead, you walk to your backyard or the local market for your produce. This greatly increases your independence while relinquishing support for an unsustainable industry. These vertical steps are also the easiest ways to begin living in line your principles. Once again, we can see the value of consistency of words and actions.

Per Bylund describes the horizontal, or extrovert strategy, as more directly related to the ideas of Konkin. The extrovert label is related to the bold choice to pursue action that the State considers to be illegal or immoral. By venturing into this territory, you are joining the ranks of the bootlegger, the moonshiner, the cannabis dealer, the guerrilla gardener, the unlicensed lawn mower, food vendor or barber, the weapons dealer, and the crypto-anarchists. When one combines the vertical and horizontal agorist strategy, an image comes into view that illustrates the steps that can be taken by a wide range of people in a variety of living situations and environments.

In the bottom left corner, we have statism and in the top right corner we have agorism. We can plot vertical actions which help lift the individual up from dependency. Perhaps your situation is better suited to vertical actions such as growing your own food, using encrypted messaging, hosting community skill shares at your house, practicing peaceful parenting tactics, providing alternatives to state welfare by crowdfunding money for community projects and feeding the homeless, or simply cleaning up the neighborhood. Each of these steps move the individual (*and in the long-term, the community*) vertically towards consistency and independence. For those who are ready to become counter-economists and take on the risk of gray and black-market activity, we plot their actions both vertically and horizontally. An agorist practicing horizontally and vertically would move up and away from statism and dependency to the top right position of agorism. This means for every garden built, alternative currency used, tax avoided, skill shared, business practiced without a license, and illegal substance sold, the individual can plot their progress moving from dependency to self-reliance and from statism to agorism.

When Konkin first espoused the concept of agorism, the consciously practicing counter-economy may have only involved a few radical libertarians, but since that time, the opportunities for black and gray market exchanges have grown immensely. As the state's weaknesses become apparent, it will become safer for the masses to begin exiting the former economy and joining the counter-economy. This is the truly freed market, or agora, of which Konkin spoke.

Now that we have outlined the vertical and horizontal agorist strategy derived from the work of Karl Hess and Samuel Konkin, we must elaborate further on a concept that we hope will become widely adopted and adapted to many different communities. This is the aforementioned concept of Freedom Cells. Freedom Cells are peer-to-peer groups made up of 7 to 9 people (with 8 being ideal) organizing themselves in a decentralized manner with the collective goal of asserting the sovereignty of group members through peaceful resistance and the creation of alternative institutions. Freedom Cells could be seen as a very specific type of mutual aid group, where agorism and counter-economics play a key role. The name comes as a response to state propaganda around "Terror Cells." We are consciously choosing to reclaim the language and build cells that spread freedom. Also, FC's act like cells in a body that are performing important tasks individually while also serving the goal of the larger organism. In our vision, every FC is playing a vital role of spreading counter-economic activity and agorist philosophy while also forming a part of the larger network that will foster exchange of ideas and products between cells.

The number of 8 participants is drawn from the research of Bob Podolsky and his book *Flourish!: An Alternative to Government and Other Hierarchies*. Podolsky is the protege of researcher John David Garcia, who spent twenty years researching how to maximize the creativity of a group of people working together on a joint project. After performing hundreds of experiments, he came up with an optimized model based on groups of 8 that he called an Octet or Octologue. The idea being that a shortage of individuals would leave the group limited in capability, but with too many people the group is bogged down with disorganization and lack of focus. Podoslky recommends forming Octologues made up of 4 men and 4 women guided by specific ethical tenets.

Although Freedom Cells are also promoted as groups of 8 individuals collaborating together, they differ from Octologues in that they are heavily focused on decentralization. So while Bob Podolsky has outlined a detailed vision of how an Octologue should operate, we hope to provide examples of applications for FC's without telling other FC's how to operate. The needs of each community will naturally differ. Beyond a general agreement to respect each other's right to be free of coercion, we believe the FC's should not be monopolized by the vision of a single cell. We caution the reader to remember that our ideas are a guide, but not the final word on the literally limitless possibilities.

In the beginning, individuals can work together to accomplish goals such as every group member having 3 months' worth of storable food, encrypted communication, a bug out plan, and ensuring participants have access to firearms (or some form of self-defense) and know how to use them safely and proficiently. All the while, cell members make themselves readily available to render mutual aid to their cell, in whatever form that may come. Once you have established 7-9 people within a FC, each individual should be encouraged to then go on their own and start another FC, especially if the original members are not living in close proximity to one another. Living reasonably close to each other will allow for a quick response time in emergency situations. Once again, every member of the FC's should be encouraged to start additional cells.

Eventually, the original would be connected to 7 or 9 additional cells, through each individual member for a total of 70-90 people. Imagine the strength and influence these cells could exert once they are connected in the digital world via FreedomCells.org and in the physical world where possible. The creation of the Freedom Cell Network could also serve as a social network for traveling agorists looking to do business in the counter-economy with other like minds. Through building and supporting alternatives such as local food networks, health services, mutual defense groups, and peer-to-peer economies and communication networks, FC's will be better able to disconnect and decouple themselves from state institutions they deem unworthy of their support. Once groups become large enough in numbers, it becomes quite possible for participants to opt out in mass and secure their liberty.

This is the model we have been following in Houston with The Houston Free Thinkers activist community and The Free Thinker House community space. We began by building gardens and selling the crops via Next Door. We are also selling juice and kombucha tea using fruits harvested from trees of neighbors who understand our goals. We started with a small group of about 3 to 4 people meeting and discussing the goals and themes of our cell. The goal is to have skills and knowledge diffused throughout the group. This way, if one person leaves the group the knowledge is not taken from the cell. For example, knowing that every cell member can perform CPR, use encrypted communications, shoot a gun, or communicate the Agorist message may be important for your cell. Obviously, certain individuals will be more skilled or knowledgeable in some areas, but there are foundational skills and information that should be common among all cell members.

Our group has also used the structure to educate each other on specific topics of interest. Perhaps your FC meets and agrees to learn everything available on permaculture or a particular philosophical concept. You divide the topic up among your cell and return two weeks later to educate each other. Or maybe your cell joins the Cell411 app and responds to emergency alerts in your community. Several cells could join together to cop watch or actively resist and disarm violent police or other agents of the state. A Freedom Cell could connect with other cells for a covertly organized guerrilla gardening action. With the constant barrage of fake news coming from the establishment media, a FC could quickly research and debunk incoming propaganda. FC's can organize alternative exchange networks that encourage local artisans and entrepreneurs to come sell their unregulated crafts and accept alternative currencies. In a "Shit Hits the Fan" scenario, FC's could have prearranged bug out locations stocked with supplies. If several FC's were equally prepared, you now find yourself with a small community of empowered individuals as opposed to being forced to defend yourself alone.

These are the pockets of agorism that Konkin predicted would come as the counter-economy outcompeted the statist economy. While Konkin outlined his theory of getting from statism to agorism, he did not explore in detail the answer to how this would happen. We believe Freedom Cells are at least part of the equation. Konkin was correct in his prediction that the state would not hesitate to smash down any agorist who dared venture into the counter-economy too quickly or too boldly. This can plainly be seen in the punishment of Ross Ulbricht, the accused "criminal mastermind" of the Silk Road online marketplace.

Ulbricht helped people from all around the world do black-market business without paying a single dime to the government of their respective homeland. Ulbricht and his apparent admin alter-ego Dread Pirate Roberts both expressed an affinity for the philosophy of agorism. When he was sentenced to three life terms in January 2015, the judge called his opposition to government and economic restriction "dangerous" and declared that she must make sure no one dares to "take up his flag." The state was quite literally terrified that the Silk Road allowed individuals to do business without their involvement. For all their alleged concern about the safety of drugs purchased on the Silk Road, the state truly opposed UIbricht because it was a real-world practice in counter-economics designed to take power away from the state. In fact, drugs purchased on the Silk Road were far safer than those found on the street due to the reputation based rating and review system that was built into the site. Additionally, the online market removed the possibility of violence during the transaction, a danger that is all too real when buying drugs on the street.

Remember, we cannot defeat the Federal Reserve (or other central banks) by using their currency, this will only empower them. We must create and support alternatives to the state's monopolies whenever possible. It will take brave agorists venturing into uncharted territories, making mistakes, occasionally falling victim to the state's law, and learning how to better our approach. We need these pioneers to lay the groundwork so that others in the future will not have to face the same difficulties. As these trail blazers light the way, we also expect to see a growth of free communities and freedom networks around the world.

We have a vision of thousands of interlocking autonomous communities comprised of empowered individuals with a variety of unique ideas and expressions of the human experience. Communities voluntarily trading and sharing skills without the violence inherent in our current paradigm. We believe this panarchistic, polycentric world can be achieved with an organized effort to spread Agorist philosophy and increase participation in the counter-economy via Freedom Cells and vertical and horizontal agorism.

We would like to offer these "Ten tips for Building Freedom Cells" as a starting point for launching your group. Please adapt these to the specific needs of your community.

1. **Identify Potential Candidates** — are they mentally, physically, spiritually sound for your goals?

2. **Discuss Common Themes** — what are the driving forces bringing the group together?

3. **Identify Strengths and Weaknesses** — take an honest look at the strengths and weaknesses of each individual, as well as the group as a whole.

4. **Evaluate Desired Level of Freedom vs. Security** — Every individual may have a different desired level of freedom and as such, will have different aims and acceptability of risks.

5. **Set Short Term and Long-Term Goals** — What can your cell accomplish in 3 months? A year?

6. **Mindfulness Training** — Incorporate practices like Non-Violent Communication Training and group meditation into your cell.

7. **Accomplish Goals** — Document each goal successfully met by the cell or individual members

8. **Ongoing Group Education, Communication** — continuously expand your cell knowledge, skills, and supplies.

9. **Promote/Market Goals and Accomplishments** — Use the power of social media (when safe) and marketing to let the world know how much more prosperous you are in the counter-economy.

10. **Identify Strategies for Creating Income/Independence** — Leverage the power and number of your cell to create counter-economic income that can't be taxed by the State.

Chapter 4
Spontaneous Order

When one examines many of the words used to describe our society, such as democracy, freedom, representative or capitalism, you find that these words are simply abstract euphemisms which are used to disguise the true authoritarian nature of our civilization. We are supposed to believe that "we the people" are represented by corrupt politicians, and that we are "free" despite constantly being exploited and ordered around by authoritarians. Much in the same way that we are told we are "free" in our personal lives, we are also told that we are "free" in our financial lives. Nothing could be further from the truth.

No matter what political system is employed by the ruling class the people are always faced with varying levels of subjugation. The word "democracy" is used to make our oppressive political system seem more benevolent and legitimate, while the term "capitalism" is used to give the impression that we operate under a "free market" economy. Neither is true.

Despite the many definitions of capitalism, it is generally associated with the rights to private property, private production of goods, and a "free market" economy lacking in state intervention. However, although the U.S. and many other western nations are thought of as capitalist, they typically fail to respect the private property of individuals and promote heavy state regulation of economic exchanges for their own benefit, under the guise of public service.

At face value it may seem like capitalist economies represent a "free market," but when you take a look at property taxes, government subsidies for big corporations, and the legal barriers that prevent poor people from running businesses, it should become painfully obvious that a truly freed market has never existed under what most people identify as "capitalism." This is one of the many problems in associating the idea of a decentralized market of exchange with the system known as capitalism.

To those who would say the problem is a misunderstanding of capitalism we wish to reemphasize that capitalism, socialism, and communism have all been associated with authoritarianism and are each contested concepts with no clear objective definition. This is an extremely important point, especially considering the fact that so many anarchists are attached to one of these terms. Some are attached to the term socialism because they align with the stated goals of socialism, such as ending poverty. Meanwhile, others are attached to the term capitalism because they align with its stated goals of free enterprise and private property. However, with both of these systems, the stated goals are vastly different from the ends they achieve. For this reason and many others, these terms should be abandoned when discussing future concepts of non-statist economic systems.

The system that we have in place today, whether superficially appearing to be socialist or capitalist, could more accurately be called corporatism, mercantilism or cartelism. These words describe a system where the elite use their power in government to control the rest of society and prop up their corporate partners by eliminating competition through the political system. The monolithic corporations that now exist would have never been able to grow into what they are today without the help of government intervention and protection. Without government intervention, the infamous lobbyists in Washington would become obsolete because they would lose their power to influence and manipulate the marketplace through bribes or coercion. Many of the world's biggest and most predatory corporations have been able to develop massive monopolies and avoid any type of legal consequences for their destructive behavior because the government gives them an unfair advantage.

In today's system, we don't have independent businesses working on a level playing field. Instead we are left with a few massive corporations and cartels that use their power in government to maintain their monopolies and stomp out their competition. This is the very definition of fascism — the merger of state and corporate power — and it has become the dominant economic system in the world. Looking back through history, we can see that an elitist parasite class has always sought to use any available source of influence, from politics to religion, to take advantage of the people that they are claiming to protect.

Most of the "leaders" throughout the world propagandize the people into believing they live in a free and democratic society. This illusion pushes the masses to take their grievances to the polls like good citizens rather than taking their concerns into the streets or creating solutions that could actually make an impact. Currently one of the most totalitarian nations on Earth is called the "Democratic Republic of North Korea." Likewise, the government in America and the European Union are some of the most fascist regimes in history, yet claim to operate under systems of "capitalism" or "democratic socialism." It's a political word game that's designed to disguise the truth.

Almost every economic analysis in the world is dictated by the ideas of two long-dead aristocrats. On one end of the spectrum, you have Karl Marx representing the labor theory of value and communism. Adam Smith can be found on the other end representing capitalism and "classical economics." Our whole way of doing business on this planet has changed very little since the time of these two men, and that could very well be the root of our problem.

Imagine how much we could accomplish if a few people in every city across the world wrote their own economic manifestos and gathered to respectfully discuss their ideas. The masses refuse to accept last generation iPods and video games, but without much thought, accept ways of living that are centuries old. It's time for us to work together to create strategies where everyone can meet their needs without violating the rights of others.

Capitalism and socialism are both terms that have been tainted by government and statism. They are terms that have been drug through the mud for hundreds of years and mean very different things to many different people. These differences in definition often make discussion of these terms impossible (especially on the internet!) We understand one could make the same argument regarding anarchism and it's unfortunate association with violence. While it is true that certain schools of anarchists who view violent revolution as a legitimate tactic, they are not the majority. Most freedom loving anarchists want to radically alter the systems of governance we have today, but do not advocate the force and violence we have seen displayed by those calling themselves socialists, capitalists, and communists.

Much of the money that is collected through taxation is used to line the pockets of politicians and establish bureaucracies that add to the size and power of government. A very small fraction actually ends up being spent on worthwhile public services. It should be obvious that if given the opportunity to allocate their own resources among themselves, communities would be able to provide services that are far superior to those that are forcefully imposed by central planners. Quite simply, our world does not need authority figures to dictate the course of human history.

The brutality and callousness of past regimes should serve as a constant reminder of how dangerous it is to give people authority over the lives of others. Rulers of the past have taken the credit for the hard work of the average people who have built civilizations on their command, leaving behind a historical myth that claims humanity owes its entire progression to kings, priests, politicians, and other authoritarians. In reality, we have the ingenuity of our ancestors to thank, not the tyrants who rode on their backs. The history books may glorify warlords, monarchs and aristocrats as being the founders of our modern way of life, but this is only the result of the victorious warlords writing the history books.

Many world-changing inventions, enlightening philosophies, and leaps in human development have been brought forth by those who spent their lives under the boots of authority, not those wearing the boots. Historically, authority figures have actually done their best to hinder this process and prevent the general population from empowering themselves with technology and philosophy.

The power structures of the past were well aware that the peasants had the potential to rise above oppression peacefully through the advancement of philosophy and development of advanced technology. This was very pronounced during the times of the Middle Ages where people could lose their lives on counts of witchcraft if they were caught developing unknown technology or discussing any philosophy that may have undermined the existing establishment. Frederick Douglass stated that when he was a slave in the American south, he was not allowed to learn how to read a calendar, or even know how old he was. The power structures of the world today use very similar strategies. They prevent research into alternative energy and alternative medical treatments, and stifle technological advancement with stiff regulations and intellectual property laws.

There have been periods in history of significantly less government intervention in the economy, but these situations could hardly be referred to as "free market." As long as we are subject to central banks, government-mandated currency, taxation, bailouts, and regulations, we are dealing with a very tightly controlled market, not a free one. The government mandated school curriculum and corporate media tell us that economic regulations are necessary to keep people safe from the corporations who have monopolized the economy. This is a clever trick because most people fail to take a few steps back to see that these corporations have been empowered and protected by the government in the first place. In fact, many corporations are exempt from many of the regulations and taxes that are hoisted upon the smaller businesses who are trying to compete. If they are not entirely exempt, they are certainly equipped to deal with the regulatory hurdles that keep most poor entrepreneurs out of the marketplace.

These are the policies that have created the completely unjust and unsustainable economic environment that has forced so many people into poverty and despair. Companies like Monsanto and Goldman Sachs would not survive a day in a truly freed market that lacked the political mechanisms they currently use to stomp out competition and stay on top. They would be forced to depend on the support of the community and the integrity of their product. Fortunately, in the face of more honest and efficient entrepreneurs, corporations like Monsanto would be exposed and fall flat on their faces. The very concept of a "corporation" is a government-created entity which acts as a legal shield to keep CEOs from being held accountable for the messes they create. These legal loopholes have allowed the monopolization of certain industries, creating megacorporations that no legitimate small business can possibly contend with. The state education system and corporate media keep the public in the dark by failing to acknowledge that our current economic model is a result of government intervention.

In a world where people were actually allowed to trade freely without third party intervention, everyone would be an entrepreneur. Sure, workers would still be needed, but our guess is that in a free society most labor jobs would be filled with people trying to earn extra money—working a summer job, getting some startup money for their own business, a teen working their first job, and things of that nature. It seems that the "wage-slave" model of working a dead end job for your entire life is due to a lack of choices currently in the marketplace. There is something to be said for picking up a skill and sticking with it throughout the years, but in a truly decentralized and free economy there would be more of a potential to start your own business which could then employ others.

A group of entrepreneurs would also have more freedom to band together and form a commune, co-op, or mutualist enterprise. We believe that a freed market would favor nonhierarchical worker owned businesses. People are always free to enter whichever types of arrangements they prefer, but we predict that most people would likely prefer not working under authoritarian bosses. This preference for non-authoritarian work would lead some to gravitate towards horizontally owned businesses or entrepreneurship. Even in today's industries, businesses where workers have a share in the spoils of the company tend to be far more successful and offer better customer service because the employees have more of an incentive to do a good job rather than just punching a clock. In fact, in the past few years, worker-owned businesses have already begun to outnumber corporations worldwide, although this transformation is not so obvious in the United States.

The point is that without the state intervention and the propping up of corporations that do nothing but feed the consumerist frenzy, we would see a decrease in the need for pointless labor. We reject the notion that being a worker simply for the sake of work is virtuous. When it came to the working class, Konkin also argued that the state stifled innovation and entrepreneurship which kept the working-class busy doing meaningless busy work. He called workers and peasants, *"an embarrassing relic from a previous age at best and look forward to the day that they will die out from lack of market demand."* Indeed, with technological growth pushing farther towards automation, the menial jobs done by most workers could be done by artificial intelligence, paving the way for existing workers to become entrepreneurs.

In the world we are describing, the quality of life and creativity on the planet would explode and create a dynamic civilization with the potential for peace and abundance. Different currencies could be tested all throughout the world while new ways of doing business and structuring society would develop in different areas until the optimum solution for health and well-being was discovered. These ideas would be voluntarily adopted by the masses because of the value added to their lives. This vision is possible.

By now it *should* be common sense that initiating violence greatly diminishes the quality of any situation or relationship. Violence may seem to be a strong word to describe government policy, but legitimized threats of violence backed by the guns and prisons of the State are still acts of violence. If you disobey the government for too long or with too much fanfare, the end result is ultimately your death. By breaking the laws of the government, you will likely find yourself in their court system. If you choose not to participate, they can send out men with guns to your house to take you away and put you in a cage. At that point if you refuse to go they will use force on you, and if you attempt to defend yourself you will be killed.

The state wants the public to believe that only a guilty party resists an arrest. But what if that arrest was really an unjust kidnapping? Who is to say that the court issuing the charges is legitimate? Were the courts and laws in Soviet Russia or Nazi Germany legitimate? Were the people who disobeyed them guilty of a crime? Putting on a uniform and working for the king, the sheriff, or the president does not grant you the right to kick down the doors of nonviolent people and attempt to kidnap them.

This systemic violence disrupts the process of spontaneous order by stifling humans will power and creativity. Spontaneous order is a way of describing the complex building process that takes place all throughout nature, as well as in interactions between human beings. When applied to human interaction, this building process is set into motion by people trying to solve problems and improve their quality of life.

Human beings have an incredible ability to find solutions for any problems that may stand in our way. Just as a rushing river will forge a new path around a boulder that has fallen in its midst, groups of voluntarily cooperating people (Freedom Cells) will naturally find a way around any roadblock when they have a desire to do so.

The phrase "*Where there is a will, there is a way*" is extremely relevant in this context and describes the process of spontaneous order and self-organization in a most concise way. It can be difficult for some to see this unfolding in nature because of how our day-to-day lives are compartmentalized and separated from our actual needs. Due to this compartmentalization, many of us have come to believe that there will be no food if the grocery store closes down, there will be no electricity without a government power grid, and that there will be no safety without the king's guards patrolling the community. However, all of these needs can be handled more proficiently by the open hearts and strong minds in our community. Without a state to hold us back, we will witness spontaneous order and self-organization within the agora.

Chapter 5
Agorism is not Anarcho-Capitalism

The goal of this essay is threefold. First, we will identify the key concepts which outline the philosophy of agorism and the strategy of counter-economics, as outlined by Konkin in *The New Libertarian Manifesto* and An *Agorist Primer*. Second, we will illustrate how radicals of all stripes can utilize the strategy of counter-economics, as described by Konkin, without necessarily endorsing his philosophy of agorism and its specific tenets. Finally, we will describe what sets agorism apart from anarcho-capitalism and other schools of thought. We will show that although the counter-economic strategy can be utilized by nearly any individual, agorism itself is not simply a strain or subset of anarcho-capitalism, as some believe, but rather, it a unique political philosophy of its own which can be used by anarchists of any economic background.

Before we dive in, allow us to briefly explain the inspiration for the title of this essay and the essay itself. As we will demonstrate, the agorist message and counter-economic strategy can be of use to any individual who finds themselves in pursuit of a freer, just, and ethical world. However, the reason the title focuses on anarcho-capitalism is because we have noticed a trend in "right-libertarian"/AnCap social media circles where individuals claim to support the ideas of Konkin and his agorism, yet also express a distaste for left-libertarianism. Our goal is to help readers with this viewpoint understand the essential role Konkin and his "new libertarianism," or agorism, played in developing the American left-libertarian movement.

Agorism As Consistent Libertarianism

Let's start by getting an understanding of Konkin's vision. Konkin called for the creation of a revolutionary movement led by workers and entrepreneurs voluntarily cooperating in economic exchanges that take place outside of the state's grasp. He called this movement The New Libertarian Alliance. Konkin based his revolutionary ideas on a foundation of libertarianism in the vein of Rothbard and the American individualist anarchists before him. In *The New Libertarian Manifesto* Konkin writes: "*Where the State divides and conquers its opposition, libertarianism unites and liberates. Where the State beclouds, libertarianism clarifies; where the State conceals, Libertarianism uncovers; where the State pardons, Libertarianism accuses.*

"*Libertarianism elaborates an entire philosophy from one simple premise: initiatory violence or its threat (coercion) is wrong (immoral, evil, bad, supremely impractical, etc.) and is forbidden; nothing else is.*

"Libertarianism, as developed to this point, discovered the problem and defined the solution: the State vs. the Market. The Market is the sum of all voluntary human action. If one acts non-coercively, one is part of the Market. Thus did Economics become part of libertarianism." From this, Konkin developed his views on property:

"Libertarianism investigated the nature of man to explain his rights deriving from non-coercion. It immediately followed that man (woman, child, Martian, etc.) had an absolute right to this life and other property—and no other.

"All theft is violence initiation, either the use of force to take property away involuntarily or to prevent receipt of goods or return of payment for those goods which were freely transferred by agreement."

Konkin became involved in the burgeoning libertarian movement in the late sixties. At this point the lovers of liberty were beginning to recognize the potential for a national movement of anti-statist, pro-market radicals. In the midst of this opportunity, Konkin saw libertarian activists being lured into "get liberty quick" schemes in the name of pragmatism, such as electoral politics. In a counter-attack to the enemies of liberty, Konkin outlined a new philosophy that he believed was simply the result of applying libertarian principles to their most consistent and logical ends.

"The basic principle which leads a libertarian from statism to his free society is the same which the founders of libertarianism used to discover the theory itself. That principle is consistency. Thus, the consistent application of the theory of libertarianism to every action the individual libertarian takes creates the libertarian society.

"Many thinkers have expressed the need for consistency between means and ends and not all of them were libertarians. Ironically, many statists have claimed inconsistency between laudable ends and contemptible means; yet when their true ends of greater power and oppression were understood, their means are found to be quite consistent. It is part of the statist mystique to confuse the necessity of ends-means consistency; it is thus the most crucial activity of the libertarian theorist to expose inconsistencies. Many theorists have done so admirably, but we have attempted and most failed to describe the consistent means and ends combination of libertarianism.

"New Libertarianism (agorism) cannot be discredited without Liberty or Reality (or both) being discredited, only an incorrect formulation."

For Konkin, a truly libertarian society would be agorist— *"Libertarian in theory and free market in practice."* This society would include respect for justly acquired property, voluntary cooperation between entrepreneurs and producers, and replacing all of the state's "services" with private competition among individuals and collectives.

"Libertarian analysis shows us that the State is responsible for any damage to in-

nocents it alleges the 'selfish tax evader' has incurred; and the 'services' the State 'provides' us are illusory. But even so, there must be more than lonely resistance cleverly concealed or 'dropping out'? If a political party or revolutionary army is inappropriate and self-defeating for libertarian goals, what collective action works? The answer is agorism."

The goal of agorism is to replace all non-consensual, coercive relationships with voluntary relationships based on mutual benefit via entrepreneurship in the black and gray markets. This shuffling of "large collections of humanity from statist society to the agora" was "true revolutionary activity." According to Konkin, agorists should not launch "attacks" on the state. "We are strictly defensive," Konkin wrote in An Agorist Primer.

Further, Konkin described an agorist as "one who lives counter-economically without guilt for his or her heroic, day-to-day actions, with the old libertarian morality of never violating another's person or property." The philosophy stresses the importance of taking action. "An agorist is one who lives agorism. Accept no counterfeits. There are agorists "trying to live up to it." There are, of course, liars who will claim to be anything. As Yoda said so succinctly, 'Do. Or do not. There is no try.' That's Agorism."

Counter-Economics as Defined by Konkin

If Agorism is Konkin's premiere philosophical contribution, his recognition of counter-economics as the path towards agorism is equally important. The term counter-economics can be attributed to the time and period in which Konkin developed his ideas. "Counter-Culture was a popular phrase, one of the only lasting victories of the "hippies." Counter-Economics implied that the "revolution wasn't finished" and that the Economic System needed to undergo the same upending as the culture had," Konkin wrote.

As defined above, the black and gray markets are part of the counter-economy, which Konkin defined as "All (non-coercive) human action committed in defiance of the State." In line with the principles of non-aggression, Konkin labels initiatory violence in the form of theft or murder as the "red market," the one type of activity that is shunned in his counter-economy. Konkin explains that as the State's repressive and oppressive activities increase, the people will begin seeking economic alternatives to state regulation and interference. This provides an opportunity for forward-thinking agorists to launch and support counter-economic businesses and activity. Konkin believed that once the counter-economy had progressed to the point where entrepreneurs were providing the public with protection and security services that could rival or defend against the state, the agorist revolution would be complete.

"Slowly but steadily we will move to the free society turning more counter-economists onto libertarianism and more libertarians onto counter-economics, finally *integrating theory and practice. The counter-economy will grow and spread to the next step we saw in our trip backward, with an ever-larger agorist sub-society embedded in the statist society. Some agorists may even condense into discernible districts and ghettos and predominate in islands or space colonies. At this point, the question of protection and defense will become important,"* Konkin wrote. (3)

"Eventually, of course, after a period of increasingly rapid change of this kind, the "underground" will break into and displace the "overground"; the state will wither away into irrelevance, its taxpayers, soldiers, and law-enforcement people having deserted it for the marketplace; and we'll be left with a free, agorist society," Konkin wrote. (4)

Counter-Economics as a Tool for All Radicals

Konkin envisioned a world of decentralized, peer-to-peer communities consciously and voluntarily doing business in the counter-economy as a means towards ending the state and liberating the people. The range of (and opportunity for) counter-economic activity has only increased with the expansion of the internet and decentralized technology like cryptocurrencies. Konkin discussed various forms of counter-economic activity including, using cash to avoid detection, barter, investing in precious metals, undocumented employment, use of illicit and illegal drugs and medicines, prostitution, bootlegging, gambling, weapons dealing, or simply providing a service while accepting payment in non-statist currencies.

The possibilities are essentially endless and should be welcomed by all radicals who are seeking alternatives to statism and the status quo. Any individual or collective who recognizes the economic monopoly that is maintained by the continued use of the Federal Reserve note should be supportive of counter-economic measures and investing in creating alternatives. Whether your idea of economic freedom is collective ownership or individualist in nature, agorism offers an opportunity for communes, mutual banks, time stores, and marketplaces based in the counter-economy. This will allow all non-statist counter-economic ventures to cooperate and compete in the pursuit of a freer society. As we note in our first book, there is an opportunity for the creation of an agorist-mutualist alliance and some agorist theorists are even calling for an agorist-syndicalist alliance. Quite simply, if you want to abolish the state and the privileged class who benefit from its existence, create alternatives to the current paradigm and outgrow the archaic institutions of yesterday.

We should note that Konkin was critical of communism. In *"Counter-Economics: Our Means,"* he writes, *"the anti-market commune defies the only enforceable law—the law of nature. The basic organizational structure of society (above the family) is not the commune (or tribe or extended tribe or state) but the agora. No matter how many wish communism to work and devote themselves to it, it will fail. They can hold back agorism indefinitely by great effort, but when*

they let go, the "flow' or 'invisible hand' or 'tides of history' or 'profit incentive' or
'doing what comes naturally' or 'spontaneity' will carry society inexorably closer to
the pure agora." (3)

Understanding Konkin's Vision of Agorism

It is important to distinguish counter-economic activity from full on agorist activity. While one may be a drug dealer, sex worker, arms dealer, barber
without a license, or other underground entrepreneur, it does not follow that
one is also a consciously practicing counter-economist or agorist. Generally,
economic activity in the black and gray markets is always counter-economic
because it is untaxed and removes the state from the situation. But, without
the awareness of agorist philosophy and conscious effort to remove economic
power away from the state, one is simply breaking the state's law. While flout-
ing the state's laws against victimless crimes is a commendable act, it does not
make one an agorist. In short, you can support and participate in counter-
economic ventures without wholeheartedly embracing Konkin's ideas, but you
would not be an agorist.

*So, what differentiates agorism from anarcho-capitalism and other forms of mar-
ket anarchism?*

As noted earlier, Konkin was a vital part of the establishment of the left-libertarian movement of the 1960s, 70s, and 80s. The Movement of the Libertarian
Left was born of Konkin's experiences working with Murray Rothbard and
Karl Hess on Left and Right, a journal dedicated to bringing together the
anti-statist "right" and new left of the late 60s. These experiences greatly influenced Konkin's thinking and development of agorism. When asked why
he chose to identify as a "libertarian left" or left libertarian, Konkin said he
was "to the left" of Rothbard, so it became natural to refer to his movement
as left-libertarian. He also noted his interest in continuing "Rothbard's 1960-
69 alliance with the anti-nuke, then anti-war New Left."

*"Among important figures in the development of the modern libertarian movement,
Konkin stands out in his insistence that libertarianism rightly conceived belongs
on the radical left wing of the political spectrum,"* writes David S. D'Amato for
Libertarianism.org *"His Movement of the Libertarian Left, founded as a coalition of leftist free marketers, resisted the association of libertarianism with conservatism. Further positioning it on the left, agorism embraces the notion of class
war and entails a distinctly libertarian analysis of class struggle and stratification."*

When asked about the main differences between left-libertarian/agorism and
anarcho-capitalism, Konkin said, *"In theory, those calling themselves anarcho-
capitalists do not differ drastically from agorists; both claim to want anarchy (statelessness, and we pretty much agree on the definition of the State as a monopoly of
legitimized coercion, borrowed from Rand and reinforced by Rothbard). But the*

moment we apply the ideology to the real world (as the Marxoids say, "Actually Existing Capitalism") we diverge on several points immediately."

In Konkin's words, *"the "Anarcho-capitalists" tend to conflate the Innovator (Entrepreneur) and Capitalist, much as the Marxoids and cruder collectivists do. Agorists are strict Rothbardians, and, I would argue in this case, even more Rothbardian than Rothbard, who still had some of the older confusion in his thinking."* Konkin also said the AnCaps of his time had a tendency to *"believe in involvement with existing political parties"* and using the *"U.S. Defense complex to fight communism,"* terrorism, or any other misguided cause. While it may be said that AnCaps who support the Defense Department are a minority in 2017, the point does illustrate that since the beginning of the agorist movement there has been an effort to segregate from the AnCap element. With a growing segment of today's AnCap movement being in favor of using state violence to enforce immigration and "protect" cultural conservatism, it makes perfect sense that Konkin wanted to separate himself and his movement from such positions, despite the overlap between the two philosophies.

Konkin believed *"A lot more than statism would need to be eliminated from individual consciousness"* for a truly free society to exist. Based on this statement (and his writings elsewhere) it seems clear that Konkin espoused a "thick" libertarianism that fights for collective liberation through individual means and does not end its analysis at statism or property rights. Indeed, Konkin specifically wrote about the oppression waged against women and the gay community, something often ignored or explicitly avoided by many AnCaps. Another difference between Konkian libertarianism and that of "right libertarians," is the issue of class. Although the right typically avoid class-based analyses, Konkin helped develop what has become known as "The Agorist Class Theory." The Agorist Class Theory refutes Marx's communist class theory and recognizes the differences between non-statist entrepreneurs and statist capitalists.

Konkin elaborated on these ideas in an interview and in discussions on the left-libertarian Yahoo group. Again he stressed the importance of separating the *"non-innovators and pro-statist Capitalists"* from the *"non-statist Capitalists (in the sense of holders of capital, not necessarily ideologically aware),"* calling them *"neutral drone-like non-innovators."* Additionally, Konkin made favorable comments towards workers' movements. In the left-libertarian Yahoo Group, Konkin said he approved of the Industrial Workers of the World's (IWW) attempt to recruit libertarians. Konkin said he wanted *"to remind old MLL members and inform newbies that, free market and pro-entrepreneur as we are, MLL supports genuine anarcho-syndicalist unions which consistently refuse to collaborate with the State. (In North America, that's the IWW and nothing else I know of.)"* He noted that the IWW split with the U.S. Socialist Party for the same reasons his MLL split with the U.S. Libertarian Party— *"a rejection of parliamentarianism for direct action."* Konkin also disagreed with conflating the terms "free enterprise" and "capitalism" with the "free market."

"Capitalism means the ideology (ism) of capital or capitalists," he wrote. *"Before Marx came along, the pure free-marketeer Thomas Hodgskin had already used the term capitalism as a pejorative; capitalists were trying to use coercion—the State—to restrict the market. Capitalism, then, does not describe a free market but a form of statism, like communism. Free enterprise can only exist in a free market."*

Konkin referred to his movement as "revolutionary" and "radical," terms that are generally used to describe left-leaning movements, and rejected by "right libertarians" and conservatives. The use of terminology from the new left was not a mistake. Konkin was consciously making an effort to distinguish his brand of "revolutionary market anarchism" from the growing anarcho-capitalism movement, which came to be associated with political action and cultural conservatism. In his time, Konkin saw many Ancaps as "sell-outs" who avoided revolutionary activity due to its social and legal risks while opting for ineffectual, vanilla lifestyles, more in line with the conformity of mainstream, statist society.

In conclusion, Samuel E. Konkin III successfully created an extension of libertarian philosophy by utilizing tactics that are consistent from theory to application (Counter-Economics) while providing a path towards a freer society. He made efforts to acknowledge the differences between his movement and others, but at the same time recognizing that the counter-economic attack can be waged by a wide spectrum of anti-statists. If we can successfully create a panarchist alliance of counter-economists, we may yet construct a truly freed market that allows free experimentation and trade between different schools of thought. In this space we will see the conscious agorist movement flourish.

Chapter 6
On Non-Voting

Despite our distaste for electoral politics, we feel the need to remind potential voters that there are vastly more important and empowering ways to spend your time and energy than voting for a president. However, this is not just a mindless attack on the status quo. This is part of our strategy of spreading anti-state and pro-empowerment rhetoric. This strategy seems more important than ever because Americans are (once again) divided in their support for candidates who seem like polar opposites but are actually both seeking to use the power of the state to achieve their goals.

Every election cycle, the dead stream media fills first time voters heads with propaganda designed to make them feel like they are changing the world. There is an abundance of "Meet the new generation that is changing the presidential election" and similar headlines. Don't forget that the last generation that supposedly "changed the world" via the presidential election gave us Obama, who gave us more war, more surveillance, drone bombings, continued robbery by the banksters, and some would argue that electing a Democrat (especially the first black president) pacified the anti-war movement that was reaching millions in the early 2000s.

This is, of course, if you actually believe that presidents are voted in. Presidents are selected, not elected. You are not truly electing a president. We could say that the electoral college elects presidents and the popular vote does not matter. We could also note that voting machines are easily hacked and rigged. Additionally, based on how the Republican and Democratic establishments treat "outsider" candidates it has become clear that no one will ever become president unless they have agreed to toe the party line.

You will not find us voting for these parties because it should be painfully obvious that the elections are rigged. It's all a facade. Just think of it as a sad, boring entertainment and your life will be much better off.

We can already hear the naysayers, *"But, if you don't vote how will your voice be heard?", "If you don't vote you have no right to complain!" People died for the right to vote, if you don't vote you are giving your power away!" or "Non-voting is childish, just because you can't get your way you won't play!"*

We choose not to vote because it is immoral to use force (under the guise of government) to enact our particular vision for the rest of society. Even if we didn't have a philosophical problem with voting, we don't see a single candidate that represents our values or goals. Why should we be forced to participate or be shamed when the available options are extremely lacking?

We choose not to vote because the time it takes to research candidates and vote is better spent elsewhere, namely in our communities. We find value and results when we apply our energy and passion into the local community and create solutions that empower us and those closest to us. Although we have philosophical arguments against voting, we do think those who focus their energies locally may find opportunities where organizing and voting can be effective to reduce government intrusion in their lives. However, we absolutely do not think that voting (on any level) should be used to force your particular solutions on other free humans.

We also want to stress that there is no "political revolution" taking place. The very idea is an oxymoron. Specifically, the idea of an electoral revolution is preposterous. However, this does not mean that there is no role for political activism. As Steven Horowitz has brilliantly pointed out, politics is more than elections and voting. Horowitz writes:

"When we write a letter to the editor, share a story or a meme on social media, talk about US foreign policy with friends over a drink, or step into our classrooms to teach economics to college students, we are being political. Every time we engage in the conversation about what is wrong with the world we live in and how we might make it better, wealthier, more just, or more peaceful, we are being political. Elections and voting are neither the most important elements of politics nor the sum total thereof. That's too narrow a conception and one that even libertarians should reject. If anything, we understand correctly that voting might be the least important and least effective kind of political action."

A true revolution—an evolution that propels humanity forward—is not going to come from the ballot box. The establishment would like you to believe such a thing is possible—that voting for a president is power—but this is actually an act of giving away your power. However, this is not a message of doom and gloom. This is a message of empowerment. YOU ARE POWER. The moment we stop giving away our power and believing that this system offers us any hope for a better future, the sooner we can embrace and heal ourselves and our communities. From there we will flourish.

Do not assume that non-voting and removing yourself from the system means apathy or failure. By removing ourselves from the systems we do not support and building new alternatives outside of the state apparatus, we are creating the world we want. We need propagation of this message as much as we need creation of agorist alternatives to the statist economy.

We also need active non-compliance/resistance campaigns at every level, on every front. We believe agorist methods and the creation of pockets of agoras and Freedom Cells are at least part of the solution towards a better world.

We are not simply preaching from behind a computer screen. These are real world strategies that we have embodied and will continue to employ throughout our lives.

We believe the United States is at a pivotal moment where the population will decide whether they want to play the game and put their faith in another candidate for another election—or pursue a more direct path to liberation. Our goal is not to shame those who vote but to encourage each of us to find ways in which we can directly engage and empower our communities rather than simply putting faith in politicians. We fully believe that we are capable of creating new systems of organization and abundance that have the potential to radically enhance our experience of liberty.

PART 2—OUR VISION OF A STATELESS SOCIETY

Chapter 7
Providing Public Services Peacefully

The time has come to start thinking unconventionally when considering alternatives to the current methods of funding community projects. As it stands right now, our civilization is forced to fund projects involuntarily through coercive taxation. The force and violence involved with the collection of taxes is only scratching the surface of the negative consequences that this practice has on our society. Let's take a moment to hash out the implications of coercive taxation.

Since the government is allowed to extract money from the people by force, this guarantees they will have funds for any project they want, even if those projects are unpopular with taxpayers. This is because the public has no choice but to pay taxes, therefore they have no say in how their money is used. Thus, the taxpaying public (*and not the agorist!*) end up paying for their own oppression and unjust wars around the world. Sure, there are some social welfare programs that assist people, but the cost of these projects are a tiny fraction of the money that is actually received via taxation. Most of the money that is stolen through taxation is used for bureaucratic budgets, collection enforcement, and the gluttony of federal and state governments. So while a portion of the revenue is being used for beneficial projects, a majority of the money is still being wasted or used for nefarious purposes. Imagine a thief giving you five dollars while also taking a hundred dollars from your back pocket.

One of the most common complaints about the government is that it does not truly serve the public. The reason for this is simple: the government gets paid regardless of whether or not the people are satisfied. This means they have no incentive to actually listen to the public they depend on for funding. Likewise, the disharmony between the state and citizen inevitably leads to mismanagement, violence and corruption. On the other hand, if community projects were funded through voluntary means people would only pay for the services they wanted. This would likely lead to a lack of funding and the eventual collapse of authoritarian governments as they were faced with either extracting funding from the public using physical force or adjusting their own behavior. Under these circumstances wars would be prevented, small businesses would have an easier time competing in the marketplace, and trillions of dollars in wasted overhead would either be back with its rightful owners or used in beneficial social projects and programs. If someone wanted to invade territories halfway around the world or put together an oppressive bureaucracy like the Department of Homeland Security, they would lose funding because most people would not willingly support their authoritarian adventures. This is the whole concept behind voluntarily funding community projects: good service will render payment from the public, while poor service will lead to a lack of a customer base and thus a lack of funding.

There is an unbelievable amount of fear directed at this concept because for most of history our civilizations have been propelled by violence, instead of a balance of compassion and logic. Immediately upon hearing about these ideas of doing away with coercive taxation, many people who are new to the idea will immediately scoff, *"if taxes were not collected under threat of force then no one would pay them! There will be chaos and the poor will die in the streets!"* It's time to recognize that forced taxation isn't working for the average person and ideas like *"the consent of the governed"* and *"the social contract"* are complete fallacies.

We must acknowledge that there is a growing discontent among Americans. The two corporate political parties are losing support and people are losing faith in the system itself. Do we really think that the public would choose to sign a contract agreeing to have one third of their earnings stolen to pay for the government's actions? If not, then it surely cannot be said that the system of involuntary taxation is any type of consensual relationship. And if the relationship is not consensual and voluntary, then it is not legitimate.

If tax revenue was put into projects of value to the people, they would be more likely to voluntarily contribute money. Although our culture projects a pretty bleak view of human nature, our world is filled with a diverse spectrum of people who are kind and care a great deal about their neighbors. Recent studies have even shown that compassion might be hard-wired into the human genome. Einstein believed that, *"If people are good only because they fear punishment, and hope for reward, then we are a sorry lot indeed."* So while it is true that people are naturally driven by incentives, most people also exercise empathy for their fellow human beings and are driven to help others when possible. In fact, helping others and the emotional reward it provides is often the incentive needed to drive people to help others. In fact, in 2010, people gave over 290.89 billion dollars to charity. This is after the public has already been mugged for one third of their income by the government, and in the middle of the worst economic conditions since the Great Depression. Imagine how much they would have given had they been able to keep all of their income and had the reassurance of knowing their money was actually being spent correctly. Not to mention, imagine if all the money the public gives to wasted political campaigns was redirected to projects that the community actually wanted.

There is currently a lack of confidence in the ability of charities to support our needs—and with good reason. Many charities have succumbed to the corruption of our culture of dominance and become part of the non-profit industrial complex, doing very little to help, and pocketing a lot of money. In many cases, it would be best to bypass the middlemen altogether and give money directly to people in need. However, even considering this corruption, charities still perform more honestly than governments. According to 2008 data from *Charity Navigator*, an average of 80-85% of the money that is donated to charities actually ends up in the hands of the needy. That same report goes on to quote several sources who found that the government takes over 70% of all tax revenue collected and uses it for their own public funds, salaries, military projects, and wasteful bureaucracies. They also found that less than 30% of public tax revenue is actually spent on the public. It was even suggested by 1984 U.S. Grace Commission that nearly every dollar of income tax collected in America funds political corruption and pays the debt to the Federal Reserve. So even in today's world of "subpar charities" those charities outcompete the State when it comes to improving the condition and lives of those in need.

There is no need to force compassion and anyone who claims that charity must be forced does not have your best interest at heart. The myth that the public benefits from taxation is just an elaborate advertising scheme that attempts to justify its existence. Even mobster Al Capone ran soup kitchens in Chicago so the people would overlook his crimes and see him as a charitable man. The government takes the same approach by spending some of their pocket change on welfare programs and community projects, but all of this is only done out of an obligation to maintain the appearance of effective management of tax revenue. In a free society where public services and community projects were funded voluntarily, there could be various community groups that gather to discuss the issues important to the community at large. These meetings could be open to everyone and facilitated by alternating community members. Meetings could also take place online with identifies confirmed on a blockchain. These brainstorming sessions would allow the community to present suggestions for the allocation of resources. All suggestions would need to comply with the sovereignty of the individual. As mentioned earlier, FreedomCells.org could help organize these meetings.

There could be essential life-saving programs that would always be receiving donations, and available to everyone in the community—whether they donate or not. Since these areas were so vital to life, they would likely receive the funding needed due to the high value of the service. For example, water treatment plants, fire fighters, or community gardens would have no problem with funding because they are in high demand.

When it comes to community defense, the public generally blindly puts their faith in the police and military. As with all other mechanisms of the state, these organizations are monopolies rife with corruption and inefficiency. Despite these obvious truths, the propagandized masses continue to credit these institutions for holding our society together. The popular misconception is that without forcing people to pay for these monopolies there would be chaos and danger. However, other models for community defense are entirely possible without the need for state-sanctioned theft. Under the current paradigm, if you are upset about police corruption you cannot simply stop giving them your tax dollars and search for another security provider. Instead of waiting for the state to fix the problems, there are private citizens taking matters into their own hands by organizing to provide security for their community. A great example of a currently existing alternative to the police can be found in Detroit. To counter the notorious corruption and ridiculously long police response times, Dale Brown formed the "Threat Management Center" in areas of Detroit where police don't answer 911 calls. Brown's organization fights crime, offers free protection for victims of domestic violence, and is also able to service poor areas of Detroit for free by charging a premium to work security in the city's richest neighborhoods.

Two other important areas of debate related to providing services in a world without involuntary taxation are the roads and the courts. When it comes to courts, the vast majority of civil disputes, especially in the world of business, are actually handled by nongovernment arbitration services. There is no reason why criminal cases cannot be handled in the same fashion. Anarchists who do not wish to use force to collect money for "the public good" are often asked, *"who will build the roads?"* Apparently, there are those who believe in the absence of the State humanity will suddenly become incapable of laying down a dirt path or connecting roads into an interstate freeway. These people discuss the creation of government roads as if the construction was simply due to the kindness of government and not made possible by the theft of taxation. However, what the government really does is collect money from private citizens under the threat of violence, then use that money to employ those very same citizens to build infrastructure. The reality is that the people could build infrastructure themselves for less money if they coordinated with neighbors and other communities. In other words, if they just cut out the middleman. This exact scenario played out in 2009 on Hawaii's Kauai Island when private citizens performed a 4 million road repair job for free in 8 days. Beyond the basic necessities, a myriad of secondary programs and services from transportation, internet, and space exploration could also be funded through voluntary donations from the community. Remember, as a result of the lack of overhead and enforcement costs which inflate all bureaucratic budgets this would likely be cheap in comparison to the prices that we see today on public projects.

Many anarchists on the left still have a tendency to support taxation because they see it as the only way of correcting the massive inequality in the world, but taxes empower the government, not the poor. Taxation has been around since the dawn of government but has done nothing to reverse the massive inequality that has always existed, in fact, inequality continues to grow at an alarming pace even as taxation increases. Money from taxes is used to build and maintain the institutions that keep the class structure in place and keep people in poverty. Feeding and housing the poor, and correcting the massive inequality in this world are goals that should be shared by anarchists, but we should not be trusting our enemy to solve these problems when they created them in the first place.

Some may be concerned that it would be hard to achieve community goals on a voluntary basis, but this would actually improve the efficiency and value of public services. Oftentimes government funded jobs don't even see completion! It is unbelievably common for Western governments to start popular programs during election years to gain public support, only to later pull the plug so the funds can be used for wars or bailouts. This kind of manipulative behavior takes place all the time. However, when there is a project that has enough support, it will usually receive sufficient donations from individuals, businesses and charity organizations to keep the program operating. This can clearly be seen in the explosion of online crowdfunding websites and campaigns. We also saw this in the US in 2011, when the government pulled the plug on funding for the SETI space program in the midst of a half-dozen wars and major austerity measures. This was a program that the public felt so strongly about that over 2,000 donations were received in a single week, easily surpassing their goal of 200,000.

If we think about this same problem presenting itself in the potential free society that we are discussing, we can easily assume that it can be solved in a similar fashion. Except this time around, there will be far less overhead and people will have more to give to the cause, thus ensuring a greater success rate than we see today under the rule of the State. If people stopped contributing to a certain program, that program would put out word to its supporters to raise the extra funds needed to carry on the project. This is the wonderful thing about how our species self-organizes and uses their intelligence and resources to solve problems when they appear.

When a need arises in a community, people naturally and spontaneously come together to take care of what needs to be done. They don't need a bureaucrat with a gun in their face forcing them to do it. For our species to have a future, we must start thinking about more peaceful ways of doing business. We must stop justifying the use of violence in all circumstances — even "soft-core" violence like government legislation, taxation and indoctrination.

Chapter 8
Stewardship of the Earth

Regardless of your thoughts on anarchist or statist theory, every single human being on this planet needs clean water and the fruits of the Earth to survive. The Earth is our home and our source of life and it is not something that is promised or guaranteed. This simple fact has been overlooked by our species as unsustainable practices continue to destroy our planet for the short-term gains of an elite few.

The negative relationship that our species has with the Mother Earth is without a doubt driven by the authoritarian control structures and economic systems that dominate the world. If there was an award for the planet's biggest polluters, the governments and militaries of the world would undoubtedly take the prize, along with their corporate friends. In addition to making a mess of the world on their own, global governments suppress clean and renewable energy technology, which in turn forces the rest of us to use unhealthy products that damage our bodies and environment.

There are several competing philosophical views when it comes to the environment and the concept of ownership. We cannot deny that our species' time here on this planet is finite, while the Earth will be here for many, many future generations. With that being the case, it hardly makes sense to consider ourselves the owners of the land, the water, or other resources which predate and will outlast our existence. We take a view of the ownership of the Earth that could be more correctly termed stewardship. Essentially, each of us is a caretaker of the life on this planet, whether we choose to accept the role or not. This does not mean that all claims to property should be abandoned, but it does imply a certain amount of personal responsibility in relation to the living standards of future generations. We must acknowledge that for much of recent history humanity has been a poor caretaker of the planet. Still, we reject the notion that government bureaucracy is the answer to destruction of the environment.

Ironically enough, it is the governments and international governing bodies in charge of protecting the environment who are largely responsible for the dismal condition of our habitat. It is often the state and scientific establishment that push the propaganda that the average citizen is the source of all of our environmental woes. In June 2015, a group of scientists from Stanford University, Princeton University, the University of California, Berkeley, and others warned that the Earth is experiencing a sixth mass extinction era. They called for fast action to save endangered species and habitats. The scientists claimed that species are disappearing at up to about 100 times faster than the normal rate between mass extinctions, known as the background rate. Their study was published in the journal Science Advances.

The researchers told Stanford that their estimates were conservative and that the situation may be much worse than previously believed. "*We emphasize that our calculations very likely underestimate the severity of the extinction crisis, because our aim was to place a realistic lower bound on humanity's impact on biodiversity,*" they wrote. Paul Ehrlich, the Bing Professor of Population Studies in Biology, a senior fellow at the Stanford Woods Institute for the Environment, and co-author of the study said, "*[The study] shows without any significant doubt that we are now entering the sixth great mass extinction event.*"

Of course, it is absolutely important for free hearts and minds to strive to live an existence that is in balance and harmony with the planet and all the life we share this space with, and it is true that this is not currently happening. Environmental damage is taking place, but the study ignores the impact government institutions have on the environment and it places the blame solely on the average consumer. While it is true the average consumer does play a role in environmental pollution, their impact is minuscule in comparison to that of governments and major corporations. Also, one of the reasons the average consumer uses toxic products in the first place is because more sustainable alternatives are forced off the market.

Also, Professor Ehrlich's involvement might set off a few alarms for those familiar with the topic of eugenics. Eugenics is the belief that humans can be "improved" or controlled through genetic or social engineering. In 1981, Ehrlich wrote the book, *Extinction: The Causes and Consequences of the Disappearance of Species*. Before that, Ehrlich cowrote *Ecoscience*, which sheds some light on his ideas. Published in 1977 with John Holdren, former Science Czar for the Obama Administration, *Ecoscience* promotes a number of radical ideas for dealing with the world's population. Some of these ideas include forced abortions enforced by a global police force, which requires the loss of individual sovereignty. Quite simply, these people want the public to believe that humanity is a disease, something to be managed, controlled, or eliminated.

The same people responsible for most of this environmental degradation also create nature based foundations and other phony environmental organizations. These organizations are used to stash money and often advance eugenics depopulation programs. The ruling class understands that human beings naturally have an interest in preserving the environment and that most people will typically not question or criticize actions taken in the name of environmental protection. The latest scheme of the ruling class is exploiting environmentalism and fears of "global warming" to establish a carbon credit taxing system. The rationale of this theory is that human beings are creating environmental destruction via their use of carbon, so the suggested solution is to tax the average person and control their energy use. If climate change is actually a result of man-made carbon output then surely taxation wouldn't be a realistic solution, yet according to the establishment this is the ONLY possible solution.

Yet, the average citizens aren't responsible for the majority of the world's environmental destruction, nor are they responsible for the majority of the world's carbon output. In fact, the 50 largest transport sea vessels produce more carbon than all the cars in the world. These are military vessels, oil tankers and other transport vehicles for corporations and governments.

Howard Zinn's incredible research in *"A People's History of the United States of America"* reveals that, *"In 1992 more than 100 countries participated in the earth summit environmental conference in Brazil. Statistics showed that the armed forces of the world were responsible for two thirds of the gases that deplete the ozone layer. But when it was suggested that the earth summit consider the effect of the military on environmental degradation the United States delegation objected and the suggestion was defeated."* The general public is not to blame for the environmental crisis that stands before us. We have inherited it from the careless governments and corporations who suppress alternative energy sources and are responsible for the vast majority of the world's pollution.

The perpetrators of these crimes place the blame everywhere but themselves, and use their political power so they can actually benefit from all the destruction they are causing. Al Gore was one of the most prominent spokesman for the carbon-based global warming theory. He is also one of the primary advocates for a worldwide carbon tax and is closely involved with businesses that stand to reap large profits as a result of possible carbon tax schemes. He says his motivations are to reduce the energy uses of the general public, but according to the Tennessee Center for Policy Research, he has a mansion in the Belle Meade area of Tennessee which consumes more electricity every month than the average American household uses in an entire year.

When this information went public, he defended himself by saying that he pays a "carbon offset," but what he didn't say is that he paid it through a company that he owned called Generation Investment Management. In other words, he paid the money to himself! Al Gore became a proponent of a carbon tax via his good friend and founder of the embattled Enron Corporation, Ken Lay. This makes perfect sense considering the fact that Enron was an energy company which had very close ties in Washington, and was notorious for concocting deceitful schemes to fleece the public out of their hard-earned money.

To make matters worse, most of the evidence paints a picture quite different from the "official" stance on global warming. The earth's temperature and climate has been changing and fluctuating since the beginning of time on account of various factors, namely solar activity. Drastic changes in weather have been recorded throughout history and some would argue these changes are a natural process. To claim that a natural process that has been happening forever is evidence of a recent threat defies logic. Since the "Climategate" scandal broke in November of 2009, the carbon-based global warming theory has lost support and is now under extreme public scrutiny. Although politicians and mainstream media sources claim that there is some sort of a scientific consensus on this topic, there still exists a reasonable amount of skepticism within the scientific community itself.

While all of this discussion and controversy is taking place over this very specific theory, there is a list of other environmental issues that are being ignored. Our energy resources are being poorly mismanaged by the organizations that control them. These governments and corporations are destroying the planet and placing the blame on us so they can justify making us foot the bill. The abundant use and lack of long-term studies on genetic engineering and pesticides has created new species of weeds and pests that pose an unprecedented threat to our ecosystem. Toxic radiation and pollution have become commonplace in our everyday environment, mostly due to corporate carelessness and military exercises. There are very serious environmental issues that we need to correct, but it's not limited to one chemical compound and we aren't going to solve anything by taxing the average consumer.

Without a doubt, the Earth is suffering. The planet is ravaged with environmental disasters, loss of important ecosystems and species, and a population that seems increasingly ignorant to the impact it is having on the rock they call home. Every free mind should work to live in harmony with this planet and reduce the impact of our existence on this beautiful, unique place we call Earth. That is without question. What we should question, however, are the motives for governments and other parasitic classes who promote the idea that humanity is the problem that needs to be corrected.

Another recent environmental issue which divided activists (particularly the American Libertarian movement) was the 2016 fight against the Dakota Access Pipeline near Cannonball, North Dakota. The DAPL, alternatively known as the Bakken Pipeline, is owned by the Dallas, Texas-based corporation Energy Transfer Partners. The pipeline is slated to stretch 1,172 miles upon completion and transport crude oil from the Bakken fields of North Dakota to Patoka, Illinois. The project is set to cross the Missouri River not far from the Standing Rock Sioux Reservation in North Dakota. The Standing Rock Sioux claim that the U.S. Army Corps of Engineers violated the National Historic Preservation Act by not properly consulting them before approving the project. The Sioux filed suit against the Army Corp and in April 2016 launched the Sacred Stone Spirit Camp as a site of resistance to the pipeline. Protesters, allies, and journalists came from all around the world in support of the Spirit Camp, as well as additional camps that were launched in support including the

Red Warrior Camp, Rosebud camp, and Oceti Sakowin. Beginning in August 2016 the number of tribes and indigenous communities standing in solidarity with the Standing Rock Sioux grew to over 500. The coming together of such a large number of tribes, many of whom have been enemies in the past, was a historic event in itself.

Beyond the lack of consultation with the natives, the water protectors (as the Sioux and allies prefer to be called) were fighting against the property claims of the U.S. government. Technically (according to the U.S. government) the water protectors in the Oceti Sakowin camp north of the Cannonball River were on private property owned by the U.S. In October 2016, the protectors launched an additional camp closer to the construction of the pipeline. The Sioux called this the "Treaty" or "Frontline Camp" named for the 1851 Laramie Treaty under which the Sioux still maintained ownership of the land. The Sioux stated that they were implementing their own form of eminent domain and retaking the area because the U.S. government has failed to abide by its own treaties.

In order to prevent the completion of the pipeline, which the Sioux and water protectors see as not only a violation of treaties, but an attack on the water and planet, the camps were willing to risk arrest by using direct action to physically stop the construction of the pipeline. Some critics of the water protectors argue that they are in the wrong for going on private property and "forcing" the cops to use violence in defense of said property. We completely disagree with this misguided view. Anarcho-capitalists, libertarians, conservatives, and other propertarians who take this position are completely ignoring the history of broken treaties between the U.S. and indigenous communities of the landmass currently known as North America. This is particularly disturbing to see coming from followers of Austrian economist Murray Rothbard. Drawing on John Locke's homesteading proviso, Rothbard argued that individuals who mix their labor with unused property can become the legitimate owners. "*The homesteading principle means that the way that unowned property gets into private ownership is by the principle that this property justly belongs to the person who finds, occupies, and transforms it by his labor,*" Rothbard wrote in "*Confiscation and the Homestead Principle,*" (The Libertarian Forum, June 15, 1969). "*This is clear in the case of the pioneer and virgin land. But what of the case of stolen property?*"

Rothbard goes on to say that when dealing with stolen property one must make an effort to find the legitimate owner. This means the original person who homesteaded the land or the person who legitimately acquired the property from that original owner. If unable to locate the original owner, the person who was last in possession of the property without the need for statist privilege becomes the proper owner. While we have criticisms of other stances taken by Rothbard (particularly his stances on agorism, cultural issues, and his later adoption of paleo-conservatism) we agree with him on this issue. This means that Energy Transfer Partners, the U.S. Army Corp of Engineers, and private citizens who sold their land for the pipeline cannot be considered the legitimate owners of the land in question. In particular, not when this land has historically been used by the Sioux nation and was only acquired by any agency of the U.S. government through violent wars and broken treaties. Rothbard also responds to the critics who believe that the water protectors should respect the private property rights of the oil company and attempt to fight the battle in court.

"*What of the myriad of corporations which are integral parts of the military-industrial complex, which not only get over half or sometimes virtually all their revenue from the government but also participate in mass murder? What are their credentials to 'private' property? Surely less than zero. As eager lobbyists for these contracts and subsidies, as cofounders of the garrison state, they deserve confiscation and reversion of their property to the genuine private sector as rapidly as possible. To say that their 'private' property must be respected is to say that the property stolen by the horse thief and the murdered must be 'respected,'*" Rothbard wrote.

Frankly, these corporations do not have rights and should not be granted the same property protections as people. Without subsidies and state granted privilege, these corporations would not be able to maintain their monopoly on energy. The corporate Oilgarchy and their state partners also work together to suppress alternative energy technologies that have the potential to outcompete the oil barons. Another point of contention in the DAPL debate has been the fact that the movement views itself as defenders of the sacred Mother Earth and natural resources. The fight between the water protectors and the Oilgarchy is best seen as a cultural divide. The indigenous people of this planet tend to think in terms of the principle of the 7th generation. This means that one considers the effects of their actions on not only the next generation, but the 7 coming generations. This perspective differs greatly from the opposing view that could be termed the "Modern" or "Western" worldview which tends to focus exclusively on the here and now. It is this type of thinking that perpetuates the use of oil and other invasive, unsustainable products.

The water protectors, specifically the indigenous communities, are fulfilling their spiritual commitment to defend the land and the water. Many of them do not care about debates over whether the direct action was a violation of property norms. These are individuals who are often willing to die in defense of the planet. We believe this is an honorable position that could be supported while still being consistent about not initiating force or even violating property rights. For example, one could argue that a homesteader who causes irreversible harm to their property is initiating force against future generations of property owners and the planet itself. Additionally, damage done to one piece of property will undoubtedly lead to contamination of adjacent properties due to the interconnected nature of the environment. What this means is that polluters themselves are actually committing the first act of aggression, and would thus open themselves up to consequences from their neighbors.

We believe this position is sound based on property claims as well as an argument for defending the undefendable. In book 1 of this series, we mention the need for humanity to rethink our relationships with non-human animals and the planet. We discussed the implications of consciousness and rights applied to animals and the environment. Although some will argue that animals are incapable of rational thought and therefore incapable of being considered anything other than property, we have come to the conclusion that animals should be given equal status to children, the elderly, adults with diminished mental capacity, or similar vulnerable groups incapable of self-defense and reason. With each of the groups, it is generally accepted that a guardian or agent of the vulnerable individual would be justified in defending them against the initiation of force. This same logic can be applied to animals and potentially the Earth, in reasonable circumstances.

For example, if you witness your neighbor abusing their dog for no good reason you may feel called upon to ask them to cease and desist. If that fails you could gather your freedom cell and issue a warning. If that also fails to end the violence, you may consider physically removing the dog from the abusive owner. If the owner views his dog as property, he may consider you to be aggressive upon his legitimate claim to ownership and choose to respond violently. At this point we have two individuals who believe they are in the right. This situation could be arbitrated between competing insurance agencies, but would likely lead to one agency recognizing the rights of animals and the other agency denying such protections. Until there is a global shift in the perspective of our relationship with animals, we are likely to see a continued debate over whether they are property. Still, we were drawn to anarchism because we desire a world without systematic, publicly accepted violence. Viewing animals as property to be used for entertainment is the type of thinking that leads to orcas trapped in captivity at Sea World, and miserable animals held prisoner in zoos. *Should we not hold ourselves to a higher standard and live a compassionate life in balance with the animals and the environment?*

We are not advocating a fascist vegan takeover where every individual is forced to abandon meat eating. In fact, one of the authors of this book is vegan, and the other is not. We don't have any intention of sending one another to the gulags or re-education camps. However, we do advocate a more conscious relationship with the animal nations and the Earth. We also call on those concerned with dangers to the environment and animals to boycott factory farming industries, including most mainstream restaurants, and non-organic, non-local produce which involve the heavy use of dangerous pesticides. Mass factory farms are damaging to the surrounding environments and also perpetuate the disturbing slavery and abuse of animals bred to feed the human population. Not to mention that animal agriculture is responsible for a large portion of greenhouse gas emissions. If you want to fight deforestation and carbon emissions, stop supporting animal agriculture.

Statism is also responsible for propping up the corporations involved in industrial farming and animal agriculture. Without statism and with an increase in the counter-economy and agorist localization, factory farms (and the abuse to the environment and animals caused by them) would be greatly reduced. If we grow the urban farming and backyard gardening movements, we could decrease the need for such unsustainable and violent industries. This won't be a perfect vegan world where no one eats meat, but it would greatly reduce the acceptable level of violence used against animals and the Earth.

Our final point relates to the question of who is best suited to tend to the local environment. The common refrain from the authorities is that the people are ill-equipped to handle management of local resources and protection of the environment. We are told that without a government the environment would become sold off to the highest bidder and polluted. However, recent research seems to contradict these claims. A July 2014 report from the World Resources Institute and the Rights and Resources Initiative found that communities take better care of forests than governments. The report, *Securing Rights, Combating Climate Change*, reviewed over 130 earlier studies in 14 countries to see the effect of community management of resources. According to the report, areas of the Brazilian Amazon under control of the indigenous communities saw a deforestation rate of 0.6 % while government-held areas were at 7%. In Guatemala, the rate of forest loss in government-protected areas was 20 times that in areas under community control. The World Resources Institute report confirms a 2012 analysis by the Institute of Ecology which found that on average, government-protected tropical forests were cut down about four times as fast as community-managed ones. Finally, the work of Elinor Ostrom perfectly illustrates the benefits of community environmentalism versus state environmentalism. Ostrom, winner of the Nobel prize for economics in 2009, found that problems with resource management occur when outside forces, including governments and well-meaning conservationists, intervene.

It is clear that humanity needs to reevaluate our relationship with the planet and all of its inhabitants. Rather than looking to governments or elites to save the day, we should be focused on how we can take action that will defend the livelihood of those living today and future unborn generations. This action may sometimes involve directly challenging the mechanisms of power that attempt to damage and control the planet in ways that affect our very existence. We should strive to remain consistent with our goal of not initiating violence while at the same time standing strong as warriors in defense of the Earth.

Chapter 9
The Authoritarian Right and Left

There are several different examples of political spectrums in use today. Most people in the U.S. measure the political parties and philosophies across a horizontal line, from liberal to conservative. Others see the political spectrum as a square with totalitarianism in the top corner and freedom in the opposing corner. We tend to disagree with most political spectrums because they misunderstand the eternal struggle of freedom versus tyranny and mistakenly believe that either the right or left side is closer to freedom, or that one is better than the other. This tyranny manifests itself as non-voluntary communism, statism, fascism, imperialism, and any other form of authoritarianism. The opposite of all these power schemes is anarchism.

In the realm of politics, economics, and religion there exists many "false dichotomies" in which there seems to be a narrow field of two options to choose from. In reality, there is actually a larger set of possibilities beyond the pre-approved guidelines. In other words, you are asked to choose between black and white, leaving you to think that the only colors in existence are black, white and maybe gray, when in reality there is a whole palette of different shades and tints that are completely left out of the discussion. The statement, *"If you're not with us, then you're against us"* is a classic false dichotomy, because it only presents two options, both of which amount to violence, while completely neglecting the possibility of remaining neutral. Likewise, the traditional left/right paradigm is also a false dichotomy which forces people to choose between two seemingly different, but equally authoritarian sides.

Anarchists should not make the mistake of believing that they are a part of "the left" or "the right." These terms are skewed beyond repair and have different meanings in different nations and at different points in history. Alliances with right and left have failed every time because ultimately the followers of the corporate political parties are still playing into the mainstream paradigm. This leaves them open to manipulation and adopting what Konkin called antiprinciples. The mainstream left and right will always sell out the principled, but misguided anarchists who seek alliances with one side over the other. We should absolutely reach out to both the right and the left and attempt to bring our message to them as much as possible, but we must be careful not to sacrifice our principles. We should work to bring them towards our principled stance. Rather than believing the answer lies in one end of the political spectrum, freedom minded individuals should work to ally with like minds from all sides. The danger is in believing that one end of the spectrum holds the one path to liberty and that the other side is the problem. This is the same false dichotomy that we sought to escape when we first abandoned the left/right paradigm and mainstream politics.

After waking up to the reality that the Democratic and Republican parties are controlled, many free thinkers have taken to a life of activism in hopes of changing the world. However, many of these people who broke through the mainstream left/right paradigm are now falling for another false paradigm leading to the same cycle of frustration and division that is seen in the mainstream political circus. The legitimate frustration felt by those seeking solutions has caused some on both the left and the right to become even more extreme in their dogmas and in their support of government. These individuals fail to remain consistent and instead fall prey to the deception of statism once more.

An interesting aspect of the political spectrum in America is the fact that it is constantly changing and shifting. In America, Democrats and Republicans regularly trade positions and switch stances on important issues. For example, for a period of time after World War II, prior to the red scare and the Cold War, the Republicans were known to take strong anti-war positions. The red scare and Vietnam War pushed conservatives towards a more pro-war position while the Democrats reacted in opposition, and subsequently became known as the anti-war party during the era of the new left. In reality, neither corporate party is truly anti-war. They simply adopt anti-war rhetoric to gain the support of people who wanted peace. In terms of economic policy, "liberals" were traditionally advocates of free markets, while in today's political climate most identifying with that label advocate strong government control of the economy. What this tells us is that both ends of the spectrum do not stand on principles, but are constantly manipulated by media hype, the whims of politicians, and calls for "pragmatism" in the face of both real and imagined political or cultural enemies.

In America, this has resulted in what has come to be known as the "Alt-Right" on one side and the "Social Justice Warriors" (SJWs) on the other. Many of those who now identify as Alt-Right came out of the 2008 Tea Party movement and the subsequent growth of the American Libertarian movement fueled by Presidential candidate Ron Paul. The former congressman from Texas was a student of Murray Rothbard and has actually been very outspoken against the Alt-Right (and SJWs). After the Libertarian movement failed to capture the presidency and end statism, many activists found themselves disillusioned with not only the political system, but with libertarian principles. Whether these people ever truly understood the message is debatable, but in the end this crowd went on to support Trump and has come to be associated with wanting to violently impose their vision of "freedom." The Alt-Right has become obsessive with combating their enemies: leftists, commies, "cucks", SJWs and anyone else who does not support their heavy-handed vision of society. In their obsession with their enemies, they have lost sight of the goal of freedom.

On the other side of the spectrum are the social justice warriors, the hyper-vigilant group who weaponizes identity politics to win elections and seeks to use the force of government to censor free speech in the name of political correctness. Of course, we stand against bigotry of all kinds as well, and many of the ideas espoused in this series do support what could be interpreted as "social justice," but what we oppose is how these ideas are leveraged politically and how the movement behind them chooses to aggressively engage with anyone who isn't perceived as an ally.

This movement's roots are in the progressives that believed the election of Barack Obama in 2008 was their moment. After eight years of expanding the wars, the surveillance and police state, targeting whistleblowers, and corporatism, the progressives lost faith in Obama. Many of this same crowd had their bubbles burst once more in the summer of 2016 when "Independent" Democratic Presidential candidate Bernie Sanders handed his revolution over to the Democratic nominee, Hillary Clinton, and did the same in 2020 for former Vice President Joe Biden. Instead of working on solutions to the systemic problems that they correctly identify, they often spend their time focusing on microaggressions, "call out culture," and advocating for more diverse overlords. Just like the Alt-Right, they have become so obsessed with their "enemy" that they have lost sight of developing solutions to the two-party system.

The left and right fear one another so much that they end up embracing the rhetoric of dictators in order to vanquish their political enemies and save their version of civilization. It is common for those on the left to venerate historical dictators like Stalin or Mao, and now increasingly common for the alt-right to embrace murderers like Chile's former dictator Augusto Pinochet. In fact, many in the alt-right, and even some confused anarcho-capitalists have recently been promoting the idea of throwing political opponents or "counter-revolutionaries" out of helicopters into the ocean, an inhumane practice that was notoriously employed during Pinochet's reign of terror. They justify this outright call for violence by citing insidious libertarian infiltrator Hans-Hermann Hoppe's "physical removal" proposal. Hoppe is a conservative monarchist who masquerades as an anarchist and espouses authoritarian views that are in total opposition to true libertarian values. In his book "*Democracy, The God That Failed*" Hoppe outlines his vision of a "free" society:

> "*One may say innumerable things and promote almost any idea under the sun, but naturally no one is permitted to advocate ideas contrary to the very covenant of preserving and protecting private property, such as democracy and communism. There can be no tolerance toward democrats and communists in a libertarian social order. They will have to be physically separated and removed from society.*"

Hoppe goes on to express his distaste for "alternative," nontraditional lifestyles:

"Likewise, in a covenant founded for the purpose of protecting family and kin, there can be no tolerance toward those habitually promoting lifestyles incompatible with this goal. They—the advocates of alternative, non-family and kin-centred lifestyles such as, for instance, individual hedonism, parasitism, nature-environment worship, homosexuality, or communism—will have to be physically removed from society, too, if one is to maintain a libertarian order."

Of course, in a truly free society operating under libertarian norms it would be permissible for an individual to choose what type of people they prefer to live near. Their preferences might even resemble Hoppe's vision. However, what Hoppe is describing is obviously a dictatorship, yet his supporters will insist that these types of aggressive tactics towards political enemies are necessary in order to save "western civilization." Hoppe's supporters have said that he is being misinterpreted, that he is only describing a vision for his ideal covenant community, but it seems fairly clear he imagines physically removing people from his ideal society, not just his own property.

It is important to point out that Hoppe has a massive body of work, most of which does not promote this type of hateful strategy of exclusion, but these passages soil the rest of his work, and leave a dark cloud over libertarianism as a whole, so we cannot with a clear conscience reference or promote his work in a positive light.

One common refrain from the alt-right is that they are here to save western civilization, or white culture, or European values, while disparaging "Eastern civilization." This outlook tends to mask bigoted views and completely ignores the violence of the West and the accomplishments of the East. In reality, both eastern and western cultures are responsible for great achievements and systematic violence. Furthermore, as detailed in Gavin Menzies's book, *1434: The Year a Magnificent Chinese Fleet Sailed to Italy and Ignited the Renaissance*, the European Renaissance that western nationalists hold up as a point of superiority was actually a gift from China. The concepts and inventions that were developed in Europe during the Renaissance were not the independent work of Europeans as mainstream history urges us to believe. Instead, this was merely a time when the less advanced Europeans came into contact with more sophisticated cultures and learned from them. Yet, members of the alt-right still believe that western cultures have a monopoly on "civilization."

Essentially, the philosophy of the alt-right is that state violence or private violence is justifiable and necessary against political opponents who have ideologies that are deemed to be threatening or dangerous. According to their logic, the ideologies of their political enemies, whether it be communism, environmentalism or whatever, are viewed as acts of aggression in themselves, and thus they believe that they would be defending themselves by using violence against their enemies. While it may be true that certain ideologies can be precursors for acts of aggression, simply holding an idea is not an act of aggression, and does not warrant a forceful response. If we follow that line of reasoning, we will have constant conflict and we will see the end of the progress which liberty has allowed humankind to experience.

This illogical sophism is not exclusive to the right either, leftists are regularly justifying violence against political enemies who have not aggressed against them, but have merely espoused views which they find threatening. This was seen clearly during protests surrounding the 2017 inauguration when white supremacist Richard Spencer was punched by a black-bloc protester while he was being interviewed on the street. The attack was largely celebrated by left-leaning activists who felt that Spencer's ideology was an act of violence which justified a forceful response. This is, of course, the same argument that the authoritarian right uses to justify violence against their political enemies. Spencer's ideas may be absolutely disgusting, but if we allow violence to be used against his ideas, then that means anyone can arbitrarily decide that an idea is a threat to their existence, and then use philosophy to justify violence on any person they choose.

On the other hand, when Richard Spencer crosses the line from simply talking about having a white separatist community to wanting to physically remove or exterminate people of color, that takes a step closer to what we call aggression. No physical act of violence has been taken, but a threat has been issued. When someone has made it clear they want to use violence against you, do you allow them to grow in influence to the point that they might actually be able to get away with violence? Or do you preemptively attack them to stop their growth? And at what point do you decide to move? Should it be once they have become backed by the force of law? If so, we would argue that criminals are already in power and thus violence could be justified against them. We do not think such an action would achieve the goal of a free and ethical society thought, so we choose not to initiate force. But some might propose that statism is such a threat that they should use violence against those who vote. On the other end of the spectrum someone might say that Anarchists are a threat to "law and order" so violence is justified against them. You see where we are going with this. This is a slippery slope that leads to barbarism and a reversal of our progress as a species. Remember, good ideas do not require force. We can convert hearts and minds with reason and logic, as well as leading by example.

Just after the attack on Spencer at the 2017 inauguration, he attempted to infiltrate the International Students for Liberty Convention, and notable libertarians in attendance showed us exactly how someone like him should be handled. When Spencer attempted to set up his own speech outside the event, he was confronted by a large group of conference attendees, including Jeffrey Tucker, Will Coley, and others, who challenged Spencer's ideas, and told him that his fascist views were not welcome at that property. Spencer called for a police escort and quickly left the building without incident.

Both the Alt-Right and the SJWs are guilty of collectivizing their enemy and refusing to judge each individual according to their own behavior. This division can even be seen within the alternative and independent media. Journalist outlets once responsible for hard-hitting investigative news are now simply perpetuating the same false dichotomy while pretending to be anti-establishment, as they too have fallen victim to the trap of division. Sadly, the alternative media has become no different than the divisive corporate media, with extremists on both ends having endless arguments and rarely discussing solutions.

In the end, the mainstream political left is manipulated by their compassion while the right is manipulated through their desire for independence. Compassion and a pursuit of independence are both admirable qualities, but both can be used against us. The right perceives compassion as negative because they can see how the left is manipulated, but at the same time, they do not see how they are being manipulated through their desire for independence. Likewise, the left perceives independence as negative because they see how it is used to manipulate their political enemies, but they cannot see how their compassion is used against them.

Both sides play into the hands of the establishment by advocating violence and division, and in this sense these groups work towards the same ends despite any apparent superficial differences. It is possible for rational people to be both compassionate and independent without being manipulated by government or being divided among one another.

The hate and division seen in politics should make one thing extremely clear: It is not a good idea to force large populations of people in a specific geographical location to live under the same rules, adhere to the same culture, fund the same projects and so on. People are unique individuals with a broad spectrum of beliefs and values. For optimum peace and prosperity each of these unique individuals should be able to live according to those beliefs and values, so long as they do not impede on their neighbor's freedom to do the same.

Chapter 10
Identifying the Alt-Right Infection

The aim of this essay is to call attention to the individuals who helped promote the entryism of Alt-Right, Nationalist, and even fascist leanings into the American libertarian and anarchist movements. We will draw some conclusions as to how this type of thinking came to infect a movement based on self-ownership, individualism, anti-authoritarianism, and respect for justly acquired or homesteaded private property.

Before we explore the attempts at creating a fusion of alt-right activism with the American libertarian movement, it's important to define these terms. When we are speaking about the American Libertarian movement, we are speaking of those who range from libertarian-leaning conservatives who may vote for the Libertarian Party (or even the Republican Party) to Rothbardian Anarcho-Capitalists, agorists, voluntaryists, and abolitionists. Within this movement there exists wide ranging, varied paths which bring individuals to the philosophy of libertarianism. Some came to the ideas because they want less government in their lives. Others came because they hope to abolish the government completely. Some found their way through a deontological, or natural-rights libertarian worldview. Others simply want to be left alone. Generally though, these individuals found their way to a philosophy which promotes self-ownership, individual liberty, anti-authoritarianism, and respect for justly acquired private property.

When we speak of the Alt-Right, we are referencing the now-infamous sector of American politics that not only rejects mainstream right-wing politics, but take their calls to "Make America Great Again" to another level by declaring that all of Western Civilization, or white culture, or European values (however they arbitrarily define it) is under attack and must be saved. The Alt-Right claims it is attempting to save the West from the supposedly evil forces of multiculturalism, communism, and mass immigration.

Many of these individuals espouse a desire to have a strongman in power (Trump, for some) to remove the enemies of liberty as they see them, and instill a sense of law and order. This movement is definitely varied and still finding itself, but, generally, you find white supremacists and nationalists, paleoconservatives and paleo-libertarians, traditionalists, and other obscure groups who hate the left-wing and feel left out or deliberately ignored by the political establishment. There are also those within this group who blame their problems on and call for the removal (and sometimes murder) of immigrants, Muslims, Mexicans and Jews.

And, yes, as many in the media have noticed, it is true that there are former libertarians currently embracing the Alt-Right message. (Check out the search results for "alt-right" and "libertarianism") This is because the Alt-Right has taken some of the basic libertarian values—non-intervention, anti-globalism, respect for private property (well, at least for some)—and attempted to juxtapose them with their inherently divisive rhetoric. We don't subscribe to the notion that Libertarianism is some type of gateway or pipeline to the alt-right or fascism, but we do think there are few people who deserve part of the blame for pushing American libertarians (young and old) into joining this collectivist populist front of the extreme right wing.

Walter Block

First, we saw Walter Block (a libertarian thought leader who is already problematic in other areas) promote the idea of "Libertarians for Trump" based on the assumption that Trump was the least worst option. Block repeated the same faulty logic we often hear from the dead stream media and activists lacking in principle: Trump would be better than Hillary. If Block's words are to be taken at face value then this is one hell of a case of misreading the tea leaves. Even worse, Block launched this group in March of 2016, several months before Trump won the election. We would argue it is the work of thinkers like Block that helped influence some libertarians who were (for some reason) on-the-fence about voting for Trump. We truly hope some interviewer or activist will hold Block's feet to the fire for his role in promoting Trump now that it has become crystal clear (to those with eyes and ears) that Trump is not a bastion of liberty, and ultimately, it makes no difference whether we have a Biden, Clinton, Bush, Obama, or Trump in office. Block is not an imbecile and it's difficult to chalk up his misstep as simply failed strategy given the breadth of experience he has with working with the Libertarian movement for the last 50 years.

Stefan Molyneux

Another individual responsible for swaying the minds of his followers is Stefan Molyneux. Without a doubt Molyneux formerly promoted a libertarian/voluntaryist message via his channel and website. However, in the last few years Molyneux has made very obvious shifts towards the extreme right wing. Where Molyneux once promoted peaceful parenting, debate, and philosophy as the most effective way to spread liberty, he has now become another white nationalist, race science peddling fear monger of the blogosphere. Molyneux enjoys making long presentations with charts and statistics to back up his claims and refute his critics. He can be very persuasive and make the viewer feel as if they are participating in an exercise in pure logic. But look closer and you see that Molyneux is no libertarian and does not care about universal liberty or individual liberties, so much as he cares about providing a "rational" backing for his bigoted views on Muslims, immigrants, and other groups that he claims American descendants of Europeans should fear.

The man has gone from being an outspoken anarchist or voluntaryist to espousing collectivist views and defending the establishment via Donald Trump. Despite what some would have you believe, a collectivist mindset is not compatible with libertarian values because it implies that one should be judged according to some collective identity (whether based on race, gender, nationality, age, color, ethnicity, etc.) rather than judged as an individual. Both the Alt-Right and the SJWs are guilty of collectivizing their enemy and refusing to judge each individual according to their own behavior. This does not mean that humans never see groups and that libertarians are immoral if they see groups. It does mean that every individual is worthy of liberty regardless of what collective identity they may share with others. Unfortunately, Molyneux seems to have taken a good amount of his formerly anarchist supporters with him on his journey into statism and hate.

Hans-Hermann Hoppe

Another unfortunate aspect of the Alt-Right's entryism is the influx of the immature, infantile 4chan culture of Pepe the Frog memes and fantasies of throwing their enemies out of helicopters. As noted in the previous chapter, some who identify as Alt-Right see a philosophical basis for their views in the world of Hans-Hermann Hoppe. In fact, because of Hoppe's writing, the idea of "physically removing" your enemies has become a meme in some Alt-Right and AnCap circles. The meme spawned pages like HHH Physical Removal Service. Hoppe himself even got in on the "joke" during the Mises Institute's 35th Anniversary celebration in New York City where he was seen smiling while holding a toy helicopter. Mention this to his supporters and they say, "It's just trolling!" or, my favorite, "stop pearl clutching, you leftist!"

Despite these claims, Hoppe's own words reveal how he feels. At the Mises anniversary event Hoppe stated the following during a speech titled "Coming of Age with Murray":

"The ideal of the left- or "modal"-libertarians, as Murray referred to them, of "live and let live as long as you don't aggress against anyone else," that sounds so appealing to adolescents in rebellion against parental authority and any social convention and control, may be sufficient for people living far apart and dealing and trading with each other only indirectly and from afar. But it is decidedly insufficient when it comes to people living in close proximity to each other, as neighbors and cohabitants of the same community. The peaceful cohabitation of neighbors and of people in regular direct contact with each other on some territory also requires a commonality of culture: of language, religion, custom and convention. There can be peaceful coexistence of different cultures on distant, physically separated territories, but multiculturalism, cultural heterogeneity, cannot exist in one and the same

place and territory without leading to diminishing social trust, increased conflict, and ultimately the destruction of anything resembling a libertarian social order."

It's unclear if Hoppe has ever been to a place like Houston, the 4th largest and most diverse city in the United States. Over several generations Houston's population has transformed from being a city of white middle-class workers to one in which Mexicans, Hondurans, Cubans, Vietnamese, Indian, Chinese, Ethiopian, and so many more ethnicities are represented. In fact, the L.A. Times reports:

"In 1970, about 62% of Houston's population was white. By 2010, that had shrunk to 25.6%. Over the same period, the Latino population grew from 10.6% to about 44%. Newcomers have long been part of the Houston story, a city of migrants from across the U.S. that later became a city of immigrants—and their children. From 2000 through 2013, the Houston metropolitan area's immigrant population grew at nearly twice the national rate."

Those numbers are sure to terrify the white nationalists and supremacists who believe they are being eradicated through a shift in population, but the reality is that Houston is a place with massive diversity and it has not caused the city to fall into a state of despair and conflict. There are more than 140 languages spoken in Houston and despite this lack of a commonality of language, we do not see regular conflict. The people of Houston (and other locales with diverse populations) are coexisting despite not living in "distant, physically separated territories," as Hoppe suggests. When Hoppe suggests that *"multiculturalism, cultural heterogeneity, cannot exist in one and the same place and territory without leading to diminishing social trust, increased conflict, and ultimately the destruction of anything resembling a libertarian social order,"* he ignores the reality of the diversity found within the United States. Sure, we are far from a "libertarian social order," but living in a world where we coexist, work with, and do business with people of different ethnic backgrounds does not necessarily entail a loss of trust or increase in conflict.

Hoppe would have us believe the outcome to living in diversity will always be a disaster. Rather than making an effort to reach out to others and help them understand the value of libertarian principles, Hoppe suggests physical removal and segregation. Of course, this is the right of every libertarian and every free human in general. It is immoral to force individuals to associate with those whom we choose not to. However, it would be a mistake to make assumptions about another person based on their shared ethnicity or nationality or religion or other trait. This short-sighted judgment based on arbitrary differences does not lead to a world where the individual liberty, self-ownership, and private property of an individual are respected. Hoppe's thinking leads to separating ourselves from other human beings, emphasizing an "us vs. them" mentality and a revival of the age-old view that civilization evolves through conflict.

Libertarians ought to reject this worldview and remain consistent with their support of individual autonomy and liberty.

Hoppe provided further legitimacy to the Alt-Right (at least in the eyes of his followers) when he spoke at the 12th annual meeting of the Property and Freedom Society in Bodrum, Turkey, in September 2017. In a speech titled, "Libertarianism and the Alt-Right: In Search of a Libertarian Strategy for Social Change," Hoppe explains what he believes is the connection to the Alt-Right and the paleo-conservative movement of the 1990s. Rothbard and Hoppe were both involved in the paleo-conservative movement in the 1990s.

"The Alt-Right movement is essentially the successor of the paleo-conservative movement that came to prominence in the early 1990s, with the columnist and best-selling author Patrick Buchanan as its best-known representative. It went somewhat dormant by the late 1990s, and it has recently, in light of the steadily growing damage done to America and its reputation by the successive Bush I, Clinton, Bush II and Obama administrations, reemerged more vigorously than before under the new label of the Alt-Right."

Hoppe goes on to describe the genealogy of the Alt-Right through its connection to him and the Property and Freedom Society (which he founded to express his conservative views):

"Many of the leading lights associated with the Alt-Right have appeared here at our meetings in the course of the years. Paul Gottfried, who first coined the term, Peter Brimelow, Richard Lynn, Jared Taylor, John Derbyshire, Steve Sailer and Richard Spencer. As well, Sean Gabb's name and mine are regularly mentioned in connection with the Alt-Right, and my work has been also linked with the closely related neo-reactionary movement inspired by Curtis Yarvin (aka Mencius Moldbug) and his now-defunct blog Unqualified Reservations."

We have tried (unsuccessfully) to point out these connections to different AnCaps and Libertarians who support Hoppe. They refuse to see that Rothbard's later conservative leanings and Hoppe's "rational" justifications for this type of thinking influenced thinker like Curtis Yarvin, who founded the pre-Alt-Right neo-reactionary movement under the name Mencius Moldbug. Yarvin has also been linked to the Trump campaign.

Despite the reluctance of Hoppe's followers to accept his influence on this movement, he is more forthcoming. He recognizes his role in working to move libertarianism further to the right. In Democracy, Hoppe claims that libertarians must be "uncompromising conservatives." Despite Walter Block's support for Trump, one of his better essays is called "Libertarianism is Unique and Belongs Neither to the Right nor the Left: A Critique of the Views of Long, Holcombe, and Baden on the Left, Hoppe, Feser, and Paul of the Right." The title speaks for itself and is worth your time to understand why the libertarian philosophy is rightfully placed outside of the political spectrum.

Interestingly, Hoppe notes that white nationalist Richard Spencer had previously spoken at the conference. During his talk Hoppe mentioned his disappointment with Spencer. He believed Spencer to be a lost cause—not because Spencer has called for the cleansing of non-European ethnicities in order to create a white-ethnic state. No, Hoppe was merely upset that Spencer has revealed himself as a right-wing socialist.

"When Spencer appeared here, several years ago, he still exhibited strong libertarian leanings. Unfortunately, however, this has changed and Spencer now denounces, without any qualification whatsoever, all libertarians and everything libertarian and has gone so far as to even put up with socialism, as long as it is socialism of and for only white people. What horrifying disappointment!" Block said.

John Hudak, a contributor to the website Being Libertarian, does a great job of pointing out what we consider to be some of the darker elements of Hoppe's thinking—he seems to lack empathy and compassion. He is more interested in making fun of his critics than actually engaging in debate.

"Hoppe attacks the libertarian group Students for Liberty, calling them "Stupids for Liberty" and criticizing them for their motto of "peace, love, liberty," as if peace, love, and liberty are bad things or things we shouldn't strive for," Hudak writes. *"But rather than condemning the rampant racism throughout the alt-right movement, Hoppe chooses to refer to brushing off the accusations of racism as a "strategically wise" move on their part. Though this may in fact be true, he does not address or even acknowledge the fact that there is a fair amount of racism within the alt-right."*

At this point, if there are any Alt-Right supporters still reading, they are likely saying, "Well, racism does not violate the non-aggression principle!" or that they have the right to discriminate against anyone they want on their own private property. That is true. However, if you are a bigot you will likely find yourself losing friends and business partners who choose to discriminate against such primitive thinking. The market allows for the bigots and the libertarians to voluntarily segregate or integrate, and build autonomous communities and associations based on their preferences. Some individuals may feel so wronged by the racism that they believe it must not be allowed to stand. We are not calling for punching Nazis or racists. We are calling for an awareness that these people are attempting to infiltrate the American libertarian movement and peel away as many people as they can. These right-wing collectivists are attempting to build a movement off the backs of libertarians, and any other movement with resources they can manipulate for their own ends. Don't be fooled.

The Lesser Knowns

There are other lesser-known individuals who have bought the Alt-Right rhetoric hook-line-and-sinker and used their social media echo chambers to promote the clash of civilizations. Chase Rachels, author of A Spontaneous Order: The Capitalist Case for a Stateless Society, has been working hard to shed any previous libertarian credentials he held as he shifts further towards support of nationalism and fascism. Throughout 2016 Rachels was often called to task for his tendency to support the extreme right-wing. Rachels denied this was the case and continued to deny that he was racist or pushing white nationalism. That is until Hoppe gave his recent speeches. Rachels has since come out in the open with his call for libertarians and the alt-right uniting. His website Radical Capitalist featured charming essays like, "On White Nationalism, White Supremacy, and Genocide," and "Single Mothers and Feminism Ruin Children."

In his essay For a Libertarian-Alt-Right, Rachels continues to parrot Hoppe by repeating his recent outline of how to achieve the goals of a "Libertarian Alt-Right." Hoppe's steps are as follows:

- *One: Stop mass immigration.*
- *Two: Stop attacking, killing and bombing people in foreign countries.*
- *Three: Defund the ruling elites and its intellectual bodyguards.*
- *Four: End the Federal Reserve and all central banks*
- *Five: Abolish all 'affirmative action' and 'non-discrimination' laws and regulations*
- *Six: Crush the "Anti-Fascist" Mob.*
- *Seven: Crush the street criminals and gangs.*
- *Eight: Get rid of all welfare parasites and bums.*
- *Nine: Get the State out of education.*
- *Ten: Don't put your trust in politics or political parties.*

Rachels says that step one is non-negotiable in order to achieve the ends of the libertarian alt-right. When you get past the first step you find goals that are actually compatible with libertarian principles—ending the wars, removing the funding for the political elite, ending the fed, abolishing regulations—and then we get to his "crush the anti-fascist mob," "crush the street criminals and gangs," and remove "welfare parasites and bums." Each of these seems like very thinly veiled digs at minorities and immigrants. Not to mention the fact that Americans of European descent also account for welfare costs. Is the answer to creating a free society to crush and rid ourselves of those who are on assistance? Is this truly a representation of libertarian values and principles? I think it's obvious that Rachels and Hoppe are not representing the philosophy as most libertarians see it.

Rachels, like Hoppe, considers himself highly rational. He has convoluted arguments attempting to justify the use of some level of state power against illegal immigrants. He also makes the preposterous claim that net taxpayers are the true owners of what is currently known as "public property" and thus should be able to restrict immigration throughout the United States. Again, John Hudak handles the argument:

"One could make a convincing argument that an individual should receive the rights to what their tax money paid for, but only if logistics are ignored. There is no way of knowing exactly where an individual's tax money went. It is possible that some net taxpayers have paid little to nothing toward the maintenance of public property, but rather had their money go toward military spending, entitlements, or even paying down the public debt. It is also practically impossible to figure out who is a "net taxpayer" and how their standing as a net taxpayer relates to others (whether they deserve more compensation than their neighbor, for instance)."

Not to mention, deciding who gets paid what would necessitate a centralized institution to handle such claims. This would lead to the creation of another state. Our view on borders is that the time has come to abandon terms like open and closed borders in favor of decentralized borders (more on that in chapter 13). We believe individuals like Rachels and Hoppe attempt to use libertarianism and its logical arguments and conclusions to justify their pre-existing bigotry and bias towards other individuals from different cultures, ethnicities, and traditions.

Rachels has also shown he is willing to exploit existing racist symbols and codes for a cheap joke, or to wink at/dog whistle to the racist elements of the Alt-Right. For example, in a post on the Radical Capitalist Facebook page, Rachels took the popular white supremacist phrase "1488" and adopted it to fit Hoppe and the Alt-Right. Fourteen is a reference to the 14 words ("We must secure the existence of our people and a future for white children") promoted by prominent white supremacist David Lane. The 88 can refer to a quote from Mein Kampf or Lane's essay 88 Precepts. Alternatively, it can also be used to refer to "H", the 8th letter of the alphabet, and stand for HH, or Heil Hitler. Rachels has modified 1488 to 14888, or "There can be no tolerance to democrats and communists in a libertarian social order," and Hans Herman Hoppe.

Sadly, Rachels—A supposedly pure voluntaryist who claimed to believe that the initiation of force made you a statist, no matter the excuse—has now joined the rank-and-file Alt-Right.

Conclusion: Liberty Grows Through Individual Action

These individuals are a part of the reason for the misconception that there is any valid connection between the libertarian philosophy and the Alt-Right.

Individuals like Walter Block used their credibility among the movement to promote a Trump victory while Stefan Molyneux used his platform to promote Trump, as well as give voice to guests who peddle race science and promote an inevitable clash of civilizations. We also place blame on Stephan Kinsella, Lew Rockwell, and Jeff Deist for their silence on the presence of racists and bigots, and for tacitly promoting the cause by pretending it's simply a joke to trigger leftists.

As previously stated, we do not believe Hoppe's focus on saving western civilization, crushing the anti-fascists, or removing "welfare parasites" should be the focus of any libertarian platform. All of these men are either lost in the lie that immigrants are going to hurt them or take their jobs, or they are deceitfully pushing statism and authoritarianism to further some other agenda. We do not care to speculate. We already know their view of the world leads to division and conflict. These men continue to spread the idea that our current predicament can be reduced to left vs. right, Alt-Right vs. AntiFa, etc. They need conflict in order to spread their ideology, get clicks, and seize power. This is why Hoppe and others attempt to reduce libertarianism to be exclusively about private property and the reduction of conflict related to the scarcity of resources. While establishing norms does help reduce conflict over resources, this is not the focus of libertarianism. The philosophy starts with an understanding of self-ownership. From there one derives the concept of ownership of goods and products created by the self, as well as property which was homesteaded. This, along with some respect for the non-initiation of force, is the foundation of libertarianism in America.

It should be clear that the Alt-Right's preference for tradition or conservatism does not mean that all libertarians with conservative leanings are racists or bigots or Alt-Right. However, the aforementioned men are at best confused former libertarians and at worst they are authoritarians and racists biding their time while using libertarianism as cover. Be cautious of supporting them.

We must continue to guard against the undercover statists and authoritarians and work to keep this philosophy focused on empowering the lives of all individuals so they may manifest the life of their choosing. This message grows by living the principles in our daily lives and limiting our involvement and support of the State. Libertarianism will not grow if the libertarian movement chooses to align with the Alt-Right. This does not mean the reverse—an alliance with the extreme-left wing of American politics—is necessary. It does mean that libertarians ought to remain principled and work with individuals from across the spectrum on issues where there is alignment. We can ally with and collaborate with individuals of different persuasions without diluting or abandoning our message and goals. Liberty grows one by one, as each heart and mind abandon the false promises of statism and embrace the superiority of spontaneous order, self-ownership, and non-aggression.

Chapter 11
On the Use of Force

In this series we have frequently returned to the idea that there is no single path to anarchy. This is obvious when examining the various tactics that different anarchists advocate in the quest for freedom. However, this "diversity of tactics" is another point of contention as many anarchists have strategies that are seemingly opposed to one another. Many anarchists are dogmatic and seem to think that their way—and ONLY their way—is correct. In reality, changing the world is messy and will never fit in perfectly with any group's philosophy or blueprint.

The sheer size of humanity means that changing the world will require a wide range of different tactics, possibly even coming from opposing groups. As agorists, we advocate the gradual and peaceful transition to a free society, through community empowerment, counter-economics, and self-healing. However, we are not so naive to disregard the power of more militant and potentially dangerous approaches.

This is a topic that is mostly forbidden in mainstream political discourse. Even in the history of the past century's civil rights struggles, a peaceful protest is presented as the only solution that achieved change. Clearly, there is more to the story. There were indeed peaceful protests during the Civil Rights era which made an impact, but there were also more militant groups, such as the Black Panthers and MOVE, who took up arms and promised to defend their neighborhoods from violent cops. Jailbreaks were also common at the time, with the Black Panthers rescuing many of their members from incarceration, including Assata Shakur. Sometimes cops were shot and killed in the process, although this was certainly never a goal of these rescue teams.

There were also riots that occasionally developed in response to the intolerable conditions of the time. While this fact is typically sanitized by mainstream history, the Boston Tea Party and the Boston Massacre were both riots, and are seen as pivotal moments in the founding of the United States. There were agorist efforts against the state as well, with communities finding ways to divest from the system and invest in their own communities. In fact, groups like the Black Panthers participated in agorist activities by providing food, medical care, and education to people in the community for free, and far better than the free services offered by the government. These diverse efforts created a vast culture of resistance that was able to turn the tides of history to some extent. Unfortunately, some of these efforts were co-opted and many of these groups were physically and violently wiped out by the overwhelming force of the government.

Sadly, in the hierarchies that we live under, the violence that flows down-hill is invisible because it has come to be seen as "normal," or "just the way things are." Meanwhile, any violence that flows up towards those in power is seen as horrifying and unthinkable—even if it is self-defense. This is seen in both foreign and domestic policy. The number of civilian deaths caused by militaries and government law enforcement agencies far exceeds the number of deaths caused by terrorists. Fears of terrorism and gang violence are taken seriously because of the threat that they represent to the establishment, not because of the threat that they pose to innocent life. These threats are real but pale in comparison to the systemic violence of government.

"Crime," in general, is a classification that is very rarely ascribed to people in positions of power. The slightest transgressions and acts of desperation that common people commit are on constant display in the media, and are used as examples for why a power structure is needed. However, this power structure and the people that participate in it cause more pain and suffering than the criminals and terrorists they are claiming to protect us from. In reality, they only protect themselves, the class structure, and the status quo at the expense of everyone else. For example, in 2014 the Economic Policy Institute found that far more money is stolen through wage theft than robberies. The researchers looked at the data for the year of 2012 and found that about 341 million worth of property was stolen by common criminals, but at least 933 million was withheld by employers. They did not account for the many cases of wage theft that are not counted due to the victims being unable to file lawsuits. The situation is even worse when we include how much is stolen from workers through taxation.

When people in power carry out large acts of violence or theft, their actions are ignored, forgiven and excused, but those without power are held to the strictest standards and face the harshest consequences for minor offenses. This cultural narrative in which state violence is sanctioned and justified makes it very easy for the government to use extreme violence to suppress revolutionary groups, while at the same time expecting the people that they oppress to always turn the other cheek. The establishment behaves like an abusive narcissist in these situations by dealing out traumatizing abuse on a daily basis, and then acting deeply hurt and offended when someone wants to throw a fraction of that violence back in their face in a moment of frustration and desperation. For many people, the systematic violence of the state is so overwhelming on a day-to-day basis that the pain from these conditions can cause anger to manifest in the form of riots. There will be times when the state pushes too far, and people will assert their power in numbers to push back. This is a cause and effect relationship that is directly the fault of the government. When so much pressure is applied to a population that pressure will find a way to break free.

To someone who has lived a life of relative comfort within their own community, it might be difficult to understand a riot. A riot is a measure of last resort which happens when people are fed up with trying to fight the violence and oppression they experience on a daily basis. For someone who has attempted to fight injustices through the rigged legal and socially acceptable avenues, it might appear as if rioting in the streets is the only way to be seen and heard.

Riots are also about more than the issue that caused them to boil over in the first place. They are an understandable response to living with a metaphorical boot on your throat around every turn you make in your life. One reason you might see looting during the riots is because poverty is a constant grievance for much of the world's population. When someone who has been pushed to the edge sees an opportunity to address that grievance, they will take it, whether it means screaming in the streets, setting a cop car on fire, or looting a store.

Theft, violence and destruction are all that the establishment knows. However, these transgressions are hidden under the color of law so they are often harder for most people to notice. In 2003, as the United States Military was invading Iraq, the former U.S. Defense Secretary Donald Rumsfeld gave a press conference where he defended the act of looting, and described it as simply a part of the messy process of transitioning from an authoritarian regime. He pointed out that a bit of looting is somewhat understandable when a population is attempting to rise up from an authoritarian regime. Of course, Rumsfeld would not have defended these same actions if a population was rising up against his regime, but his words would still ring true if that were the case.

"The task we've got ahead of us now is an awkward one … It's untidy. And freedom's untidy. And free people are free to make mistakes and commit crimes and do bad things. They're also free to live their lives and do wonderful things. And that's what's going to happen here. And for suddenly the biggest problem in the world to be looting is really notable. While no one condones looting, on the other hand, one can understand the pent-up feelings that may result from decades of repression and people who have had members of their family killed by that regime, for them to be taking their feelings out on that regime. And I don't think there's anyone in any of those pictures … (who wouldn't) accept it as part of the price of getting from a repressed regime to freedom."

—U.S. Secretary of Defense Donald Rumsfeld, April 11, 2003

While we understand the motivations and reasoning behind some who choose to riot and/or loot, we do not believe rioting and looting is always going to be an effective long-term strategy. In fact, the state will often have undercover agents act as provocateurs who commit random acts of violence that can be used as justification for violence against peaceful protesters. The point is that the issue is not as simple as many anarchists believe it to be. As usual, the most interesting lessons to be learned are found in the shades of gray that exist beyond the dogma.

Anarchists on the left typically take the position in support of targeted property damage and looting, while propertarian-anarchists find any violations of property to be morally reprehensible. This division is unsurprising considering that the issue of property is the primary source of debate between these two camps. Most AnCaps seem to passively approve when government is targeted for acts of vandalism, but will remove their support for the entire movement if someone breaks the window of a business during the same riot. However, AnCaps seem to have no problem overlooking this type of collateral damage when observing uprisings in places like Hong Kong, where the fight is against a communist police state, which they perceive as inherently worse than a capitalist police state. Even some mainstream conservatives described the protesters in Hong Kong's 2019 riots as freedom fighters, even though they set buildings and police cars on fire and shot arrows at the cops with homemade bows.

Most people seem to support violent uprisings against oppressive dictatorships, but everyone has different standards of what classifies as a dictatorship, and these standards are informed by a person's own personal bias and beliefs. It is important to recognize how much our perspectives on these issues are shaped by our personal experiences in the society that we live in. There are exceptions to this generalization, but people who are comfortable or have advantages within the current control structure are much more likely to feel threatened by militant tactics like riots, than people who don't have much to lose.

Whether activists who advocate different strategies realize it or not, their disparate efforts often work in tandem to erode the power of the state even when they aren't intentionally cooperating. As agorists we understand that committing "illegal" acts is sometimes the only way to live free or set change into motion. We understand that those who riot or loot feel as if they are finally being heard after being ignored for so long, or taking back from a society that they feel took so much from them. We also understand the importance of considering how your tactics will be viewed by the larger population. If our goal is to build a massive, inclusive movement of abolitionists, anarchists, agorists, and rebels, we need to think about how our actions will be viewed by the public at large. We must not lose sight of our goal to liberate the hearts and minds of humanity while remaining true to our principles. In one moment of passion, all of our efforts at building coalitions can go up in flames. As with all things, it is important to achieve balance through understanding the nuances of controversial topics such as the use of force.

Chapter 12

Panarchist Experiments: Can Propertarians & Non-Propertarians Coexist?

Centuries ago, most people would have thought it was impossible for two people who belong to two different religions to be neighbors, yet it happens every day in modern society. In this same way, it is possible to envision a future world where neighbors have different concepts of economics, culture, and politics, and are still able to live in peace. If we aim to create a stateless society, we must understand the potential hurdles and pitfalls that we may experience along the way. As we have studied revolutionary movements of the past, several areas of concern have consistently appeared in our research. We hope to remedy these complex situations by providing a balanced perspective into how people of varying beliefs can coexist.

As we have made clear in the previous chapters, we believe society is capable of spontaneously organizing without the need for central authority or government. However, one of the biggest roadblocks to achieving this goal comes from within the "radical" movements themselves. Namely, the conflict between those who believe private ownership of property is itself an act of violence or theft, and those who believe private property norms are the key to a free society. These different camps have vastly different ideas about economics and culture, which puts them at odds and make it very difficult to form alliances, despite a common enemy in the state. However, these differences are not irreconcilable, and it could be possible for these groups to live side by side if they both adopted an attitude of mutual respect.

Regarding the title of this chapter, *Can Propertarians and Non-Propertarians Coexist?*, we do not intend to argue in favor of complete private ownership or total communal ownership of resources. Our goal is to illustrate that coexistence based on mutual respect and a recognition of individual sovereignty is possible. Many anarchists of the past have sought to determine who is right or wrong in property claims, and who has the moral high ground. These contributions are valuable, but they have already been discussed at great length in various social circles and publications. Our goal here is not to determine blame or moral high ground, but to predict how free humans would handle disputes in the most civil way possible, since peaceful resolution is in everyone's best interest. This is not to say that morality is relative or a matter of opinion, morality is a very real and objective thing that centers around the use of force. However, we recognize that not everyone is going to share the same views on topics like this, so it is important to determine how this disagreement could be rectified peacefully.

We believe in panarchism, a true marketplace of ideas where all forms of governance and anarcho-hyphens can compete and cooperate to their liking. During the transitionary period between the state's total collapse and the establishment of new free communities and collectives, there is great potential for a power vacuum as opposing groups attempt to gain a foothold in the post-state world. However, we predict that this potentially violent period will be short as people realize that peace and cohabitation is in their own self-interest.

If the battle with the state is particularly grave, it is highly unlikely that the people will want to continue to wage bloody conflicts among themselves. This is not to say that conflicts will be non-existent, but we believe mutual respect will make for more manageable conflict resolution. The anarchists involved in the Spanish revolution of 1936 were ultimately crushed by competing factions of communists and statists. This lesson should not be forgotten. Still, we should strive for common ground because the other option is endless conflict. The world is a beautifully diverse place and will always be so. If we cannot compassionately debate differences of opinion, we are doomed to repeat our violent past. As noted in the last chapter, authoritarians of all stripes buy into the illusion that they can force the world to conform to their particular worldview and values, but this is an impossible task, even if one end in the conflict does have the moral high ground.

So then, how do we go about achieving this state of mutual respect and healthy conflict resolution? We believe the answer lies in the work of Josiah Warren, America's first individualist anarchist, abolitionist, and founder of anarchist intentional communities. Under his leadership, the community of Modern Times, New York lasted several years with thousands of residents without maintaining a police force or court system.

Modern Times was also unique in that it did not end in failure as many homesteads did, but instead it was swallowed up by the growing United States. Warren espoused a philosophy based on what he called *The Sovereignty of the Individual*, a principle which recognized the value in individualism and stressed the need for mutual respect of other free individuals' right to be free from coercion. He stressed that individuals living in a complex society have interlocking interests and as such, there will be conflicts and there will have to be compromises. Warren was adamant that free people should not impose their will on others and instead allow diversity to reign.

According to Warren, "*Liberty, then, is the sovereignty of the individual, and never shall man know liberty until each and every individual is acknowledged to be the only legitimate sovereign of his or her person, time, and property, each living and acting at his own cost; and not until we live in a society where each can exercise his right of sovereignty at all times without clashing with or violating that of others.*"

With this principle in mind, let us examine a few scenarios involving conflicting views of property and see if there is a possibility for coexistence. These scenarios represent some of the common objections and most difficult questions to answer. This is not a strategy for reaching anarchy or overturning the current system, that will be discussed in later chapters, this is merely an exploration of how people with different ideas could live peacefully in the same vicinity once we already get there.

First, imagine the state has dissolved and people are free to organize and homestead without intervention. In the absence of the state, a variety of organizations, from co-ops to insurance companies, would compete to provide protection and insure people's property against theft or harm. Now, Imagine we have two adjacent plots of land, plot A and plot B. Plot A is occupied by a farming family, their house, and their crops, all of which they acquired through their own labor. The farmers on plot A support private ownership of property. Plot B is unoccupied. However, prior to the state's collapse the land had been sold to someone who owned the title but never actually homesteaded or made changes to the land. One day, a group of anarcho-communists discovers the two plots of land and decides to homestead plot B. The AnComs begin planting crops, building shelters, and altering the lay of the land. The farmers from plot A are friends with the prior owner who holds the title to plot B so they decide to question the AnComs about their new settlement. The AnComs insist that it's obvious that no one has lived on or made use of the land and they declare themselves the rightful stewards. Is it legitimate for the AnComs to occupy and homestead plot B?

If the previous owner has no plans to return to dispute and it is clear that no one's sovereignty will be violated in the process, we believe plot B could be homesteaded without the need for conflict. Also, if the title holder to plot B came into possession of the land with the assistance of any state privilege then it was not justly acquired and therefore not a legitimate claim. To satisfy this argument one would need to make reasonable effort to determine whether the property in question was in use. This leads us to a major issue with deciding land claims of this nature: the arguments tend to venture into arbitrary territory which makes it difficult to establish norms. For example, how long must one wait before homesteading someone else's unused property? And what qualifies as unused? Also, who decides how much land is "too much" for one person? How do we answer these questions while respecting the sovereignty of each individual?

We think this is an important time to reiterate the need for spontaneous order and discretion based on mutual respect. What we mean is that in a truly free society without a central authority there is no way to force or coerce every single person to live according to the property norms of your choosing. The vast human experience guarantees that we are not always going to agree on complex moral issues, and with that being the case, it is best to find a way to handle these issues without hurting people or throwing them in cages. Of course, there will be rare occasions where violent and unreasonable people will need to be subdued or isolated, but that would be the exception to the rule in a world where people are attempting to avoid the use of oppressive tactics seen throughout history. There is also the problem of how currently existing inequities would carry over into a post-state world, but we believe that the current class structure would begin to disintegrate immediately without a government to protect it. Furthermore, most of the wealth and power that the ruling class has in the modern world are built upon the legal fictions and social constructs that we have indicted in this book. A collapse of the state and authoritarian culture would not bring about an entirely clean slate, but it would bring humanity closer to that goal than we have ever been before.

We imagine a world where some communities implement private property norms and others have property arrangements that resemble unowned or community ownership. How will each and every conflict play out with such a patchwork of norms? Only the individuals involved in each particular situation can decide. Unless AnComs and AnCaps are prepared to yield the force of the state to ensure their specific property views are the new monopoly, we'd better get used to mutual respect and compromise. A one-size-fits-all solution is already a part of the problem we face today.

Let's look at one more example to see how these conflicts might be resolved. What happens if the title holder to plot B returns to find the AnComs living on his land? The title holder tells the AnComs he has been waiting for the right time before he chose to build on the land. The AnComs say that they found the land unused and believe they now have a stronger claim due to homesteading. Who has the stronger claim? How do we resolve this conflict without resorting to violence? Many anarchist thinkers have suggested competing arbitration agencies which would be responsible for sorting out conflicts. The AnCaps may use some type of insurance agency, while the AnComs may have a free community organization to handle disputes. The two agencies would consider the claims and attempt to resolve the conflict as impartial third parties. In the event that the two agencies cannot resolve the conflict to the satisfaction of their customers, or attempt to take sides, there could be entirely impartial groups that have members in both communities, and more groups could be brought in for very serious or difficult rulings. Obviously, this increases the possibility of conflict, but in the end, we believe the lack of incentives for war will deter individuals from pursuing this path. Especially, as humanity grows to accept the sovereignty of each individual. These conflict resolution entities will be influenced by public opinion and market demand to resolve these situations as peacefully as possible because their social standing will be negatively impacted by stories of violence, especially in the age of livestream and YouTube.

Conflicts that happen within a certain community with shared beliefs would be easy to resolve, but situations like the one described in this chapter are much more difficult because there is a disagreement in values in addition to the initial dispute. If communities with different values are within proximity to one another, they are going to need to agree on a few basic quality-of-life standards to allow for genuine conflict resolution. The specifics of these standards will likely vary depending on the culture of the region.

Again, we stress that the above situations are entirely theoretical. We have no way of knowing how free people will choose to self-organize and handle dispute resolution. There will always be conflicts and differences of opinion. It is up to each of us to hold ourselves to a higher standard and strive to always respect the sovereignty of other individuals and use our best discretion in each case of conflict. Even if the whole of society is forced to accept one specific dogma, there will always be dissenters and the only way to stop the dissent is to enact totalitarian control. We can either have freedom to disagree and peacefully resolve conflicts, or we can continue the cycle of violence and coercion. It has been said that ideas which are worthy do not require force or violence to implement. If one stands by their beliefs wholeheartedly, they should be able to respectfully debate the merits and potential failures without resorting to violence.

Chapter 13
The Revolutionary Potential of "Illegal" Immigrants

We are going to take a look at one more area of conflict among students of radical political philosophy. After examining differences of opinion on property and the environment, we believe it is essential to discuss the arguments around borders and immigration. We start by considering several key questions. What would migration look like in the absence of the state? How does a society's view on property affect the view of immigration? Would there still be a class of people known as "illegals"?

Traditionally, libertarian and anarchist positions on borders have favored an "open border" solution. This would be in contrast to a "closed border" with immigration controls. This is naturally in line with anarchism considering the fact that governments implement and control borders, and anarchists seek to abolish governments. However, recently some anarcho-capitalists and libertarians have argued for closed borders. They believe private property norms justify forcibly restricting the movement of other free humans, even beyond the borders of their own property. The AltRight takes it a step further and argues that the State may even be a necessary evil in order to save "western civilization" and "traditional values" from an "invasion" of immigrants.

The discussion on borders often centers around whether or not immigrants will have access to "public property" while visiting. Closed border advocates argue that in a stateless society based on private property norms, immigrants would not be welcome unless they were explicitly invited or had employment opportunities. If the immigrant is not invited or does not have a contractual agreement, they would not be allowed to occupy private property. Since the closed border/ private property advocates believe there will be no such thing as "public property" in a free society, they argue that immigrants without an invitation will have nowhere to go and will thus be trespassing and subject to physical removal. We argue that in the absence of the state, land currently known as "public property" (or land controlled by the government) would revert to unowned property. This would allow for individuals to travel across or homestead on this previously government held land. Those who argue that taxpayers should have the first claim to this land ignore the reality that failing to join the counter-economy and continuing to fund the state is not a noble act. Taxpayers and agorists are equally enslaved under the statist system, but when the state collapses, favors will not be paid to those who extended the life of the state by failing to withdraw financial support. We find it laughable that "anarchists" would suggest that paying taxes is honorable and deserving of special privileges in the post-state world. Sure, we are all forced to pay taxes under the threat of violence, and the fact that people pay under duress should not be held against them, but at the same time, those who have the courage to take the risk certainly deserve an extra level of respect and admiration.

One major roadblock in the borders debate is the use of faulty terminology. A valid objection to the concept of public property is the association of the concept with government controlled property. However, we do not think public property needs to be exclusively thought of as government property. In his essay *In Defense of Public Space*, libertarian thinker Roderick T. Long discusses the problems with the public and private debate:

"When we think of public property, we think of government property. But this has not traditionally been the case. Throughout history, legal doctrine has recognized, alongside property owned by the organized public (that is, the public as organized into a state and represented by government officials), an additional category of property owned by the unorganized public. This was a property that the public at large was deemed to have a right of access to, but without any presumption that government would be involved in the matter at all.

I have no interest in defending public property in the sense of property belonging to the organized public (i.e., the state). In fact, I do not think government property is public property at all; it is really the private property of an agency calling itself the government. What I wish to defend is the idea of property rights inherent in the unorganized public."

It seems as if the time has come to abandon terms like open and closed borders in favor of decentralized borders. We imagine a free society with decentralized borders would consist of a mixture of open borders, closed borders, public property, private property and unowned land. We believe a network of competing public and private spaces which allow for freedom of movement is most consistent with the sovereignty of the individual.

Regardless of theoretical concerns, government borders are a utopian idea to begin with, especially when considering areas as large as Europe and the United States. In most of the world (and especially in Western countries), governments can't even secure their own prisons and airports, which increasingly resemble fortresses. Furthermore, creating an effective and staffed wall for the border of the U.S. is barely even physically or financially possible. Over the course of a three-year project, the U.S. government spent 2.4 billion to build 670 miles of very unimpressive fencing along the Mexican border. Considering the U.S. shares roughly 6,000 miles of international borders, it would cost 19 billion to construct a small, unimpressive fence along that entire border. This figure does not include the cost of staffing the fence, or the costs that would come along with making a fence large enough, the barbed wires, weapons, and a buffer zone. These additional expenses could easily double or triple the cost of the project.

Not to mention this militarized border would require an expansion of the already bloated police and surveillance states. Currently, most of the U.S. border is not even fenced or staffed with the military, and there has been no major disaster as a result. Some would argue the violence along borders, particularly the southern border between the U.S. and Mexico, is an example of a major disaster that could be remedied with tighter border controls. However, it is the state and its insistence on intervening in the free movement of humans and cross-border exchange of goods which fuels the cartels and gangs that cluster around distribution points along the border. The blame should be placed on the restriction of movement that comes along with closed borders, not a lack of border control. Even if a massive wall were built and soldiers were staffed every few feet, the closed border would create a demand for immigration, and thus a huge financial incentive for soldiers and government workers to use their positions to smuggle people inside. This is exactly why drugs and contraband flow through prisons, behind many layers of walls and barbed wire. Even at airports, which are now as secure as prisons, people are still capable of sneaking guns and other prohibited items onto flights.

Some of the fascists formerly masquerading as anarchists argue that allowing open borders will lead to a flood of foreigners who lack an understanding of the cultural norms of the nation-state. Even if we are to ignore the fact that the nation-state is a fictitious creation, we should not stray from principle based on fears and assumptions about the future. These proponents of closed borders argue against immigration because they believe the migrants will vote for statism and the welfare state. If these migrants are allowed to enter we will see statism grow and libertarianism die, they argue. These pro-border "libertarians" are effectively calling for pre-crime laws and profiling in the name of protecting borders, which is a blatant contradiction of libertarian values. Ironically enough, many of the modern libertarians that advocate for closed borders belong to the Ludwig Von Mises Institute, an academic institution dedicated to continuing the legacy of Ludwig Von Mises, the founder of Austrian economics. Mises was a Jewish refugee during World War II and would have likely been killed by closed-border policies.

Just as the statists will argue in favor of a surveillance state to prevent terrorism, the border-thumper will try to ban movement in the name of saving "Western Civilization." Whether the argument for a closed border is coming from the left or the right, it is based on the worldview of central planners who do not have faith in the power of individuals to self-organize.

Our final suggestion on the topic of immigration and borders may sound like heresy to some, but we believe it offers the only possibility of creating harmony among free people and thus, furthering our opportunities for a world without a state. Conversation. Conversation and compassionate communication are needed on the part of both the local population and the migrants. Even in the State-controlled world we have today we should oppose granting the state power over border control. Opponents of open borders are so adamant that immigrants from non-Western nations (i.e., those with predominantly brown skin) are going to be statists, leftists, or leeches of the welfare state, that they are willing to support the state to enforce borders. They refuse to search for common ground with their brothers and sisters who happen to be born on a different piece of land.

As anarchists, we should oppose closed and State-controlled borders. As agorists, we should strive to form alliances with immigrants and teach them the value of remaining unregistered by the state and operating in the counter-economy. For an example of the potential for converting "illegal" immigrants to revolutionary agorists, let's reexamine Peru's informal economy as mentioned in chapter 2. In *The Other Path*, Hernando De Soto notes that in the 1970s Peru's rural population began flooding into the cities. The migrants moved en masse from the countryside to the cities, causing the migrant population in Lima, Peru to explode from 300,000 to 1.9 million between 1940 and 1981. The migrants left the countryside to escape poor living conditions and in search of financial opportunities in the big cities. Upon arriving, the migrants were greeted with hostility from people within the borders of their own nation.

De Soto notes that "*the greatest hostility the migrants encountered was from the legal system.*" The barriers the migrants faced within the cities seemed to be a result of statism and interference in the market, but also policies aimed at discriminating against the rural, indigenous populations of Peru. "*Quite simply, Peru's legal institutions had been developed over the years to meet the needs and bolster the privileges of certain dominant groups in the cities and to isolate the peasants geographically in rural areas*," De Soto writes. Ultimately, the formerly rural population recognized that the legal system was designed to exclude them and "*discovered that they must compete not only against people but also against the system.*"

It is this reality of state-enforced barriers to entry in the marketplace that drove the migrants to join the "informal economy." They chose to purposefully and voluntarily break the law in pursuit of financial gain and a better standard of living. Imagine if a collection of Freedom Cells dedicated themselves to welcoming and allying with incoming "illegal" immigrants in an effort to help them understand the value of the informal or counter-economy. This "Agorist Welcoming Committee" could help connect immigrants to an underground network of black and gray market services, including access to community healthcare and untaxed employment. By choosing to relinquish fear-driven xenophobia, the *Conscious Agorist Movement* could create a cadre of self-aware immigrant agorists capable of wielding their collective economic power. Individuals are unpredictable, and there is no telling how people are going to act or behave once they move someplace new. Perhaps this fear of the unknown is what pushes many to make assumptions about strangers. Regardless, we have the power to influence newcomers in our communities, and in the case of immigrants, they are prone to favor counter-economic activity since there are so many legal restrictions preventing them from entering the statist economy. The revolution is in the conversations and we should seize every opportunity to organize with immigrants to overthrow statist, authoritarian borders.

PART 3 — CREATING CONSCIOUS AGORAS

The goal of this final part of the Manifesto of the Free Humans pertains to both of our specific preferences for a Conscious Agora existing in a stateless society. It is important to remember that we do not believe in one-size-fits-all models, and are not attempting to state that every free, conscious agora should organize in the fashion described in the following pages. Obviously, our subjective preferences are contained in these chapters, but we see our ideal intentional community as existing among the myriad of diverse, unique communities that will exist in a truly freed marketplace of ideas. We encourage the reader to take our words and review them and compare to your own values and principles. Do our ideas measure up to your vision? If not, please take what you can learn from our efforts and adapt it to your community's specific needs.

We believe in freedom and thus we believe in diversity. Our vision of an intentional community will be one among the many coexisting communities, microstates, communes, neighborhoods, and other yet-to-be-discovered ways of self-organizing. The actual formation of such a community is slated to begin in early 2020. We will spend the next four years building towards this goal via the Freedom Cell movement. While the political system continues to disappoint the masses, Freedom Cells and agorism offer a bright future.

The next three chapters explain the Points of Unity for this coming intentional community: Sovereignty of the Individual, *PermAgora*, and Mindfulness. The triangle on the following page represents the culmination of these three principles. When combined with a counter-economic strategy, these principles lead to the realization of the Conscious Agora.

Chapter 14
Sovereignty of the Individual

W hen imagining our ideal community, there are several considerations to make. As we have discussed, there is a vast spectrum of opinions regarding property, the environment, immigration, and the organizational structure society will take. No matter the agenda item, our first question is always: *does the action impede upon another free person's right to live free from coercion and violence?* Those in favor of animal equality could also expand the question to ask, do my actions prevent *any life* from living free of coercion and violence?

Whichever principle you start with, the goal is the reduction of violence and oppression in our everyday lives. This is a foundational principle for the establishment of a Conscious Agora. As mentioned earlier, this principle is known as the *sovereignty of the individual* and was first expounded by Josiah Warren in the 1840s. In his book *Partisans of Freedom: A Study in American Anarchism*, William O. Reichert describes Warren as the "chief architect of libertarianism." Despite his best efforts, many modern anarchists are oblivious to his powerful body of work.

Warren wholeheartedly believed that any action taken to limit the rights of the individual was immoral and would lead to strife. In his manifesto he writes:

"The forming of societies or any other artificial combinations IS the first, greatest, and most fatal mistake ever committed by legislators and by reformers. That all these combinations require the surrender of the natural sovereignty of the INDIVIDUAL over her or his person, time, property and responsibilities, to the government of the combination. That this tends to prostrate the individual--To reduce him to a mere piece of a machine; involving others in responsibility for his acts, and being involved in responsibilities for the acts and sentiments of his associates; he lives & acts, without proper control over his own affairs, without certainty as to the results of his actions, and almost without brains that he dares to use on his own account; and consequently never realizes the great objects for which society is professedly formed."

Warren came to these conclusions after his experiences with Robert Owen, a British social reform activist who had launched a utopian community in Scotland before coming to America to launch another community in New Harmony, Indiana. Warren was living in Cincinnati, Ohio until he decided move his whole family to New Harmony to join Owen's community. The decision would greatly affect his philosophical path. Warren would later note that New Harmony failed due to the decision to put communal interests above that of each individual. With his newfound appreciation for individuality, Warren left New Harmony in 1927 and headed back to Cincinnati to further develop his theories. In 1847, Warren established a community known as Utopia just thirty miles from Cincinnati. Finally, in 1850, Warren went to New York and established Modern Times on Long Island. The community was successful for several years under the direction of Josiah Warren and his theories. Eventually, Modern Times would evolve into the city known as Brentwood. The town was described as a thriving community with a printing plant, a carriage factory, and a furniture factory. A place where every house had a garden, every person was free to live as they pleased, and there were no police, courts, jails, or even a single recorded crime. Residents reported that conflicts were handled by isolating or refusing to do business with those who chose to violate the sovereignty of other individuals.

All of this was made possible because Josiah Warren founded the community on the basic understanding that every individual's right to self-ownership would be respected. "*The great principle of human elevation was perceived to be the SOVEREIGNTY OF EVERY INDIVIDUAL over his or her Person and Time and Property and Responsibilities,*" Warren wrote. He also believed that only through a process called "Disconnection" could an individual untangle their connections to other human beings and truly respect the sovereignty of the individual. Warren extended his individualist vision to economics, stating that a version of the Labor Theory of Value, or what he called Equitable Commerce, ensured that unequal exchanges did not take place. In this way, Warren can be seen as the earliest proponent of mutualist economics. Although we favor the subjective theory of value, we appreciate Josiah Warren's development of concepts like Time Banking and Labor Hours, which he arrived at through his Equitable Commerce theory. Ultimately, we completely accept the sovereignty of every individual to organize their economic transactions how they please, regardless of our own personal preferences.

It is Warren's Sovereignty of the Individual that will guide the intentional community we plan to establish. This will require purchasing land and, unfortunately, paying property taxes. Of course, agorists should always strive to opt out of taxation. However, in the current political climate it seems inevitable that free humans will be best served with a piece of land with which to build for the future and propagate the message of freedom. By purchasing land before the state collapses or is defeated, we hope to be proactive in our efforts to build the counter-economy and the coming agora. It has become increasingly difficult to sit by and live among "mainstream" society, all the while contributing to unsustainable systems that do not serve to harmonize relationships between the inhabitants of this planet.

The hope is that we are able to gain a foothold on a piece of land and continue to propagate the agorist message until the state becomes weak enough (and the agora strong enough) that our community decides we are no longer under threat to pay property taxes, a strategy we will explore in detail later in this section. The freedom of land also allows a Freedom Cell to grow their own food, cultivate independence via counter-economic activity, and maintain a level of privacy from governments and their loyalists. A Freedom Cell could use the land to build community centers for hosting meet-ups, counter-economic markets, radical music festivals, skill shares, and cell building.

Within this free agora each member of the Freedom Cell will be free to make a living as they please (provided they respect individual sovereignty), use any currency they choose, grow what food they want, and build whatever home they choose. Obviously, a community can decide to only permit vegans, for example, or allow only sustainable methods of building to be used, but each individual entering into the community will be made fully aware of any contractual obligations that may exist. Our main goal is to establish that every single person choosing to live within the walls of our community is free to do as they please, provided they are not harming anyone else. The intentional community that will begin in 2020 only has two other stipulations for potential community members, both of which make up the remaining corners of our triangle.

Chapter 15
PermAgora

A key aspect of The Conscious Resistance is that humanity needs to re-evaluate the nature of our interpersonal relationships and connections. Not only when it comes to each other, but our relationship with animals and the planet itself. The morality of our relationship with the planet and animals should be reviewed, and in fact, must be reviewed if we want to survive with any type of prosperity. If the goal is consistency, we must take the time to examine and challenge every one of our preconceived notions of the world. Ultimately, this comes down to an individual choosing to review and adjust their own behaviors and actions, not only in relation to taxation and voting, but every single one of our daily habits which are not aligned with our principles.

When imagining our ideal community, we do not envision a place where the land is exploited, polluted, and stripped of the finite resources located within the Earth. We have no intention of living in a community where the Earth is viewed as an object to dominate, a means to an end, or a backdrop to our consumerist lifestyles. Refusing to initiate violence in our relationships should extend to all our relationships, including the relationship with this planet. These realizations led us to the next corner of the triangle: *PermAgora*, or sustainability. We wish to create an intentional community that honors the sovereignty of every individual to be free to make their own choices provided they harm no other. In our community, this would extend to our philosophy on the environment. This means that any permanent resident or visitor to this community would be voluntarily choosing to live in harmony with the environment and community at large. We are not interested in forcing other free humans outside our community to live as we choose in this ideal intentional community. Instead, we hope to live as an example of what is possible when conscious individuals choose to change their own behavior without the need for threats from the state or other forms of coercion.

A great example of living in a low-impact lifestyle without the force of law is the environmental activist and adventurist Rob Greenfield. He is known for taking on extreme adventures in order to highlight environmental damage and waste. Greenfield has taken several bicycle tours across the U.S., dumpster diving in every city and small town he stopped in. Greenfield estimates that he has dumpster dived in over 2,000 dumpsters in over 25 states. In 2016, he launched his "Trash Me" project which saw him spend a month wearing all of the trash he created. Using a special suit, he walked around for 30 days with bags of trash attached to him. All of this was done to raise awareness about important aspects of the fight for a healthier species and planet. The best part of all? Greenfield is not out there calling for government intervention. He recognizes that the only way to heal the planet is through individual awareness and action. Hopefully, with the help of people like Rob, we can help inspire our species to action before our time on this planet expires.

Within our intentional community, sustainable practices will be employed in the process of building shelter, growing food, and working with animals. Sustainable means using technologies and practices that do not deplete resources and create as little waste as possible. We imagine a community living in harmony with the environment and leading low-impact lifestyles. Some activists have also begun calling for "regenerative" practices that not only sustain the environment, but regenerate the soil and return it to its naturally healthy state. In this way, "Regenerative Activism" might be thought of as taking actions that sustain and regenerate the health of the individual, as well as the community at large. When we began researching sustainable practices and experimenting with urban farming, we consistently found references to Permaculture.

Permaculture is a portmanteau of permanent agriculture and culture. It refers to an approach to designing communities and perennial agricultural systems based on relationships found in nature. It has also expanded into a philosophy on how we interact with the world. Permaculture systems have the potential to be far more productive and much less energy intensive than conventional agriculture. Permaculture was first developed by Austrian farmer Sepp Holzer on his own farm in the early 1960s and then further theoretically developed by Australians Bill Mollison and David Holmgren during the 1970s. Essential to Permaculture is the idea that agricultural systems should not require a lot of work to maintain, they should improve the land, and produce in ways that provide for humans, animals, and other local ecosystems.

There are three ethics central to permaculture philosophy: earth care, people care, and fair share. Earth care means to rebuild the natural capital of the environment and to take care of the soil. People care simply means caring for family, community companionship, and self. This also involves self-reliance and working to reduce the production and consumption of unnecessary material resources. Fair share means to voluntarily set limits on consumption and redistribute the surplus back into the community. This is not a call for centralized management of resources, but instead a recognition of the need for self-organizing among sovereign individuals. In a truly freed market individuals will prefer to do business with communities operating with sustainability and environmental awareness in mind. Those who practice unsustainable practices and environmental destruction will quickly lose support and economic power.

In his book, *Permaculture: Principles and Pathways beyond Sustainability*, David Holmgren expanded on the permaculture philosophy with the addition of 12 principles. We will not be examining each principle individually, however, they are provided to emphasize the mentality behind the philosophy of permaculture.

1. Observe and Interact
2. Catch and Store Energy
3. Obtain a Yield
4. Apply Self-Regulation and Accept Feedback
5. Use and Value Renewable Resources and Services
6. Produce No Waste
7. Design From Patterns to Details
8. Integrate Rather Than Segregate
9. Use Small and Slow Solutions
10. Use and Value Diversity
11. Use Edges and Value the Marginal
12. Creatively Use and Respond to Change

Permaculture can be viewed as a less forceful, more mindful, approach to living off the land. Agorism is also a less forceful, mindful approach applied to economics and exchange. Both philosophies encourage creation and building. When combined together we get *PermAgora*, the synthesis of permaculture and agorism and the application of both approaches simultaneously. PermAgora is a developing school of thought based on the research of permaculture student Eric McCool. In Eric's words, "*The goal is the restoration of the natural systems of the planet, and changes in our way of life so that we need not be dominated by violence and coercion.*" To remove the violence and coercion from every aspect of our lives we must adopt new ways of thinking about the environment. The coming Conscious Agora will benefit from an alliance of Freedom Cells practicing PermAgora. We hope to lead the way.

Chapter 16
Strong Hearts and Revolutionary Minds

The next essential piece of the triangle of liberation is the concept of "Mindfulness." This simple concept could be also be termed "mindful awareness" or simply, awareness. Mindfulness represents the reality that we must apply a sense of heightened awareness, a constantly self-aware state of mind, to every one of our actions if we hope to continue the spiritual evolution of our species. Throughout The Conscious Resistance series, we have stressed that achieving peace and freedom is a task that requires more than just knowledge or logic. Compassion and communication skills are also essential if one is attempting to create positive change in the world. In past generations, people on different ends of political and religious spectrums have seen each other as mortal enemies. This behavior has negatively impacted living standards on all sides (except those ruling from above). When groups with divergent views are able to set aside their differences, the standard of living is typically elevated on all sides. When groups are locked in endless war or conflict everyone suffers, except, once again, those ruling from above. Oftentimes, feuds and conflicts continue due to manipulation from the establishment. Sometimes, these disputes are simply the result of inflated egos on both sides. In many cases, people seem more concerned with being right than finding solutions. It is this mentality that we are working to heal.

The term "The Conscious Resistance" was born out of an awareness that the world is in a state of imbalance due to the influence of small groups of elitists working to use the state and corporate power to live off the fruits of the rest of the world. It was also born from our individual realization that those who wish to control and manipulate others do so because of their own pain. That pain is absorbed by the population and then turned into fear and anger. This results in states of anxiety and disharmony which allows for the continued manipulation at the hands of the same fearful elite. Our ambition is to lead the way by being open and vulnerable about our own struggles and triumphs. For the two of us this means incorporating meditation, positive affirmations, visualization, and other practices into our message of anarchism. Because of this decision to focus on healing and interpersonal relationships, The Conscious Resistance could also be referred to as *Holistic Anarchism*.

The term holistic is related to the theory known as Holism, which argues that *"the universe and nature should be viewed in terms of interacting wholes (as of living organisms) that are more than the mere sum of elementary particles."* Holistic is defined as "relating to or concerned with wholes or with complete systems rather than with the analysis of, treatment of, or dissection into parts." For example, holistic medicine typically treats the entire body and mind in an attempt to address the root of an illness as opposed to only focusing on treating symptoms. The field of Holistic ecology examines humanity and the environment as a single system. When examining whole systems rather than the individual pieces of a particular problem, you are likely to come away with a completely different perspective and thus, a different solution than you would find when studying the individual components.

Holistic anarchism posits that the end of statism and authoritarianism will not come by examination of political and economic theory alone. The fight against the state should be viewed holistically, meaning we should view the problem in terms of the whole system. This means reflecting on all the forms of oppression faced by the free people of our world. This also means being honest about the ways our personal habits and prejudices are contributing to the oppression we see. By understanding the fight against the state as a battle with many arenas, and choosing to reflect on the steps we can take as individuals, we are employing holistic anarchism. Ultimately, it is not just the tyrants in office, or the theft of taxation that is keeping us from being free. It is our own self-limiting thoughts and actions which truly hold us back.

In *Finding Freedom in an Age of Confusion*, we explored the concept of Nonviolent Communication (NVC), a conflict resolution technique that was promoted by activist and psychologist Marshall Rosenberg. The premise of NVC is simple: instead of arguing about who is right or wrong, and who must win or lose, people should strive to have win-win interactions by focusing on ensuring that the needs of each person are met. The goal is to find solutions to problems by addressing the unmet needs of everyone in the equation. Again, from a holistic anarchist perspective the way we communicate with other free people is equally important to making sure our arguments are sound. It's extremely difficult to have a rational discussion when both parties feel their concerns are not being heard. Such a battle of insecurities is not likely to lead to a better understanding of one another. How can we ever hope to possibly influence others if they choose to communicate with anger, aggression, or impatience? We recognize that human connection is essential on the path to liberty. We lead by example and learn to communicate without violence, condescension, or passive aggressive tendencies.

Daryl Davis is a shining example of how the power of love, understanding and compassion can overcome the darkness of hate and bigotry. Davis, a black, 58-year-old blues musician and author, has managed to successfully convince hundreds of racists to quit the KKK. Davis goes deep behind enemy lines to Klan rallies and white supremacist meetings and attempts to make friends with people who hate him. Davis says he has been doing it for over 30 years. He is even responsible for single-handedly causing the entire Maryland chapter of the KKK to dissolve. Years ago, Davis began seeking out members of the KKK so he could learn more about racism first-hand. In the beginning, his initial goal was just to try to gain some type of understanding of why these people choose to be racist. On at least two separate occasions has had to defend himself from violent Klan members. Most often, though, these meetings happen without any incident. While there are plenty of tense moments, the interactions between Davis and the racists he encounters are surprisingly pleasant. Instead of focusing heavily on race and areas of disagreement, Davis instead tries to focus on areas of agreement and steers the conversation towards common ground.

"If you spend just five minutes with your arch enemy, you will discover that you have something in common, and if you spend ten minutes, you'll find you have something else in common," he says.

Davis has a closet filled with Klansman uniforms, all of them given to him by friends and former Klansman who quit the racist cult as a result of their friendship. One KKK member and Baltimore City Police officer even gave Davis both his Klansman uniform and his police officer's uniform. The approach that Davis has taken in converting racists into friends is the same approach that anarchists can use to turn statists into free thinking human beings.

One such anarchist attempting to find common ground is Sterlin Lujan. Rather than holistic or conscious anarchism, he refers to his approach as "relationalism" or relational anarchism. Lujan, also known as the "Psychologic Anarchist," is a professional writer, editor, research assistant, and aspiring counseling psychologist with a BA in psychology. In his essay Anarchy and Emotion Pt. 2, Luxan explains his viewpoint:

"I call it relationalism. It is the philosophy that promotes absence of rulers and total freedom through relationships and social healing, rather than through the traditional routes of argumentation, persuasion, or economic theorizing. Current conceptions of anarchism have been hyper focused on the LEM Axis. That is, they are geared toward solving Logical, Economic, and Moral problems of society and government."

Instead, Luxan suggests employing empathy when dealing with others.

"If people are attuned to each other's feelings, there is less of an opportunity for violence and aggression to erupt. This is the application of the therapeutic alliance to society-at-large for building a freer, more psychologically stable world. In order to build a social order based on logical, moral, or economic truths, humans must first grapple with their emotional worlds and how they relate and interact with all people. They must learn to heal each other through being together and uniting, in much the same way that a counselor helps a client get better through their mutually agreed upon alliance. In this sense, the philosophy of relationalism sees the anarchist as a social healer that creates communities and nurtures love."

Luxan's relationalism is perfectly aligned with our message of holistic anarchism. We applaud his efforts to explore the intersection of anarchism and psychology, in the same way we have explored anarchism and spirituality. Our hope is that the message of freedom and empowerment will continue to grow until there exist anarchists in a variety of fields of research, each pushing for true freedom through the filter of their particular area of expertise.

The evolution of consciousness is absolutely necessary for true, lasting freedom to be achieved. We boldly stand by our positions and arguments made in this series, but the reality is that none of the solutions presented will succeed if the broken and confused people of this world refuse to do the necessary internal work for individual healing to transpire.

The insecurities, doubts, and fears will differ person to person, so a holistic self-assessment is needed to decipher where to begin your healing process. If we want to heal the deeper root causes which allow violence to be perpetuated among our species, we must be willing to face ourselves. If we fail to recognize healing and personal growth as a vital part of the fight for a freer, ethical world we are setting ourselves up for failure. Our only hope in creating a free society based on mutual aid, voluntary association, and individual sovereignty is to embark upon a path of mindfulness, reflection, forgiveness, acceptance, healing, empowerment, and finally, self-actualization. These seven steps are the ongoing path towards The Conscious Resistance.

Chapter 17
Mobility vs. Homesteading

It is a wonderful experience to witness the beautiful expressions of diversity that spring forth as individuals pursue their own version of freedom. After all, freedom is a personal and individual experience. There is no one size fits all models or path to freedom; the outcome depends on individual preferences and circumstances. This principle holds true with the agorist lifestyle and engaging in counter-economics. Although we are describing what an intentional community may look like from our perspective, some freedom seekers view mobility as the ultimate expression of freedom and may choose to live nomadic lifestyles. Others may choose to opt out of community or neighborhood living and live the life of a hermit. All of these paths are valid and compatible with agorism.

When creating the ideal living situation, many variables must be taken into consideration. *Where do you want to live? How many people will live with you? What kind of community do you want? Where will you get your food? How will you make an income or provide for basic necessities?*

For some individuals, organizing into Freedom Cells will naturally lead to forming communities and communal living. Some will choose to live in the same neighborhoods or towns, as in the Texas Freedom Grounds, and others will choose to share land. But what of those who say they don't want to live one place? What about the restless travelers and the noble nomads who would rather live life on the road? Is there a better opportunity to realize freedom in your life and the life of your family by choosing to live nowhere and everywhere?

One of the main reasons we argue for establishing a community with land to tend and defend is the ability to grow your own food and produce your own goods. Growing your own food is a huge step towards independence. Although some creative folks have engineered ways to grow food on top of vehicles, it is extremely difficult to sustain yourself this way. Also, having a piece of land allows for the building of shelters and structures which can store supplies, food, and everything you need to survive an emergency. Granted, one could simply rent out a storage space and keep all these items stored until needed, but what happens when the *shit* hits the fan and you are on the road, thousands of miles away from your survival supplies?

We believe it is essential for Freedom Cells to begin thinking about having a location to rendezvous in the event of an emergency. If you live in the city, this might include two places; one within the city as a meeting point, and another meeting place outside of the city limits, ideally on a piece of land where you have supplies waiting. If you find yourself on the road during an emergency, you may have trouble finding a safe place to stay and supplies to sustain you. Hopefully, we will soon have a large Freedom Cell Network across the globe that will ensure none of our brothers and sisters go without help. On the other hand, if you and your family are living in a bus, RV, or simply towing your tiny house everywhere you go, you have a certain level of freedom that landowners do not. Two great examples of nomadic anarchist families are the Blushes in Austin, Texas and The Undocumented Humans in Arizona. Most of the families and individuals we know who are living the nomadic life say they enjoy a level of freedom they did not know while paying rent on land, houses, or apartments. There may be times when an emergency requires bugging out of your house or land. The ability to have your house and your vehicle in one machine is definitely a benefit in this situation. Nomads with vehicles will likely have most of their important possessions with them, and will not be faced with the difficult choice of what to take and what to leave behind.

Some free people will prefer solitary travel, either in their vehicles or as hitchhiking adventurers living off the counter-economy. Others will want to be more secluded and choose to homestead land in the wilderness, far away from other homes and communities. Perhaps this person prefers the independence of seclusion, or they have social anxiety or other issues that make a rural lifestyle preferable. Although the hermits might not be directly connected to a community by physical proximity, they can be connected digitally through FreedomCells.org or other online groups that allow for organizing and exchanging with other freedom-minded individuals.

Whether your path finds you hiding out in caves, sailing on the freedom fleet, nomading on the bus, relaxing in the neighborhood, or living in a community of thousands, the goal is freedom. No matter what living situation you choose there are dozens of methods to participate in the counter-economy. Our preferred place of residence should not prevent us from establishing a powerful alliance of interconnected and interlocking Freedom Cells and free communities.

Chapter 18
Getting Off the Control Grid and Defending the Agora

When discussing the idea of a free society, one of the most frequently asked questions is *"how do we get from here to there?"* The transition is without a doubt the most challenging step on the path to freedom, but throughout this book we have laid the foundation for a possible future. Now, we will end this journey by exploring how we can sever our involuntary relationship with the state, once and for all. Our goal is to establish alternative ways of living prior to our emancipation from government. These alternatives are the lifeboats that will allow us to escape the sinking ship. This is where the importance of Freedom Cells, counter-economics and competing with state services and institutions comes into play.

As free-thinking people begin to create free communities in geographical regions that are still disputed or claimed by governments, there will be a need for self-defense. Some free humans will also want to agitate the existing government in hopes of weakening it and spurring on its demise. Our primary focus should be on growing the counter-economy and agora and we do this by reducing our dependence and support of the existing government. We need a sustained, coordinated campaign of noncooperation, tax resistance, counter-economic activity, and mass opting out of the structures operated by state and corporate power. This should be done in tandem with a push for individual healing, community building, and compassionate activism.

We believe tax resistance is absolutely necessary to weaken the state. Those invested in the counter-economy are already taking sales tax away from the state and if you can make your money "off the books" or "under the table" do not hesitate. If you can be paid in alternative currencies even better. Every cent you take from the state is a victory on the path to realizing the Conscious Agora. Some Freedom Cells may choose to continue to pay their taxes, or avoid the income tax and sales tax when possible, until the time arrives where the state is too weak to pursue them or they are capable of defending themselves from thieving tax collectors. Connected cells and communities may choose to band together to coordinate an organized tax resistance campaign to further agitate and weaken the state.

If we work diligently, we can make a coordinated tax resistance campaign go viral across Freedom Cells spread throughout the U.S. If we are able to prevent the state from taking funds that equal the annual defense budget, we believe the state will take notice of their waning influence and power.

The U.S. government's revenue from federal, state, and local sources were estimated to be 7 trillion during 2016. About 4.6 trillion of that comes from income and payroll taxes, the exact taxes one avoids by joining the counter-economy. During 2016, the Department of Defense (responsible for the U.S. military) had a budget of 582 billion. As the numbers show, it would only require a loss of less than one trillion dollars in income and payroll taxes to remove the budget for the Department of Defense. This would make it difficult (not impossible) for the state to continue to wage war and it would send a message that the people are getting organized. The state will be forced to have the Federal Reserve print massive sums of money which will only hasten the push towards hyperinflation and economic chaos. Amidst this chaos, the agorists will jump into action and offer counter-economic services and assistance to those who chose not to prepare. The state could also take money away from popular government services like welfare, veteran assistance, etc., and redirect it towards the war effort but this is also likely to be an unpopular move. Will the people really stand by and do nothing as their government takes the services they have become accustomed to in the name of more war? Let's hope not. Either way, this will serve to weaken the power and influence of the State.

As the existing government's economic power and support wither away, it will be more difficult for them to hire enforcers to follow their arbitrary orders, and formerly proud law-abiding, tax-paying citizens will flock to the underground economy. As this process takes places, the tables will turn and there will be a shift of power between the free people and the governments. The state would no longer have the upper hand in terms of raw physical strength. The drones, tanks, and other machinery of death will no longer be affordable for tyrants now that their formerly compliant tax cattle began to leave the farm by withdrawing their support for the system. Likewise, the soldiers and police forces who support oppression and suppression of revolution will have to rethink following orders once the propaganda of the state is destroyed. In fact, even in today's political climate, the government is having increasing difficulty finding people to fly their drones and wear their badges. On January 4, 2015, Air Force Chief of Staff General Mark Welsh sent an internal memo to General Herbert "Hawk" Carlisle complaining about drone pilots quitting in record numbers. Welsh said he feared that this exodus could cripple drone "combat readiness" for years to come. Indeed, military and police forces are constantly lowering standards and raising wages in attempts to lure more people into their order following campaign. Considering this, imagine the impact that could be made if large numbers of people began rejecting the government's legitimacy and organizing to strangle its support system.

The outcomes of this strategy are real and can be seen throughout history. The counter-economy can and will overtake the state when enough people are participating. One of the most obvious and historical examples of this is seen in the fall of the Soviet Union, which was, in part, brought on by widespread smuggling, tax avoidance and other black-market activities. The underground economy was a part of everyday life for most people living in the Soviet Union, as it was actually necessary for their survival in many cases. Eventually, the ever-growing restrictions and rations on the people stimulated the growth of the counter economy, and people began to trade untaxed goods and services until the government was starved of resources and support. At the time, Berkeley economist Gerard Roland noted that in the Soviet Union, *"The logic of the second economy tended over time to undermine the logic of the command system and to lead to expanding black markets."*

This observation was later confirmed by Vladimir G. Treml and Michael V. Alexeev in their study, *The Second Economy and the Destabilization Effect of Its Growth on the State Economy in the Soviet Union: 1965-1989.* The study found that the disparity between legal income and legal spending grew significantly in the period between 1965 and 1989, meaning that people were spending much more money than they were making on the books, pointing to widespread black-market activity. In their study, Treml and Alexeev conclude that the counter economy was largely responsible for the fall of the Soviet Union.

This was done entirely by accident, simply for the sake of survival, and even under these conditions the existing government collapsed. However, without the philosophy of agorism, anarchism or even libertarianism to follow through on this accomplishment, the oppressed people of the Soviet Union allowed a new government to be formed, and fell into bondage yet again. The collapse of the Soviet Union shows us that the counter-economy can be used to weaken, or even overthrow very powerful governments, but this victory will be short-lived if people fail to follow through and apply the philosophy of agorism to their counter-economic activity.

When the state does get to a weakened point, fighting back against its agents becomes easier, and it becomes possible to physically push them back out of territories claimed by the agora. This dynamic can be seen in many developing countries where the central governments are very weak. When a protest or uprising happens in a place like this, it is not unusual to see heavily armed and equipped government agents retreat from mobs of protesters that greatly outnumber them. This is not something that is possible in the U.S. today, but it is something that could be possible once the counter-economy takes enough power away from the State.

Still, we must remember that our goal is not to initiate violence against the State. Our goal is not a violent revolution, or revolution at all. The word implies revolving and going in circles, which is exactly what we should expect should we initiate force. As Samuel Konkin commented in *the New Libertarian Manifesto*, *"never initiate any act of violence regardless how likely a 'libertarian' result may appear. To do so is to reduce yourself to a statist. There are no exceptions to this rule. Either you are fundamentally consistent or not."*

We want to abolish the state and create a world free of oppression and suffering, but we must not lose sight of ourselves in the pursuit of this goal. Every revolutionary throughout history who chose violence ended up becoming a monster and a shadow of what they pursued. Remain heart centered no matter how violent the state becomes or how divisive the political climate. We are after an evolution of hearts and minds. To sustain a long-term evolution (whether a physical fight against oppressors or a battle of hearts and minds) we must cultivate physical, mental, and spiritual strength and awareness. We believe the ideas presented in this series are a handbook which can be helpful in leading one down the path to freedom and autonomy. Finally, we are not claiming to be enlightened masters speaking of peace yet failing to embody the principles. Both of us have made plenty of mistakes and have much room to grow. However, we believe the principles and lifestyle espoused within our books are ideals to strive for. The Conscious Resistance offers the quickest way to lead our world towards a freer, ethical, and spiritually empowered world.

PART 4—UNDERSTANDING HOLISTIC ANARCHISM

We offer these final two essays as a deeper introduction into what we have come to call Holistic Activism or Holistic Anarchism. We hope the foundation we have laid will lead to a growth of the Holistic Anarchist movement.

Chapter 19
Defining Holistic Activism / Anarchism

(The following essay serves as a primer on the emerging field of Holistic Activism. More specifically, the essay introduces the concepts behind Holistic Anarchism.)

The process of becoming an activist typically begins when an individual is made aware of an injustice that strikes them to the core and moves them to act in some fashion. Once a problem has been identified, some individuals will expand further energy to identify the people and institutions they hold responsible. The individual's knowledge is expanded in a particular area, they experience discomfort from their newfound awareness, and finally, they decide to find a meaningful way to address the issue. This may take the form of holding signs in the street, writing letters, organizing email and phone blast campaigns, pursuing blogging and journalism, confronting those responsible for the problems, or taking more extreme forms of confronting power.

When applying the holistic perspective to activism, the goal is to move beyond simply identifying the problems we see in the world and move into a mode of action oriented around understanding how our individual actions and habits are contributing to the crises we see. It is a fairly simple task to point fingers at the atrocious and immoral actions unfolding around the world. A more rewarding perspective is gained by examining our individual actions. By holding ourselves accountable and asking, "How am I contributing to X?" we can make strides in aligning our thoughts and words with our actions.

In order to do this, one must consciously choose to go beyond the surface-level interpretations of political crimes, environmental destruction, rampant surveillance, the loss of civil liberties, mass extinctions, and a host of other activist concerns. A Holistic Activist identifies the injustice and begins to look for clues—much like a crime scene investigator—that contributes to a fuller understanding of the crime at hand. The Holistic Activist pays particular attention to any evidence that leads back to their own behaviors and habits. Rather than ending the effort to bring justice and morality to the world once the problem has been identified, the Holistic Activist does not stop until they can clearly see their own role in creating or contributing to the issue. Let's take a look at two particular activist movements and examine them through the Holistic Activist lens.

End the Fed & March Against Monsanto

According to the official doctrine, the Federal Reserve System is the central bank of the U.S. tasked with regulating monetary policy. In reality, "the Fed" is responsible for the constant devaluing of the U.S. dollar (or the Federal Reserve note, as it is officially known) via inflationary practices. In the few decades, millions of people have awoken to the true nature of the central banking system and began actively opposing it. Beginning in 2008, activists around the U.S. organized annual "End the Fed" rallies aimed at raising awareness regarding the economic theft and debt created by the Fed.

Activists gathered at all twelve Federal Reserve branches and sub-branches hosting speeches, rallies, marches, and selling End the Fed propaganda. The organizers spent time, energy, and money to pay speakers, pay for city permits, rent stages and booths, and promote these events. The activists identified the problem—economic theft and debt—and the institution responsible for the problems—the Federal Reserve. Did they stop to take a deeper look—a holistic look—at the situation? Overall, it would seem they did not. The organizers and activists spent months planning these events and hours hosting them. It's safe to assume their goal was to raise awareness about the problems with the Fed and discourage support of the institution. However, when the organizers paid their speakers for their time or when the vendors sold their "End the Fed" t-shirts, they more than likely exchanged Federal Reserve notes.

This is where the inconsistency in thoughts, words, and actions can be seen most clearly. From a Holistic Activist perspective, one does not achieve change or solve a problem by participating in the problem. If you want to "End the Fed," you are not likely to accomplish such a task by continuing your involvement with, use of, and tacit support for the Federal Reserve System. Quite simply, the Fed will not disappear if the people continue to play the game. A Holistic Activist would recognize their contribution to the Federal Reserve System and seek alternative means of exchange whenever possible.

Similarly, many of those participating in the March Against Monsanto experienced a disconnect between stated goals and actions. On May 25, 2013, over 300 cities around the world marched and rallied as part of the March Against Monsanto campaign. The name indicated a focus on biotechnology giant Monsanto, but the movement was a broad coalition of organic advocates, food liberty activists, and environmentalists. The participants in the March Against Monsanto included those who opposed the revolving door between the U.S. government and Monsanto, others who were generally against food made with genetically engineered ingredients, activists concerned about the abundant use of pesticides, and those concerned about the environment at large.

Unfortunately, many of the actions were explicitly focused on gathering large numbers in the streets and not enough energy was put towards education and solutions. Besides organizing in the streets to raise awareness, a Holistic Activist would also make an effort to stand for something. In this example, that would mean organizing community gardening skillshares where the marchers learn how to grow their own pesticide-free, non-GMO crops or begin volunteering at a local urban farm. This creates consistency between one's desired goals — raising awareness about the problems with Monsanto — and one's habits and actions.

Another opportunity to think holistically in this example deals with one's diet. If you were marching against Monsanto because of a desire to weaken the biotech industry, pesticide manufacturers, and/or the corporatist government, it would only make sense to limit your use of the products from these industries. This means not purchasing genetically modified products, including from grocery stores or restaurants. This could also mean only buying organic products. In addition, a Holistic Activist might begin reducing their reliance on traditional grocery stores by purchasing produce directly from farmers and gardeners at local markets. This action could be taken not only to avoid the Monsanto complex, but to lessen dependence on the unsustainable food distribution system.

This is what it means to think about activism holistically. If we each begin to take a holistic self-assessment and take a deep look at actions, we will begin to see the ways our actions are subtly allowing various injustices to continue in the world. Quite simply, when we do not account for our own inconsistencies, we work against our efforts to create a freer, ethical, and just world. This is why Holistic Activism is essential to moving into the next phase of human development and evolution. Our wisdom grows through self-reflection. As empowered individuals, and as a collective, we hold the power to free humanity from generations of bondage.

Holistic Anarchism

Anarchism is a political and social philosophy that rejects rulers and government on moral, economic, social, and/or religious grounds. It is a rich philosophy with a spectrum of schools of thought that often conflict with one another. However, anarchists generally believe that all human relationships should be free of coercion, force, and violence. Anarchists know that each human being is best equipped to rule their lives and order their affairs. Anarchists understand that communities can rely on their neighbors more often than they can rely on the government.

The Holistic perspective extends to the realm of anarchism once one acknowledges that the end of statism and authoritarianism will not come by examination of political and economic theory alone. Anarchists have a tendency to focus all of their energy on attempting to convert people via debates about the logic behind anarchism, the benefits of their particular ideal economic system, and/or the moral reasons to wave the Anarchist flag. Sterlin Lujan, writer and student of psychology, is another anarchist encouraging a shift beyond the current anarchist focus on debates. *"Current conceptions of anarchism have been hyper focused on the LEM Axis. That is, they are geared toward solving Logical, Economic, and Moral problems of society and government,"* Lujan writes.

To move beyond this hyper focus on the LEM Axis, we must engage in a holistic analysis of our struggle for freedom. By examining our personal actions and behaviors, we can begin the process of decentralizing, unplugging, and vacating the systems that are not consistent with our values and principles. The method we choose to achieve this as individuals and as communities will depend upon our ability to honestly assess our lives as we search for the root causes of our inconsistencies.

From the HolAn perspective, this process involves looking at six areas of your life: Economy, Education, Food, Energy, Communication, and Relationships. In the image below, each section represents one of these areas of your life and the two sections inside the "A" could be thought of as your internal world. Once you begin this process, you may discover other areas of your life that are inconsistent. Take on one area and one inconsistency at a time. Be patient with yourself. Actually attempting to "be the change you wish to see" is not easy work, it requires discipline and dedication. If your goal as an anarchist is to see the end of the state or the authoritarian mindset, you must take action that is consistent with these stated goals. Spend time looking at these six areas (and especially your internal world) to see where your actions are supporting statism or authoritarianism and how you might be able to remove yourself from these situations.

For example, when it comes to the economy, you may have a distaste for supporting and patronizing the Wall Street banks that caused the 2008 financial crisis, as well as numerous other crises in the last century. The Federal Reserve is responsible for the decreasing value of the U.S. dollar via inflation. It might make your stomach turn every time you conduct a transaction using a Federal Reserve note. As a HolAn, you decide to quit using the banks and switch to a credit union or hide your money in a safe or under the mattress. Even further, you decide to get involved with the silver trade, a local barter network, and cryptocurrency. Each of these gives you the option to do business without supporting the State's central banking system. When it comes to the economy, the focus on identifying consistencies and making appropriate changes naturally lends itself to the strategy of counter-economics. As we have shown in this book, counter-economics boils down to is choosing to do as much of your business outside of the mainstream economy. This allows the individual to forego contributing to the taxation system and funding the state.

When dealing with education, it is important to recognize that we live in an increasingly decentralized age where big universities and the intellectual class are not the only source of knowledge. One need not drown in thousands of dollars in debt for an education. How can we think holistically about the source and type of education we receive?

With food, a HolAn perspective would examine the source of one's food, the cost to produce the food, the type of food, and what industries one's diet is supporting. Energy involves examining the source of our power. Are you (as most modern humans) dependent on electric companies and the city government for electricity? What steps can you take to decentralize from this system?

Communication involves challenging the devices and companies we support in our desire for digital communication. Do social media platforms you support pass their customers metadata on to spy agencies? Do the cell phone companies include backdoors for covert surveillance? Activists and anarchists need to reconsider centralizing all of our communication onto platforms with close relationships to the State. We can make efforts to support and make use of encrypted platforms and generally practice a culture of security.

Finally, the HolAn platform involves understanding our words, thoughts, and actions in our personal relationships. For many anarchists, this area may seem trivial, but the reality is that each of as individuals are in the process of becoming the best versions of ourselves. We are each at different points, and though some might not yet realize it, we are here to become empowered. To do this we must work to eliminate authoritarian and statist behaviors in our professional relationships, our romantic relationships, our relationships with our parents or our children, and with our own heart and mind. If we want to rid the world of authoritarian behavior and blind submission to authority, we must work on our individual doubts, fears, and insecurities. We must also lift our brothers and sisters up by helping them recognize their own power and potential. This particular focus on relationships is the nexus of Holistic and Relational Anarchism that we will explore in the next chapter.

The foundation of HolAn is the recognition that understanding the ins and outs of the political system or mastering economic theory alone will not lead to a freer world. We must also address our internal dialogue with ourselves, our physical actions, and the habits we carry throughout our life. By devoting equal attention to these areas as we do with the LEM Axis, we are taking a balanced, holistic approach to decentralizing our lives and becoming the sovereign beings we are meant to be.

Where does Holistic Anarchism fit within the pre-existing anarchist schools?

Most current schools of anarchism define themselves based on the type of economic arrangement they wish to see in their envisioned future anarchist society. Since Holistic Anarchists consciously choose not to lead with the LEM Axis, our school cannot be named based on economics. This does not mean we eschew economic study altogether. Rather, we choose to allow each individual to draw their own conclusions based on their own holistic analysis. Our preference is for counter-economics, but we recognize that other Holistic Anarchists may decide abandoning money altogether is the solution. To each their own. That is the beauty of this practice.

With our focus on individual action, we fall under the umbrella of Individualist Anarchism. However, we do not ignore the need for the community. We simply acknowledge that "the collective" whole is best served by allowing individuals to voluntarily and spontaneously organize as they please. Holistic Anarchism also abandons all initiatory violence in pursuit of a freer world. We believe in the right to defend one's own person or property, but we do not advocate for insurrection or senseless violence. To initiate violence, even against an oppressor, is to become the monsters we seek to bring to justice.

If we actually hope to achieve our goals as activists and/or anarchists, we must take actionable steps in our lives. We cannot focus exclusively on social media activism or wait for some "leader" to come along and save the day. Every one of us must take responsibility for our thoughts, words, and actions. We must take responsibility for our own healing. We don't have to do it alone. By focusing on examining every area of our lives and rectifying our inconsistencies, we can push towards the consistent application of anarchist theory and practice. We can build compassionate and empathetic communities filled with individuals who see their own value and worth and are not susceptible to state propaganda or the barks of some authoritarian wannabe. It starts with the way we communicate with ourselves and those closest to us. It grows through the promotion of the Holistic Self-Assessment. Once the Holistic Anarchist evolution touches every corner of our world, self-governance, self-reflection, and introspection will be woven into the fabric of our lives.

Chapter 20
The Intersection of Holistic and Relational Anarchism

The goal of a Holistic Activist is to move beyond focusing on the individual battles we face and taking a look at the bigger picture with a holistic lens. This means rather than simply identifying the problems in the world, we move towards an understanding of how our individual actions and habits are contributing to the crises we see. By holding ourselves accountable, we can make strides in aligning our thoughts and words with our actions. When it comes to Anarchism, the Holistic perspective means recognizing that each human being is best equipped to rule their lives and order their affairs and acknowledging that the end of statism and authoritarianism will not come by examination of political and economic theory alone. The Holistic Anarchist thinking is similar to what Sterlin Lujan calls Relational Anarchism or Relationalism. Lujan's writing on Relationalism focuses on integrating the therapeutic findings of psychotherapy with an anarchist political philosophy. According to Lujan, "Relational Anarchism is a standalone vector or field of thought under the umbrella of anarchism. In this perspective, relationships determine levels of human freedom. The process of human interaction is more important than content."

Relational Anarchism means that the way people communicate is equally important in creating a world free of government and authoritarian rulers. Relational Anarchists promote the absence of rulers via relationships and social healing. Indeed, Luxan has come to the same conclusion as Holistic Anarchists: "Humans must first grapple with their emotional worlds" and learn to heal in order for Anarchism and self-governance to flourish. He sees the Relational Anarchist as a "social healer that creates communities and nurtures love." Where other anarchists seek to angrily berate others or condemn them as imbeciles, Lujan says relational/spiritual/ holistic/soft/compassionate anarchists want to "bring more people together and bridge economic divides."

Lujan makes an effort to draw a distinction between Relationalism and reckless abandonment of all logical thought in favor of strictly emotional responses. In Anarchy and Emotion: A Heart-Based Philosophy for Transforming Society he writes:

"In addition, Relationalism is not an appeal to emotion from a logically fallacious sense, nor a suggestion that people get carried away with their emotion and forget higher brain functioning. It is only to say that focus of anarchistic interactions should be hinged on dialogue and rapport. It is literally the idea that we can exercise rational faculties but also stay in sync with our emotions and attachment to our fellow humans."

Lujan states that although relational anarchism "contains a lot of theory and speculation," the philosophy is based on evidence from counseling psychology and attachment theory. Lujan elaborates:

"In counseling psychology, evidenced-based practice suggests people are more likely to heal not as a result of some strategy or rhetorical intervention the counselor uses, but because of the bond developed by the counselor and client."

Laurie Meyers, writing for Counseling Today, confirmed the importance of the therapeutic alliance or "counseling relationship":

In 2001, a comprehensive research summary published in the journal Psychotherapy found that a strong therapeutic alliance was more closely correlated with positive client outcomes than any specific treatment interventions."

Lujan also looks to attachment theory as evidence of the value of the relational approach. Essentially, attachment theory teaches that humans thrive when their bonds with other humans are strong. *"Not only do they thrive, but they learn how to connect with others and work through problems,"* Luxan writes. If we encourage loving, harmonious relationships we are supporting the effort to create more secure and balanced adults. These efforts could see society restructure itself around principles and values which actually empower and uplift individuals through social healing.

The Holistic and Relational Anarchism Dynamic

The Relational and Holistic Anarchist schools have much common ground and it's worth taking the time to understand how they might be of value for those seeking a more compassionate and emotionally aware approach to empowering individuals and ridding the world of authoritarianism.

First, both Relational and Holistic Anarchism encourage individuals to move beyond the narrow focus of argumentation and economic theory in their attempts to spread the Anarchist gospel. As previously noted, Luxan notes that most Anarchists are *"hyper focused on the LEM Axis. That is, they are geared toward solving Logical, Economic, and Moral problems of society and government."* Holistic Anarchism is also about moving beyond the hyperfocus on the LEM Axis and instead opting to engage in self-reflection and personal responsibility. Holistic Anarchists believe that by acknowledging the ways we are contributing to systems of oppression and statism we can begin the process of vacating the systems that are not consistent with our values and principles as anarchists.

Relational and Holistic Anarchism not only discourage the focus on the LEM axis, but both schools of thought are also focused on giving the individual tools to achieve liberation. This type of Anarchist thinking places a heavy emphasis on self-awareness or mindfulness. This could come in the form of a therapy session with a counselor or friend, time in nature, meditation exercises (in solitude or with a group), an MDMA or psilocybin trip with a close friend or partner, or simply taking time to tune in to your own thoughts. Each of these practices takes time to implement and become a habitual part of an individual's life, but we believe the effort is worth the outcome. Despite the focus on individual strategies for achieving liberation, these schools do not ignore the potential for creating mutual aid groups (freedom cells, therapeutic alliances) which help establish communities full of compassionate anarchists.

If there are any "differences" between the goals of Holistic and Relational Anarchism, it may be that HolAn is focused on a bigger picture than perhaps Lujan and his Relational Anarchism proposes. Holistic Anarchism includes a focus on relationships, but also looks at how an individual spends their money (as well as the type of money), the source of a type of food being ingested, the source of education, the source of energy and power, and all the institutions that benefit from these choices. One could argue that all of these are choices about what relationships one wishes to have and with whom so they fit in the Relational Anarchist framework. We don't dispute the point, but will emphasize that the Holistic approach involves looking at every area of our lives and trying to root out statism, authoritarianism, and generally, support for oppressive and destructive institutions which are not in line with our principles or our goals.

Healthy Relationships as a Gateway to Freedom

Relational and Holistic Anarchists recognize that until every individual is focused on building and maintaining a healthy relationship with themselves they will struggle to have truly healthy and balanced relationships with others. It is because of this that Lujan has said being an anarchist is actually making a statement about the types of relationships one wants to be involved in. Namely, voluntary, consensual relationships free of coercion. In "The Relational Anarchist Primer," Lujan writes:

"According to relational anarchists, the better humans connect with each other, the more peace and understanding that will exist between them. The greater the strength of the relationships, the less likely rulers will become necessary or begin to emerge.

"Anarchism means 'without rulers.' And besides being a political assertion, this is a psychological and relational preference. It is apolitical, based on preferred relationship standards. Instead of dispensing violence, these anarchists dispense compassion.

"The definition 'Without rulers' is a state of human interaction. It is how most people prefer to make contact with people, and how human connection unfolds when certain skill sets and forms of communication are employed. Most people do not want to be ruled. Yet they oftentimes end up in a ruler-serf dynamic as a result of cultural modes of interaction and attachment, which are generally anti-empathetic and detached."

What we recognize is that by implementing NVC techniques, becoming mindful of our own hearts and minds, and taking time to empathize with those we disagree with, we lay the foundation for a healthy discussion and sense of acceptance among our peers. It is on this foundation, in this environment of acceptance, that we will make the biggest strides towards a world without centralized authority and rulers. *"So in lieu of an infinite struggle of deciding on the best economic idea for society,"* Lujan writes. *"The relational anarchist asks everyone to come to the table and figure out how to cooperatively coexist in a state of anarchy. Indeed, the partial reason governments have maintained their power is because of the ongoing battle between 'left' and 'right.'"*

We ought to strive for common ground because the other option is endless conflict. If we cannot compassionately debate differences of opinion, we are doomed to repeat our violent past. Authoritarians of all stripes buy into the illusion that they can force the world to conform to their particular worldview and values, but this is not only immoral, it never works. Individuals do not change their habits and dead end philosophies because of violence or berating. In addition, our goal should not be to simply have our ideas and desires heard, but to make time to listen and understand the ideas and desires of those around us. So then, how do we go about achieving this state of mutual respect and healthy conflict resolution?

Nonviolent communication and the therapeutic alliances offer a great starting point for communication and dispute resolution. The mere suggestion that we might be able to coexist and possibly co-habitat with those who view the world completely different from us might be enough to cause some readers to assume we have lost our minds. However, history is full of examples of people of different religions and political beliefs coexisting. Of course, history (in the United States and elsewhere) is also rife with examples of violence and conflict. Perhaps these examples are explained, in part, by a lack of emotional maturity, proper communication skills, a scarcity mindset, and primal survival instinct? What would the world look like if we attempted to implement these holistic and relational strategies in our everyday lives?

Holistic and Relational Anarchism in Action

It's important to reiterate the need for spontaneous order and discretion based on mutual respect. In a truly free society without central authority, there is no way to force or coerce every single person to live according to the property norms of your choosing. The vast human experience guarantees that we are not always going to agree on complex moral issues, and with that being the case, it is best to find a way to handle these issues without hurting people or throwing them in cages. Of course, there will be rare occasions where violent and unreasonable people will need to be subdued or isolated, but that would be the exception to the rule in a world where people are attempting to avoid the use of oppressive tactics seen throughout history.

We imagine a world where some communities implement private property norms and others have property arrangements which resemble unowned or community ownership. How will each and every conflict play out with such a patchwork of norms? Only the individuals involved in each particular situation can decide. Unless the parties involved are prepared to wield the force of the state to ensure their specific property views are the new monopoly, we need to grow accustomed to mutual respect and compromise. A one-size-fits-all solution is already a part of the problem we face today. It is up to each of us to hold ourselves to a higher standard and strive to respect the sovereignty of other individuals always and use our best discretion in each case of conflict. Even if the whole of society is forced to accept one specific dogma, there will always be dissenters and the only way to stop the dissent is to enact totalitarian control. We can either have freedom to disagree and peacefully resolve conflicts, or we can continue the cycle of violence and coercion.

It has been said that ideas which are worthy do not require force or violence to implement. If one stands by their beliefs wholeheartedly, they should be able to respectfully debate the merits and potential failures without resorting to violence. The Relational and Holistic Anarchist schools are the most conducive to creating a world free of violence and aggression. By applying these principles one can help contribute to the evolution of hearts and minds, and grow the movement of Anarchists who practice a more compassionate aesthetic.

Onward we go, towards a Holistic and Relational future!

ABOUT THE AUTHORS, ACKNOWLEDGEMENTS & SUGGESTED READING LIST

About the Authors & Acknowledgements

Derrick Broze

Derrick Broze is an activist, investigative journalist, author, and documentary film-maker. Since 2010, Derrick has been involved in various forms of activism in Houston, Texas and around the United States. He cofounded The Houston Free Thinkers activist community in 2010 and The Conscious Resistance Network media outlet in 2013. Since 2012, Derrick has written for a variety of independent media websites, as well as freelancing for magazines. Beginning in 2015, he published 3 books with John Vibes, as well as publishing his own works, including *The Holistic Self-Assessment* and *How to Opt Out of the Technocratic State*. Derrick has written and narrated 5 mini-documentaries and 2 full-length documentary films. His next project is the 12-part documentary series, *The Pyramid of Power*. He is also planning on writing a biography of Samuel E. Konkin III, and an autobiography on his experience with drugs, addiction, depression, and prison.

John Vibes

John Vibes began his journey in activism hosting underground raves between 2008 and 2011, but also took up writing along the way. After releasing his first book, John was approached by numerous independent media organizations who invited him to be a contributing writer. Since 2011, John has worked as an independent journalist covering issues like police brutality, government corruption and the drug war. After the release of *The Conscious Resistance Trilogy*, John plans to begin working on different fiction projects, which will still carry messages similar to the ones found in these pages. John's full origin story can be found in his book *Paper Squares and Purple Stars: My Life as a Rave Outlaw*.

Acknowledgements

We would like to thank everyone who has supported our activism, journalism, and books. These essays are written with the intention of inspiring people to change the world by changing themselves. Whether this goal is achievable depends on how the individual readers integrate the information presented. If we were successful with this intention then we expect to see a growth of conscious, anti-statists in the coming decades. This book is written for those who are ready to change and those who are going to be born into a freer world.

Thank you.

Suggested Reading List

We would like to offer a "Recommended Reading" list for those interested in further study of the material which has influenced our thinking. The list contains books covering politics, philosophy, psychology, and spirituality. We believe each of these areas of research is valuable for the holistic anarchist perspective.

- *New Libertarian Manifesto*, Samuel Konkin III
- *An Agorist Primer*, Samuel Konkin III
- *The Last Whole Introduction to Agorism*, Samuel Konkin III
- *Agorist Class Theory*, Samuel Konkin III & Wally Conger
- *Men Against the State*, James J. Martin
- *The Art of Not Being Governed*, James C. Scott
- *Society Against the State*, Pierre Clastres
- *On Disobedience*, Erich Fromm
- *The Other Path*, Hermando De Soto
- *Neighborhood Power*, Karl Hess
- *Community Technology*, Karl Hess
- *Mutual Aid*, Peter Kropotkin
- *Stealth of Nations*, Robert Neuwirth
- *Human Action*, Ludwig Von Mises
- *For a New Liberty*, Murray Rothbard
- *A Beautiful Anarchy*, Jeffrey Tucker
- *Right-Wing Collectivism*, Jeffrey Tucker
- *Markets Not Capitalism*, Edited by Gary Chartier and Charles W. Johnson
- *No Treason: The Constitution of No Authority*, Lysander Spooner
- *The Individualist Anarchists*: An Anthology of Liberty, Frank H. Brooks
- *Dark Alliance*, Gary Webb
- *The Devils Chessboard*, David Talbot
- *Tragedy & Hope*, Carroll Quigley
- *The Terror Conspiracy*, Jim Marrs

- *Spirit and Resistance*, George Tinker
- *Non-Violent Communication*, Marshall Rosenberg
- *The Four Agreements*, Don Miguel Ruiz
- *The Untethered Soul*, Michael A. Singer
- *Black Elk Speaks*, James G. Neihardt
- *The Cosmic Serpent*, Jeremy Narby
- *Science Set Free*, Rupert Sheldrake
- *The Underground History of American Education*, John Taylor Gatto
- *Dumbing us Down*, John Taylor Gatto
- *Sailboat Dairies*, Michael Fielding
- *The New Jim Crow*, Michelle Alexander
- *10% Happier*, Dan Harris
- *Acid Dreams*, Oliver Wyman
- *Fool's Errand*, Scott Horton
- *Raven Rock*, Jacques Roy
- *Permanent Record*, Edward Snowden
- *Them: Adventures with Extremists*, Jon Ronson
- *Smuggler Nation*, Peter Andreas
- *Killer High*, Peter Andreas
- *Chasing the Scream*, Johann Hari
- *White Trash*, Nancy Isenberg
- *Untrue*, Wednesday Martin
- *A Renegade History of the United States*, Thaddeus Russell
- *A People's History of the United States*, Howard Zinn
- *The Color of Law*, Richard Rothstein
- *Eyes in the Sky*, Arthur Holland Michel
- *1434*, Gavin Menzies

This book is dedicated to Samuel Konkin III and Karl Hess

• • •

To find out more about The Conscious Resistance, please visit

TheConsciousResistance.com

Discovery Publisher

Discovery Publisher is a multimedia publisher whose mission is to inspire and support personal transformation, spiritual growth and awakening. We strive with every title to preserve the essential wisdom of the author, spiritual teacher, thinker, healer, and visionary artist.

CPSIA information can be obtained
at www.ICGtesting.com
Printed in the USA
LVHW040707160821
695279LV00003B/8

9 781788 944823